A MALCOLM X READER

A
MALCOLM X READER

Edited by David Gallen

Carroll & Graf Publishers, Inc.
New York

Collection copyright © 1994 by David Gallen

First Carroll & Graf edition August 1994

Carroll & Graf Publishers, Inc.
260 Fifth Avenue
New York, NY 10001

Library of Congress Cataloging-in-Publication Data

The Malcolm X reader / edited by David Gallen.—1st Carroll & Graf
   ed.
      p.   cm.
   ISBN 0-7867-0078-5 (pbk.) : $10.95 ($14.95 Can.)
   1. X, Malcolm, 1925–1965.   2. Black Muslims—Biography.   3. Afro—
Americans—Biography.   I. Gallen, David.
BP223.Z8L57635   1994
320.6'4'092—dc20
   [B]   94-4666
                                                                       CIP

Manufactured in the United States of America

Permissions

PERMISSIONS

Preface

The FBI file on Malcolm X runs to nearly four thousand pages. Early in 1991 it arrived at my desk in several cartons, and I began working on the project of editing its pages for the book that was published later that year as *Malcolm X: The FBI File*. A kind of life of Malcolm X from the FBI's point of view, the file intrigued me as much for what it did not reveal about Malcolm X (despite its length it is filled with gaps, as well as inaccuracies and bias) as it did about the Nation of Islam minister whose activities supposedly threatened America's internal security. The file became the springboard for my continued interest in the life and career of Malcolm X.

Over the next two years I researched the literature on Malcolm X and interviewed as many of his former close associates as were willing to speak with me. I produced and authored or edited four other titles relating to Malcolm X: *Malcolm X: As They Knew Him, Remembering Malcolm: The Story of Malcolm X From Inside the Muslim Mosque, Malcolm X: The Assassination,* and *Malcolm A to X*.

Meanwhile, with the twenty-fifth anniversary of Malcolm's death by assassins' bullets in Harlem's Audubon Ballroom on the Sunday afternoon of February 21, 1965, and with the release of Spike Lee's film on Malcolm in 1992, the interest in Malcolm X—and the literature on him—grew, and continues to grow. Although no single volume on Malcolm has the power or the strengths of his own *The Autobiography of Malcolm X*, recent writing places his career variously in historical, political, social, or cultural contexts as it reevaluates the legacy of perhaps the most charismatic and controversial African-American leader in this century.

In this volume I have tried to represent some of the variety in the approaches to the life and career of Malcolm X. Bruce Perry, for instance, looks at the childhood of Malcolm Little from a psychological perspective whereas journalist Louis Lomax, in a candid interview, discusses the Black Muslim movement with Minister Malcolm and theologian James Cone examines Malcolm's mission after his fall from NOI leader Elijah Muhammad's grace. The FBI file offers one version of the assassination of Malcolm X while historian Michael Friedly reconstructs the events of that fateful Harlem Sunday afternoon in light of later evidence. The volume also includes oral history and memoir as well as Malcolm's own account in the *Autobiography* of his conversion in prison to the Nation of Islam.

All the selections in *A Malcolm X Reader* have been previously published in book form or in periodicals. Except one. In October 1991 Alex Haley, who collaborated over a two-year period with Malcolm on the *Autobiography,* shared with me his thoughts and reflections on Malcolm X. This interview is among Haley's last. In it he speaks at length about their collaboration—its demands and trials and rewards—and about the trust that eventually cemented their personal relationship. He speaks warmly, with the depth of feeling that characterizes his epilogue to the *Autobiography.* And he illuminates something of the great human spirit of Malcolm X—the sincerity, the selflessness, the intelligence, the humility.

David Gallen
June 1994

Contents

"Final Views"
An Interview with Malcolm X
by Claude Lewis

"Alex Haley Remembers Malcolm X"
An Interview with David Gallen

from *Remembering Malcolm*
by Benjamin Karim
"Winter"

from *Malcolm X: The FBI File*
Section 16: March 12, 1965

from *Malcolm X: The Assassination*
by Michael Friedly
"The Assassins"

"The Children of Malcolm"
by Marshall Frady

CHRONOLOGY

May 10, 1919

Earl Little, a Baptist preacher from Georgia, marries Louise Norton in Montreal. Soon after they set up residence in Philadelphia, Pennsylvania.

1922 or 1923

Earl and Louise move with their three small children to Omaha, Nebraska.

December 1924

According to *The Autobiography of Malcolm X,* a party of hooded Ku Klux Klansmen warns Louise, then pregnant with Malcolm, to get her family out of town, as her husband is stirring up trouble in the black community with his UNIA (Universal Negro Improvement Association) "back to Africa" preachings.

May 19, 1925

Malcolm Little is born at University Hospital in Omaha.

December 1926

The Little family moves to Milwaukee, Wisconsin.

January 1928–
December 1929

Earl Little Buys a house in Lansing, Michigan, where he continues to preach. On November 7 the Littles' home is set afire and burns to the ground; the family escapes unharmed. The next month Earl Little builds a new home on the outskirts of East Lansing, Michigan.

August 1930

In Detroit, Michigan, the followers of W.D. Fard, an itinerant peddler and preacher known as "The Prophet," establish the first Temple of Islam.

September 28, 1931   Earl Little is run over by a streetcar
                       and dies; rumor holds that he was
                       murdered by the Black Legion, a
                       local white supremacist group.

January 9, 1939   Louise Little suffers a complete ner-
                       vous breakdown; she is declared le-
                       gally insane and formally committed
                       to the State Mental Hospital at Ka-
                       lamazoo, where she remains for
                       twenty-six years.

Spring 1939   Malcolm tells his favorite teacher that
                       he wants to become a lawyer; he is
                       told that "that's no realistic goal for
                       a nigger."

August 1939   A social worker recommends that
                       Malcolm be placed in a juvenile
                       home; Judge John McClellan
                       concurs.

May 1940–   Malcolm is placed in various foster
February 1941   homes in the Lansing area.

February 1941   Moves to Boston; lives with his sister
                       Ella.

1941–42   Holds a variety of jobs—among them
                       shoe shining, dishwashing, and
                       soda jerking—and works off and on
                       for the New Haven Railroad; be-
                       comes involved with Boston's under-
                       world fringe.

December 1942   Moves back to Michigan for about
                       four months.

March 1943   Moves to New York City; again
                       works for the New Haven Railroad.

October 25, 1943

U.S. Army finds Malcolm mentally disqualified for military service; he is classified 4F.

1943–44

Malcolm works intermittently on the railroad; known on the streets as Big Red, he also pushes dope, plays the numbers, peddles bootleg whiskey, and hustles. Under the stage name of Jack Carlton he works as a bar entertainer at a New York nightclub, The Lobster Pond, in July 1944. In October he returns to Boston for two months or so.

January 1945

Returns to Michigan after a holiday stint at a New York nightclub; works briefly as a busboy at the Mayfair Ballroom in East Lansing (he later claimed he danced there under the stage name of Rhythm Red) and as a waiter in a local night spot called Coral Gables.

August 1945

Moves back to New York; lives in Harlem.

December 1945

Embarks on Christmas season stealing binge in Boston with his friend Bea and her sister Joyce Caragulian, Francis "Sonny" Brown, Kora Marderosian, and Malcolm Jarvis.

January 12, 1946

Attempts to reclaim a stolen watch he left for repair at a Boston jewelry store and is arrested; indicted for carrying firearms, larceny, and breaking and entering.

February 27, 1946

Begins serving prison term at Charlestown Prison, where he initiates his own reading program in the prison library.

January 10, 1947 — Transferred to Concord Reformatory for fifteen months; during this time he is converted by a fellow inmate to the NOI (Nation of Islam) teachings of the Honorable Elijah Muhammad.

1948–52 — Transferred to Norfolk Prison Colony in March 1948 and gains access to an excellent library; transferred back to Charlestown Prison two years later, on March 23, 1950, where he serves the balance of his sentence.

August 7, 1952 — Paroled from state prison.

August 8, 1952 — Travels to Detroit; in Inkster, Michigan, gets job as a furniture salesman in a store managed by his brother Wilfred.

August 31, 1952 — Travels to Chicago, Illinois, with members of Detroit Temple No. 1 to hear the Honorable Elijah Muhammad speak.

September 1952 — Receives his X from the NOI. And thus becomes Malcolm X.

January 1953 — Leaves the furniture store for an assembly line job at the Ford Motor Company's Lincoln-Mercury Division, which he leaves for the Gar Wood factory in Detroit.

June 1953–
June 1954 — Quits Gar Wood when named the assistant minister at Detroit Temple No. 1. Becomes first minister of Bos-

ton Temple No. 11 in the winter of
1953, then in March 1954 acting minister of Philadelphia Temple No.
12; in June 1954 becomes minister of
New York Temple No. 7.

1956

Betty Sanders joins New York Temple No. 7; she is renamed Betty X.

April 14, 1957

NOI member Hinton Johnson is
beaten by New York police and
jailed; outside the 123rd Street police
station, where a contingent of Muslims from Temple No. 7 has gathered,
Malcolm demands that Johnson be
taken to hospital.

January 1958

Telephones Betty Sanders with a
marriage proposal from a gas station in Detroit on January 12; she
says yes. They are married two
days later by a justice of the peace
in Lansing. On January 19 the new-
lyweds drive back to New York and
take up residence in East Elmhurst,
Queens.

November 1958

A daughter, the first child of Betty
and Malcolm, is born; she is named
Attallah.

July 1959

A three-week tour as Elijah Muhammad's ambassador takes Malcolm
to Egypt, Mecca, Iran, Syria, and
Ghana.

July 13–17, 1959

On *News Beat* WNDT-TV Channel
13, New York, airs "The Hate That
Hate Produced," a five-part report by
Mike Wallace; it features Malcolm
X, among others, and brings the

Black Muslim movement to the attention of the general American public.

March 3, 1960

On the New York WMCA radio program *Pro and Con* William Kunstler interviews Malcolm and the Reverend William H. James on the topic "Is Black Supremacy the Answer?"

December 25, 1960

A second daughter, Qubilah, is born to Malcolm and Betty.

October 16, 1961

Malcolm appears on the NBC television program *Open Mind* with Morroe Berger, Kenneth B. Clark, Richard Haley and Constance B. Motley; the moderator is Eric P. Goldman, and the topic is "Where Is the American Negro Headed?"

April 27, 1962

NOI member Ronald Stokes is killed by police gunfire in Los Angeles mosque, and six other Muslims are wounded; the next day Malcolm is dispatched to Los Angeles by Elijah Muhammad.

December 1962

Rumors of adultery and six illegitimate children fathered by Elijah Muhammad cause numerous Muslims to leave Chicago Mosque No. 2; Malcolm speaks with three of Muhammad's former secretaries, all of whom have children by him.

1962

Ilyasah, a third daughter, is born to Betty and Malcolm.

May 1963

The *Playboy* interview, "a candid conversation with the militant

major-domo of the black muslims,''
is published in the monthly magazine. Around the same time Malcolm
is interviewed on television by
James Baldwin.

August 28, 1963   Attends the civil rights march on
Washington as an observer; com-
ments that he can't understand why
Negroes should become so excited
about a demonstration ''run by
whites in front of a statue of a president who has been dead for a hundred years and who didn't like us
when he was alive.''

November 10, 1963   Delivers his most influential speech
up to this time, ''A Message to the
Grass Roots,'' at the Northern Negro
Grass Roots Leadership Conference
in Detroit.

November 22, 1963   President John F. Kennedy is assassinated in Dallas, Texas.

December 1, 1963   At an NOI rally in New York Malcolm states that Kennedy ''never
foresaw that the chickens would
come home to roost so soon,'' despite a directive from Elijah Muhammad that no Muslim minister
comment on the assassination.

December 4, 1963   Suspended from his ministry by Elijah Muhammad for ninety days for
his remark on the death of the
president.

January 15, 1964   Visits Cassius Clay (Muhammad Ali)
for a week's vacation at his fight
camp in Miami, Florida; their friend-

ship becomes increasingly strained
thereafter.

March 8, 1964   Announces his break with Elijah Mu-
                     hammad and the NOI as well as his
                     intent to organize a "black nationalist
                     party" to heighten the political
                     consciousness of Afro-Americans.

March 9, 1964   Interviewed by Joe Durso of the New
                     York WNDT-TV Channel 13 news
                     program *The World at Ten*.

March 10, 1964   Tells *Ebony* magazine that the Black
                     Muslim leaders have "got to kill
                     me. They can't afford to let me
                     live. . . . I know where the bodies
                     are buried. And if they press me, I'll
                     exhume some."

March 10, 1964   The NOI sends Malcolm a certified
                     letter requesting that he return all
                     NOI property, including the house in
                     East Elmhurst.

March 12, 1964   At the Park Sheraton Hotel in New
                     York Malcolm holds a press con-
                     ference to announce the formation of
                     the MMI (Muslim Mosque,
                     Incorporated).

March 26, 1964   Meets Martin Luther King, Jr., face
                     to face, for the first and only time,
                     after a King news conference in the
                     U.S. Capitol.

April 8, 1964   The NOI files eviction proceedings
                     against Malcolm.

April 13–   Malcolm travels abroad; under the
May 21, 1964   name of Malik El-Shabazz, he flies

first to Frankfurt, then on to Cairo
and Jedda.

April 20, 1964

Writes of his pilgrimage to Mecca in
a letter: states that many white people he met during the pilgrimage displayed a spirit of unity and
brotherhood that provided him a new,
positive insight into race relations;
in Islam, he now feels, lies the power
to overcome racial antagonism and
to obliterate it from the heart of white
America.

April 21–30, 1964

Honored as a guest of the state by
Saudi Arabia's Prince Faisal.

April 30–
May 6, 1964

Flies to Beirut to speak at Sudanese
Cultural Center, then back to Cairo;
travels by rail to Alexandria, where
he boards airplane to Nigeria.

May 6–10, 1964

Appears on various Nigerian radio
and television programs; speaks at
the University of Ibadan.

May 10–17, 1964

Tours and lectures in Ghana; addresses the Ghanian parliament on
May 14 and on May 15 has audience
with President Kwame Nkrumah,
which Malcolm describes as his highest honor not only in Ghana but in
all of Africa.

May 17–19, 1964

Flies to Monrovia, Liberia, then to
Dakar, Senegal, and from there to
Morocco; spends his thirty-ninth
birthday in Algiers.

May 21, 1964

Returns to New York.

June 28, 1964	Announces the formation of the OAAU (Organization of Afro-American Unity), which will be committed to doing "whatever is necessary to bring the Negro struggle from the level of civil rights to the level of human rights."
July 9–November 24, 1964	Travels abroad; flies to Cairo via London under the name of Malik El-Shabazz.
July 17, 1964	Attends African Summit Conference as representative of the OAAU; appeals to the delegates of the thirty-four African nations to bring the cause of the twenty-two million black people in the United States before the United Nations.
September 1, 1964	In New York, Civil Court Judge Maurice Wahl issues order that Malcolm X must vacate residence in East Elmhurst by January 31, 1965.
September 12, 1964	"I'm Talking To You, White Man: An Autobiography by Malcolm X" is printed in the *Saturday Evening Post*.
September–November 1964	Malcolm tours Africa: by mid October he has visited eleven countries, talked with eleven heads of state, and addressed most of their parliaments; for another five weeks he will continue his tour "to better acquaint himself with the problems facing the continent," as he says in a speech in Lagos.
November 24, 1964	Returns to New York.

November 30, 1964   Flies to London for an Oxford Union debate on December 3; he speaks for the motion that "extremism in the defense of liberty is no vice, moderation in the pursuit of justice is no virtue."

December 1964   Requests interview with Claude Lewis, then of the *New York Post,* to get something "on the record."

1964   A fourth daughter, Gamilah, is born.

February 5, 1965   Flies to London, where he addresses the First Congress of the Council of African Organizations on February 8.

February 9, 1965   Flies to Paris, but is refused entry by French government officials; returns to London and on February 13 flies back to New York.

February 14, 1965   Malcolm's house in East Elmhurst is firebombed in the early morning hours.

Malcolm flies to Detroit to deliver an address at the First Annual Dignity Projection and Scholarship Award ceremony sponsored by the Afro-American Broadcasting and Recording Company at the Ford Auditorium; it is Malcolm's last major speech.

February 18, 1965   Malcolm's family is evicted.

February 20, 1965   In a telephone conversation with Alex Haley Malcolm says that "the more I keep thinking about this thing, the things that have been happening

lately, I'm not at all sure it's the
Muslims. I know what they can do,
and what they can't, and they can't
do some of the stuff recently going
on. . . . The more I keep thinking
about what happened to me in
France, I think I'm going to quit saying it's the Muslims.''

After an OAAU business meeting in
the evening, Malcolm refuses his
friend Earl Grant's invitation to spend
the night at his apartment: ''You
have a family,'' says Malcolm. ''I
don't want anyone hurt on my account. I always knew it would end
like this.''

February 21, 1965   At 3:10 P.M., just after he has begun
to address an OAAU rally at the
Audubon Ballroom, Malcolm is shot
several times; a black male later
identified as Talmadge Hayer (a.k.a.
Thomas Hagan) is arrested. Malcolm is pronounced DOA at Vanderbilt Clinic, Columbia-Presbyterian
Hospital.

February 22, 1965   Elijah Muhammad denies that he or
the NOI had anything to do with
the slaying of Malcolm X.

February 27, 1965   Malcolm's body is moved from the
Unity Funeral Home in Harlem to
Bishop Alvin S. Child's Faith Temple
Church of God in Christ at 1763
Amsterdam Avenue for the funeral
services, which are presided over
by playwright-actor Ossie Davis; approximately fifteen hundred people
attend the services, five hundred of
them outside the church itself.

Early in the afternoon Malcolm is buried at Ferncliff Cemetery, Hartsdale.

March 11, 1965

A grand jury indicts Talmadge Hayer (22), Norman 3X Butler (26), and Thomas 15X Johnson (29) for the murder of Malcolm X.

November 5, 1965

The New York Times heralds the publication of *The Autobiography of Malcolm X,* written with Alex Haley, as "an eloquent statement."

1965

Betty Shabazz gives birth to twin daughters, Malaak and Malikah.

January 12, 1966

The trial for the murder of Malcolm X opens.

March 2, 1966

Hayer testifies that he and three accomplices were hired to kill Malcolm X; he states that neither Butler nor Johnson was implicated in the slaying.

March 11, 1966

Hayer, Butler, and Johnson are convicted of murder in the first degree.

April 14, 1966

New York Supreme Court Judge Charles Marks sentences all three defendants to life imprisonment.

The Autobiography of Malcolm X *describes how day after day in 1934, a bleak Depression year, Louise Little, Malcolm's mother, would boil up a big pot of dandelion greens to feed her eleven children, all of them dizzy from hunger, and how they would daily be taunted by neighborhood kids for eating "fried grass." On luckier days they would eat cornmeal mush.*

Malcolm Little understood hunger. In many ways it defined his childhood—the hunger for food and a hunger, too, for affection, acceptance, guidance, encouragement. Malcolm Little grew up with harsh realities, and they may indeed have been far more harsh as he experienced them than they were as he remembered them in his now classic autobiography.

Speculating as to why we are who we are, Malcolm X said, "All our experiences fuse into our personalities. Everything that ever happened to us is an ingredient."

From the foster homes to Muslim mosques, from hustling on the streets to worshipping at Mecca, from Malcolm's incarceration to his martyrdom, Bruce Perry strives in his comprehensive biography of Malcolm X to document as many as possible of the ingredients that transformed a hungry child into perhaps the most charismatic spokesman for African Americans in the twentieth century. In the initial chapters of his work, carefully detailing Malcolm's early years and sometimes editing his memory, Perry offers a portrait of the child who fathered the man.

from *Malcolm*
The Life of a Man Who Changed
Black America
by Bruce Perry
from "The Formative Years"

Parental Demands

Earl Little had great expectations for his forthcoming seventh child. According to a family tradition that sprang from ancient legends ascribing magic power to the number seven, the child would be blessed with the best attributes of the ancestral bloodline. It was destined for greatness, particularly if it were male. In anticipation of the youngster's future achievements, Earl's father wrote from his Georgia farm and directed that the infant be named John, after himself.

The baby was born on May 19, 1925, in Omaha, Nebraska. "It's a boy," Earl wired his parents. "But he's white, just like mama!" The physical similarity between the newborn child and his paternal grandmother went beyond skin color. His eyes, like hers, were blue-green. His ash-blonde hair was tinged with cinnamon; hers turned reddish in the summer sun. The similarities appalled his grandmother, who despised the white blood in her veins. Her dark-skinned husband wept. No "albino" would be named after him.

The baby was christened Malcolm by his mother Louisa, who had been raised on the Caribbean island of Grenada. She had never

3

seen her Scottish father. When she was very young, her unmarried black mother had died giving birth to the last of her three illegitimate children. Louisa's dictatorial grandmother, Mary Jane Langdon, had assumed responsibility for raising her. But since Mary Jane spent considerable time away from home, her daughter Gertrude, Louisa's aunt, became Louisa's surrogate mother.

Aunt Gertie, who habitually flogged her children with straps and makeshift whips, had learned her autocratic child-rearing methods from her parents. On one occasion, her father, Jupiter, had stripped one of her teen-age sisters naked and made her kneel on the ground outside the house, where everyone could see her. Gertrude enforced her own parental decrees with similar indifference to her children's feelings. When she was away—which was much too often, according to one son—young Louisa was put in charge of the household.

Louisa apparently revenged herself by beating her young charges. Ultimately, she outgrew her usefulness to Mary Jane and Gertrude and became an economic liability. She was told she couldn't stay any longer and was sent elsewhere on the tiny British island—exactly where she cannot recall. Her memories of the ensuing period are of emptiness and loneliness. She felt so unwanted that she eventually emigrated to Montreal, where she met Malcolm's father. Earl Little—his real name was Early—was not the only man who found her exceptionally attractive. Her shiny, braided, raven-black hair hung down to her waist and contrasted vividly with her fair complexion. (She was so light-skinned that she was frequently mistaken for white.) Her figure was slim and tall, her bearing proud and erect. Her eyes, which had been sea-blue when she was younger, had turned brown except for the outer rim of the iris, which remained blue.

Earl didn't tell Louisa he had walked out on his first wife and his fist three children. Passing himself off as a widower, he married his West Indian girlfriend shortly after they met. But they did not have much in common. While Louisa had had five years of Anglican schooling, Earl was nearly illiterate. She needled him about his ignorance, which he tried to hide with pretensions of learning. They were constantly at odds.

With his new wife in tow, Earl drifted from job to job and

city to city. From Montreal, the Littles went to Philadelphia, where they had their first child, Wilfred. Soon afterward, they moved to Omaha, where Louisa gave birth to Malcolm's older sister Hilda, his brother Philbert, and then Malcolm himself.* Earl was a disciple of Marcus Garvey and was elected president of the Omaha branch of Garvey's Universal Negro Improvement Association. Louisa also joined the UNIA, which emphasized that blacks should be proud of their blackness and their African heritage. It urged them to free themselves from their dependence on whites, economically and other wise. Garvey taught that instead of integrating with whites, blacks should establish their own sovereign nation. His message was so uplifting that hundreds of thousands of American, Caribbean, and other blacks rallied to his cause. Some of them tried resettling in Africa.

Malcolm's father reportedly decided to leave Omaha after Ku Klux Klan horsemen brandishing firearms and blazing torches besieged the Littles' home, shattering the window panes with their gun butts. But Malcolm's mother—who confronted the klansmen, according to his autobiography—says the incident never occurred. Nor does her sister-in-law Rose, who lived in Omaha at the time, believe that it occurred. Rose was told by her husband that Earl had impersonated him, purchased clothing in his name, and left him to foot the bill. She also suspected that Earl had stolen the contents of her steamer trunk. But what prompted his departure from Omaha is unclear.**

In Milwaukee, the next stop on Earl's itinerary, he continued playing a prominent role at UNIA gatherings. He also drove his touring car to distant towns and villages, propagating Garvey's teachings and organizing new UNIA chapters. In Indiana Harbor, Indiana, he was evidently met with such enthusiasm that

* Malcolm was Louisa's fourth child but Earl's seventh.
** An Earl Little was convicted of larceny in Butler, Georgia, Malcolm's father's birthplace, shortly before Earl's first wife bore her third child in Talbotton, Georgia, twenty miles away. Whether this Earl Little was Malcolm's father is difficult to determine from surviving records, which indicate that the accomplice of the convicted man was named Wright Little. Earl had a cousin whose name was Wright.

he briefly served as president of that town's UNIA chapter, even though he apparently never lived there.

After Malcolm's brother Reginald was born in August 1927, the Littles trekked from Milwaukee to Albion, Michigan, where Earl's brother Jim bootlegged moonshine. When revenue agents caught up with Jim, Malcolm's father moved the family to the northwestern outskirts of Lansing, where Malcolm's younger sister Yvonne was born. The Littles purchased an aging two-story farmhouse in a semi-rural, all-white neighborhood.

By this time, Malcolm was nearly four. His reddish-blonde hair was so close-cropped it gave his head a roundish, pumpkin-shaped appearance. Though his skin had grown darker, it was still fair. The other children teased him about his "high yellow" appearance. They called him "Chink" and made fun of his bluish eyes, which seemed to change color like his mother's. "We called him a freak of nature," Yvonne recalled years later.

Malcolm's father was as dark as Malcolm was light. Though blacks who heard his crusading oratory thought he hated whites, his white neighbors had a different impression. He greeted them with smiles and gave them fresh, homegrown produce from his vegetable garden. Black acquaintances recall how he shunned them for white ones whenever he found it expedient to do so. And the son he paraded when the church deacons visited was Malcolm, his fair-skinned pride and joy. To the best of Malcolm's recollection, he was the only son his father ever took with him to the Garveyite gatherings where Earl vigorously championed the theme of black pride.

Malcolm's mother, whose American friends called her Louise, was also in conflict about color. Despite the way she extolled the ideal of black pride, she favored her lighter-skinned relatives and proudly insisted she was West Indian, not African-American. Her father, she said, was a white "prince" and plantation owner. She tried to comb the natural curl from her hair in order to make it resemble the hair of the white friends she boasted. Sometimes she scrubbed Malcolm's face and neck violently. "I can make him look almost white if I bathe him enough," she told her white neighbor Anna Stohrer. Anna felt that Louise considered Malcolm superior to her other children because of his light complexion.

But Malcolm felt otherwise, partly because his mother bent over backward to make sure he would not think his fair skin made him superior. She admonished him to get out of the house so that the sun would tan and darken his skin. He thought she favored the darker children, partly because his light skin, like hers, was a painful reminder of her illegitimacy. He felt he was her least favorite child.

Since Louise was so ambivalent about Malcolm's skin color, he could not please her any more than he could please his conflict-ridden father. He had neither parent's unqualified approval. And there was no way he could satisfy their irreconcilable demands.

Home Life

Sometimes, Earl beat Louise. He was also brutal to his children. At the slightest pretext, he beat the older ones almost savagely. If one of them violated one of his rules, he grabbed the nearest child—which one didn't seem to matter—and whaled the daylights out of him. Frequently, he administered his beatings with a sapling or a belt. "You'll kill that child, Early," Louise occasionally protested. But she never intervened. She was as afraid of her husband as her young ones were. Even some of the neighbors' children dreaded Earl Little.

Malcolm was spared the brunt of his father's brutality. Years later, he attributed the favoritism to his light skin color. Most of the beatings he received were administered by his mother, who ruled her children with an iron hand, without visible evidence of affection. Like so many autocrats, she tyrannized them the way she had been tyrannized, not only by her husband, but also by Gertrude, Jupiter, and Mary Jane Langdon. Sometimes she used a strap on Malcolm. And at times she punished him with a switch that she made him choose himself. He would try to find one that would snap, but whenever he succeeded, his mother made him fetch another, stouter one. She could hit a boy so hard with the back of her hand that it made him feel as if his head had been split open.

In a partly successful effort to discourage his mother from whipping him, Malcolm protested her beatings loudly enough for the neighbors to hear. He also rebelled in other ways. He refused to let his mother, who was a fanatic about cleanliness, bathe him. He also resisted her attempts to send him outdoors, so that the sun would darken his skin. Yet indoors, he avoided getting too close to her; whenever possible, he stayed in a different part of the house, playing marbles or poring over picture books. He was habitually surly. At times, he refused to speak to his mother. On one occasion, he reproached her for being "all witchy." Clenching his little fists, he screamed, "I could kill you."

Malcolm was learning that verbal protest could achieve results. His mother began yielding to his persistent clamor for the buttered biscuits she impatiently denied her other, less demanding youngsters. Yet his position in the household remained precarious, not only because of Louise's ambivalence about his skin color, but also because his father's favoritism toward him bred resentment in the other children.

The jealousy worked both ways, for Malcolm seemed to envy the children his mother appeared to favor. It galled him that Wilfred, who was such a responsible child, appeared to be her "angel." Malcolm's chief rival, however, was Philbert, the darkest-skinned boy in the family. Nicknamed "Blackie," Philbert was the chromatic antithesis of Malcolm, who was called "Milky." Philbert regarded himself as his mother's favorite, partly because his middle name was Norton, Louise's maiden name. The rivalry between him and Malcolm was so intense that some of their respective friends became near-enemies. Eventually, Philbert would realize that the feud was chiefly about skin color. But he couldn't bring himself to admit that the issue of color was closely linked with the issue of parental approval.

Malcolm's rivalry with Philbert spilled over into the religious sphere, where Philbert had an advantage because he was unusually devout for a youngster. Nor could Malcolm effectively compete with him physically; Philbert was two years older, sturdily built, and determined to learn how to fight back and repay his father for his brutality. Before long, boys who challenged Philbert did so at their peril. The point was made when Malcolm grabbed a hammer in an effort to defend himself against his brother. In the ensuing struggle, Philbert seized the head of the hammer, which rebounded and knocked out the inside corners of Malcolm's two upper front teeth. The inverted, V-shaped gap marred Malcolm's appearance and earned him the nickname "Toothless Blondie."

Malcolm would later deny that he had harbored negative feelings toward any of his brothers and sisters. He asserted he was "very close" to them. But Reginald, the brother to whom he said he felt closest, did not feel close to him at all; he said they communicated very little and did not share their thoughts or feelings. Yet, Reginald, plagued by an inguinal hernia that distended his scrotum until it became as large as a fist, tagged after Malcolm. Though Malcolm often dismissed him impatiently, he enjoyed teaching him and acted as his protector.

Years later, when Malcolm became a public figure, he lauded his father, a "jackleg" (self-ordained) preacher who subsisted largely on the contributions he received for the "visitin' preachin'" that he did in various black churches. He had so many rules that it was hard for his children to remember them all. But according to people who knew him, he failed to observe them himself. In addition to being brutal to his wife and children, he was notoriously unfaithful to Louise—"a natural-born whoremonger," his friend Chester Jones called him. From childhood onward, Malcolm would have great difficulty trying to decide whether to follow the path of virtue his father preached or the path of vice he often practiced.

When he wasn't propagating religion or Garvey's teachings, Earl labored at construction sites. "He worked hard when he worked,'' says his former co-worker Ray Riddle. But he did it sporadically and gave little financial or emotional support to his family. He arose late, breakfasted on what little remained in the household larder, and spent his day pontificating and preaching in the homes of his avid listeners, who fed him while his wife and children went hungry. When church dignitaries visited his home, he plied them with freshly killed chicken and made his youngsters vie for the leavings. His inability or unwillingness to provide for his children did not deter him from siring more. His aim, his wife told Anna, was to fill his household with young vassals who would do his work for him while he lounged around with fellow Masons or Knights of Pythias. "I do everything around here," she told Anna. Some of Louise's friends helped out by bringing groceries. When Earl found out, he nearly exploded, insisting that he needed no charity and could care for his own.

Earl, who was constantly telling his children they should make something of themselves, had aspirations. "He wanted to be what he couldn't be," recalls Allie Cooper, who belonged to Lansing's tightly-knit black community. In an attempt to explain away his lack of achievement, he claimed he had owned a dress store that had gone bankrupt because its white customers had boycotted it when they discovered its proprietor was black. He could have been a politician, he asserted, were it not for the fact that religion and politics don't mix. (Malcolm would one day prove him wrong.) Earl's pretensions were as transparent as his excuses. He left home dressed in business garb. In one hand, he carried a briefcase. Rapidly, he strode up and down the streets of Lansing's West Side, where most of the city's blacks lived. He told people he was operating an employment agency for jobless blacks, but a number of clients who availed themselves of his services discovered, to their dismay, that he was as unsuccessful procuring employment for them as he was for himself. He was also unable to secure financing for his scheme. Nevertheless, he behaved as if he knew all there was to know about obtaining money. "Money's no problem," he declared.

In September 1929, three months after the Littles moved into their Lansing farmhouse, they were notified that the deed to the property contained a clause stipulating, "This land shall never be rented, leased, sold to, or occupied by . . . persons other than those of the Caucasian race." The owner of the adjacent lots, a land development company that apparently believed the Littles' presence was damaging its efforts to sell to white customers, persuaded James Nicoll, who had sold the farmhouse to the Littles, to collaborate in an effort to evict them. The ensuing lawsuit was all too successful. Judge Leland Carr didn't even give the Littles time to seek new lodgings. He ordered them to vacate "forthwith" and denied them reimbursement. The judge compounded the injustice by levying all the attorneys' fees and court costs against them, despite the absence of culpability on their part. Malcolm's father shook his fist at an unjust God and refused to relinquish his home. His lawyer bought time by posting an appeal bond and serving notice that he intended to appeal to the Supreme Court of Michigan. There was little chance of success; years would elapse before the United States Supreme Court declared racially restrictive land covenants unconstitutional.

Two weeks later, on November 7, Louise warned her children not to sleep upstairs. At about two-thirty in the morning, they were awakened by Earl's shouts. The house was on fire. The Dennises, who lived to the east, had already been awakened by someone who had pounded on their door. Then came an explosion that roused the whole neighborhood. Ernie Wolf, who lived a few yards south of the Littles, peered outside and saw flames leaping fifteen or twenty feet high from the rear of the Littles' home. He pulled on some clothes and rushed outside to find Malcolm's family shivering but safe. With the help of Burt Atkins, another white neighbor, Wolf tried to rescue some furniture from the front of the blazing house. "Let it burn," barked Earl. He warned the two men to stay out of the kitchen, where, it was later discovered, the fire had begun. Joe Nicholson, who ran a grocery stand down the road, telephoned the Lansing fire department, whose firefighters refused to come because the premises lay outside the city limits. (According to Malcolm's version of what happened, the white firemen "came and stood around watching as the house burned down to the ground.") When the state police arrived, they discovered that during the

fire Malcolm's father had handed Nicholson a pistol. Earl, who
had no permit for the gun, denied it was the one that he had
fired at the white men who, he said, had started the fire. He
maintained that he had used his shotgun. But the police were
skeptical. They were equally skeptical about his assertion that
whites had set the fire. There was no need to burn down the
house to get the Littles to leave; it was common knowledge
that Judge Carr had already ordered them to vacate.

Partly because of the inconsistencies between Earl's testimony and that of his wife and Wilfred, the police jailed him
on suspicion of arson and for illegal possession of a revolver.

Subsequent examination of the charred ruins disclosed the
presence of a two-gallon oil can. Hours before the fire, Earl
had used it to buy kerosene. Louise later testified that she had
poured some of the fuel into the kitchen stove and had placed
the partly empty can behind the kitchen door. But the fire marshal found the can in the basement, beneath a set of bedsprings.
It could not have fallen there during the fire, for there was no
cellar beneath the kitchen, which had been added to the back
of the farmhouse after it was built.

Had someone inside the house moved the can to the basement
just before the fire and placed it beneath the bedsprings? Had
the same person stolen outside, knocked on the Dennises' door
to make it sound as if strangers were about, run back, and
ignited the fuel? Investigators suspected that the answer was
yes and that the person was Earl Little. But they were apparently baffled by the question of motive.*

Earl's interrogation by the police suggested a possible motive.
In the midst of his denial that he had slipped Nicholson his
revolver the night of the fire, he apparently confused him with
Nicoll, the man who had sold him the farmhouse and then
double-crossed him. Were the eviction and the fire linked? Betty
Walker, whose family sheltered the Littles immediately after
the fire, thinks they were; Earl seemed to feel that if he couldn't
have the house that was rightfully his, neither could Nicoll and
his white cohorts. Perhaps he also felt that people would be

---

*It is unclear if Earl's two fire insurance policies were still in force.

more willing to assist him financially if they thought he had been burned out rather than kicked out.

But such motives were hard to prove. After several months, the county prosecutor dismissed the arson charge.

Earl apparently quit the construction job he had held when the court handed down the eviction ruling. If he obtained another steady job, no evidence has been found to confirm it. The havoc wrought by the 1929 stock market crash soon made it nearly impossible for anyone to find employment, particularly unskilled blacks. Nevertheless, Earl managed to survive, largely on contributions from individuals and church groups whom he apparently persuaded to accept his version of the fire. The donations enabled him to move his family to what is now East Lansing, where the Littles were stoned by white neighbors. They relocated in another all-white neighborhood on Lancing's southern outskirts.

The six-acre plot of farmland they bought enabled them to raise chickens and rabbits and grow most of their own food. There are disputed reports that the Littles also received public assistance during this period. Some Lansing blacks gossiped about rumors that Malcolm's father feigned accidents in order to collect insurance. He did seem accident-prone. He was forever mashing his fingers with a hammer. On one occasion, the hammer sideswiped a nail that flew into his eye, which had to be removed. Another time, his automobile, filled with children, skidded into a ditch and overturned; miraculously, no one was seriously hurt.

Self-destructive violence seemed to abound in Earl's family. His brother Herbert committed suicide. Another brother, Oscar, was shot to death by the Pittsburgh police for wounding a white policeman who had attempted to arrest him for allegedly threatening some people with a pistol. John, the third of Earl's six brothers (two of whom had died when they were very young), was shotgunned to death as a result of a quarrel with another African-American. James, the moonshiner, was shot by a black woman whom he had assaulted. He lived to tell the tale and run afoul of the law another day.

*   *   *

Ill fortune continued to plague Earl and Louise Little. The widow who had sold them the six acres had concealed the fact that the northern three acres were encumbered by a tax lien. Malcolm's family found itself embroiled in litigation again. For the second time in eight months, they had to forfeit land they had purchased in the best of faith.

In 1931, Wesley, Louise's seventh child (Earl's tenth), was born. During the same year, Malcolm began kindergarten at Pleasant Grove Elementary School. His teacher, Olive Hicks, was well liked by the Little family, even though she later acknowledged she was somewhat afraid of blacks.

One day late in September, Malcolm returned home from school to find his parents embroiled in one of their habitual arguments. His father was determined to make a feast of one of the rabbits they raised and sold for cash. But Louise objected, not only because they needed the money, but also because she opposed eating rabbit on religious grounds. Enraged, Earl snatched a rabbit from its pen, tore off its head with his bare hands, threw the bleeding carcass at Louise's feet, and stormed out of the house. Suddenly, Malcolm's mother had a premonition that her husband was going to die. Clutching her apron, she ran after him, pleading almost hysterically for him to return. "Early! Early!" she cried. "If you go, you won't come back!" As the day wore on, Malcolm watched her become increasingly distraught, even though hours before she had confided to Anna Stohrer that she was fed up with Earl and on the verge of leaving him.

Bedtime approached without any sign of Earl. Frantically, Malcolm's mother clutched her children. Several miles away, in the no-man's-land separating Lansing from East Lansing, Malcolm's father boarded an interurban trolley. He reached for his changepurse but couldn't find it. At the next stop, he left the vehicle, perhaps to look for the purse. About twelve minutes later, another streetcar came by. There were no streetlamps and the driver failed to see him in the gloom. Minutes later, Earl was discovered lying beside the tracks. His left arm was crushed and blood gushed from his partly severed left leg, which looked as if it had been hacked open by a meat cleaver. The state police were summoned and found him still conscious. He told Trooper Laurence Baril that he had returned to the car stop just as the trolley was passing by and had tried to board the moving vehicle. But he had missed the step and had fallen under the rear wheels.

Shortly thereafter, six-year-old Malcolm awoke to the sound of his mother's screams. Officer Baril and another patrolman were in the living room, trying to calm her. They took her to the emergency room of Sparrow Hospital, where doctors were unable to save her husband. Malcolm, who knew only what he was later told about his father's death, wasn't sure what to believe about its cause. From what he and other members of the family said, his friends got the feeling that Earl's death had been accidental. But as Malcolm grew older, he began leaning towards his mother's theory that her husband had been done in by whites. Malcolm's autobiography gives the impression that his father was assassinated for political reasons by white assailants who bashed in his skull and laid him across the trolley tracks. But Trooper Baril recalls that Earl's skull was not crushed. "If it had been," he says, "Mr. Little would not have been able to explain how his injury had occurred."

Years after the streetcar ran over Earl, Malcolm would contend that his father had been killed by the hooded, black-robed members of a white hate-group called the Black Legion. But the records of the Lansing police and the Michigan state police, as well as newspaper accounts and the recollections of several of Mr. Little's black contemporaries, leave considerable doubt about whether the Legion ever operated in the Lansing area.

Some Lansingites wondered whether Earl had attempted to board the moving streetcar because some irate husband was after him. One insurance company even insisted that his death was a suicide. But the state police report, the coroner's report, and the death certificate indicate that his death was accidental.

What struck Malcolm most about his father's funeral was that it wasn't held in a church. Was this because of his unsavory reputation? Louise did her best to hide the truth from her children. "Don't tell anyone what I said about my husband," she admonished Anna Stohrer. "He was a good man." She minimized his failure to keep their bills and life insurance premiums paid up. (Some of the unpaid bills dated back a year or two, despite his admonitions about buying on credit.) Louise went into mourning and portrayed her husband as gallantly as she did her unknown father. As her children watched, Earl received in death the encomiums he had never earned in life.

The black community, many of whose members did not lament Earl Little's death, nevertheless contributed generously to his widow and orphaned children. So did the school PTA. Anna Stohrer, who had "loaned" money to Louise before, paid the overdue premium for one of Earl's two life insurance policies. It had not been cancelled because the insurance agent had advanced the sum out of his own pocket.

Not long after the funeral, Anna went to her front door and found Louise standing there with a raincoat draped over her arm, her eyes smoldering with rage. At first, Louise declined when Anna offered her a chair. Finally, hesitantly, she accepted it. Then, from beneath the coat, she withdrew a butcher knife. She began toying with it, alternately balancing the point of the blade and the tip of the handle on her knee. Suddenly, she rose and pointed the knife at Anna, who instinctively shielded herself with a chair. Just then, Anna's husband returned home through the back door. without a word, Louise hid the weapon under the coat and hurried out the front door.

When Louise was questioned about her bizarre conduct, she sought to justify it by alleging that whites had murdered Earl. This, she said, impelled her to take a white life. Her insistence that her husband had been a victim of political assassination provided her children with a father-image of which they could at last be proud. Her eagerness to blame others for Earl's death may also have been due to her premonition that her husband was about to die—a premonition that may have been a disguised wish.

Malcolm's autobiography suggests that he shared his mother's premonition. Perhaps he, too, had a guilty conscience. If so, could he relieve it by projecting his angry feelings onto imaginary assassins? His feeling that Earl had been a political martyr enabled him to portray his father as a good man. Occasionally, he buttressed the myth by asserting that Earl had been a policeman—a man who enforced, rather than broke, the law. Years later, after Malcolm Little became Malcolm X, political considerations would reinforce his tendency to idealize his father and portray him as a hero.

But in 1931, when Malcolm was six, he would not talk about his father's death. Tyrannical as Earl Little had been, his absence, according to Reginald, left the children unprotected and afraid, without a strong, reassuring hand to take command. Malcolm refused to eat. When his mother asked him why, he replied that those who try to eat disappear and never return. He also had difficulty sleeping. "Only dead people stretch out," he declared.

Boyhood Fears

Darkness terrified Malcolm; at night, he tried to wiggle beneath the slumbering brothers who shared his bed. Daytime, too, had its perils. There was the constant threat of fistfights, which he usually avoided. Even his mother, whose beatings may have contributed to his fear of physical injury, sensed his fear of combat, which caused other youngsters to claim that he was a coward. They said he was "afraid to bleed."

But fights were sometimes unavoidable. When they occurred, Malcolm defended himself as best as he could. If a stick or bottle happened to be handy, he'd use it. Otherwise, he'd try to scare his adversary with bluster, a technique he perfected as he grew older. Occasionally, he threatened boys he disliked through intermediaries, but the confrontations never materialized unless the recipient of the threat was weaker or smaller, or unless the odds were two-to-one in Malcolm's favor. (Reginald sometimes helped him out.)

Yet even during his boyhood, there was a brave, humane side to Malcolm, who defended underdogs better than he defended himself. When neighborhood bullies forced a partly disabled youngster off his bike and into a ditch, Malcolm sprang to the rescue. And he came more than once to the defense of a pint-sized classmate named John Breathour, who was no match for his larger opponents. Philbert, in turn, defended Malcolm against bigger adversaries, despite his deep-rooted differences with his brother. When Malcolm and Al Hildebridle, a tough kid who towered over the other boys, needled each other, it was Philbert who prevented the confrontations from turning violent.

But Philbert was not invincible. During a ball game, a boy named Tom Simmon took him to task for being too rough with the younger participants. The matter was settled, according to custom, atop a spur of railroad track that lay just north of the school. To everyone's surprise, Tom landed the first blow and sent Philbert tumbling down the far side of the railroad embankment. Struggling to his feet, Philbert crawled hand over hand back up the steep, rocky slope, only to be sent sprawling once more. In a flash, Malcolm was on Tom's back, despite the fact that he was older and heavier.

Some white boys picked on Malcolm for racial reasons. Others, like husky, blue-eyed Ores Whitney, defended him. Ores's family was almost as poor as Malcolm's. Nevertheless, he shared his sandwiches with Malcolm at school. A loner, Ores rarely said much to the other children. He'd stand, smile impishly, and watch them play, but he wouldn't take part. Malcolm and Ores, whose middle name was Malcolm, were considered best friends by virtually everyone who knew them. Yet they constantly bickered. No one could figure out how they could squabble so much and still like each other.

Not all the racial confrontations were initiated by whites. On one occasion, Malcolm and Reginald were threatened by blacks who tried to prevent them from passing through West Side turf in the company of white boys. One of the whites was a short, freckle-faced redhead named Bob Bebee. Malcolm, swallowing his fear, successfully stood up for himself and the others. He did it verbally; not a single blow was exchanged.

Some whites ribbed Malcolm about his skin color, calling him "Chinaman," "Snowflake," or "Eskimo." He didn't seem to mind; he just grinned. At home, however, he lamented, "They don't even know my name at school." A white friend of his named Jean———— felt that he hated his in-between skin color and wished that he could clearly identify with one race or the other. When blacks visited his home and found him frolicking with Jean, he contemptuously dismissed her as white trash and sent her away. She did not take offense because she knew he was grandstanding for his guests and would be back on good terms with her the following day.

But Malcolm turned on her again. At school one day, he learned that Jackie Alexa, whose family owned the dairy farm just south of the Littles' property, was out to get Jean. He advised Jean to avoid Jackie by using the dirt track he customarily took home from school. Then he told Jackie what he had told Jean. The result was predictable. On another occasion he chidid Jean and Geraldine Grill, another neighbor, for being cowards until they donned boxing gloves and began swinging away at each other. Like a spectator at a boxing match, he seemed to enjoy such brawls. He sided with whoever won them.

Another white girl whom Malcolm spent time with was Betty Jean Thiel. Betty was a tomboy who despised dresses and openly admitted she wanted to be a boy. The ideal present, she felt, would be a pair of blue denims with shoulder straps and copper rivets at the stress points. Like Malcolm, she had a gap between her two upper front teeth. It seemed so wide she feared it never would close.

Betty lived across the road from the Littles, a hundred yards or so to the north. She was considered "rich" because she brought her lunch to school in an empty honey can instead of wrapped in newspaper. She had more than one pair of shoes and were snow-white stockings. Most of the other white girls wore tan ones. The poorest girls wore black.

Malcolm and Betty roamed the neighborhood together. They climbed the Norway maples that commanded the Eaton Rapids road below. From a tree near the road, they sometimes suspended a tattered purse on a string. A passing motorist would spy it, emerge from his car, and bend down to snatch the prize, only to discover it eluding his grasp, as if it had life of its own. Sometimes, Malcolm and Betty "cooned" watermelon, splitting it open upon a rock and scooping out handfuls of the succulent pulp. But even on these occasions, Betty sensed, as others did, that he was not really happy. He laughed at inappropriate times—when he was taken to a surgeon to have a boil lanced, for instance.

Betty liked Malcolm and didn't hide her fondness for him. She admired his physical prowess. He could run faster than she could. He could throw stones farther and leap across the creek that bisected a corner of his yard. Frequently, he had to "rescue" her from its challenging waters. Though he never openly acknowledged that he reciprocated her affection, Malcolm appeared to like Betty—perhaps because she afforded him the unqualified approval his mother denied him. He seemed to enjoy pretending he was Betty's mate when they "played house" on the sturdy limbs of the tall maples. (There were no prescribed criteria as to who was male and who was female. They swapped roles whenever they chose.)

With Malcolm's tacit permission, Betty followed him around. She walked, not beside him, but behind him. "We didn't talk much," she later recalled. "But we must have communicated in some sort of way." Malcolm strode ahead, as if he had no need for his devoted pursuer. Now and then, he concealed himself in the chest-high brome grass, crouching like a jungle cat stalking unwary prey. As his diminutive victim passed his lair, he'd spring. Then the two would start out again, Betty trailing at a respectful distance. Years later, his political followers accorded him similar respect.

Hunger

Lansing, which had been an alternate way-station on the Underground Railroad, boasted fewer than 17,000 inhabitants at the turn of the century, and not a single paved street. But by the time the Littles moved there in 1929, it had become a thriving automotive manufacturing center. It was the proud home of the Merry Oldsmobile, the first gasoline-powered car produced in quantity in America.

During the Depression, however, automotive production plummeted to less than a quarter of what it had been. As a result, the city's residents suffered acutely. By 1933, the industrial unemployment rate for Michigan as a whole was nearly 50%. In Detroit, where the failure of two enormous banks had precipitated a state bank "holiday" (Franklin Delano Roosevelt would soon introduce a nationwide one), little children vied with each other outside one slaughterhouse to catch the discarded cattle lungs that compassionate meatpackers flung outside. A family of four on relief had to exist on sixty cents a week, plus whatever free food was available at the soup kitchens that were located at the city's fire stations. Near Lansing, in the town of Charlotte, men who were fortunate enough to find factory jobs were paid twenty-five cents per hour. Women got fifteen cents. Blacks, many of whom had migrated to Lansing because of the employment opportunities created by the

First World War and its prosperous aftermath, often received only half the wages of their white counterparts. Like everyone else, Malcolm's mother scrambled for whatever employment she could find. Her oldest daughter Hilda looked after the children. Eventually, Louise found part-time work as a seamstress. She also worked as a domestic. But as soon as her employers, who had assumed she was white, discovered she was half-black, they fired her. Malcolm never forgot how she came home crying, trying to hide her tears.

Under such conditions, it was difficult for Louise to adequately clothe her brood. In winter, Malcolm wore nothing more than a loosely knit sweater or an insubstantial jacket. The sweater, like his shirts and trousers, looked like a hand-me-down that he was not quite big enough to wear. He stood around shivering, with his gloveless hands clasped in front of him. Yet when he was offered a scarf by his friend Howard Cramer's mother, he declined it. "I'll be all right," he told her.

In summertime, when school wasn't in session, Malcolm went barefoot, for shoes were scarce. The rest of the year, he wore beat-up sneakers; snowshoes or rubber boots were out of the question, and his feet suffered constantly from the Michigan cold. Although many of the white children were just as hard up, some of them chided him about the patches in his "Raggedy Ann" clothes. Some of the blacks who were better off contemptuously called the Littles "farmers." No one, however, could poke fun at them for having dirty clothes. Louise made sure her children were among the cleanest in the neighborhood.

The house the Littles lived in, a small four-room cottage, was in no better shape than their clothing. There was no running water or indoor toilet. Furniture was sparse and the floors were rugless. A single bare lightbulb hung from the ceiling of each room. The uninsulated tar-paper shingle exterior presented virtually no barrier at all to the cold.

Even more difficult to endure than the cold was the hunger, which intensified as the Depression deepened. Every few days, Malcolm and Reginald walked two miles to the Peter Pan bakery. The stale surplus bread they purchased there kept them alive. Whenever possible, Malcolm's overworked mother made it into breadburgers or bread pudding. But at times, they had no bread at all; Louise and her children had to subsist on dandelion greens.

During lunchtime at school, Malcolm sat by himself in a cafeteria corner, furtively pushing two pieces of sandwich bread into his mouth. Between them lay a grayish ooze resembling cat food. Sometimes, there was nothing between the slices but the wild leeks Malcolm gathered on the way to school. One day, a girl who sat beside him in class burst into tears because of the odor. So instructions were given for leek sandwiches to be confiscated and burned.

Some of Malcolm's schoolmates, all of whom were white, tried their best to help out. One hoodwinked her mother into believing she needed more food and passed the extra along to him. Another girl shared her oranges and apples with him. Malcolm repaid her with nickel candy bars that he bought with money he earned delivering newspapers. Two other girls who lived in the neighborhood invited Malcolm and Philbert into their home to share grapefruit. The boys reluctantly turned the offer down; their mother had given strict orders not to "embarrass" whites by eating at their tables.

It was degrading to have to accept handouts. In the school cafeteria, Malcolm would let the food offerings sit, as if he didn't want them. But when he did let himself eat, he wolfed the food down with both hands. Being a beggar was particularly humiliating at Christmas time, when each pupil contributed a small gift that was placed in a kitty and distributed by lot. Malcolm was unable to contribute. The other children insisted that he receive a present anyway, but when the gifts were handed out, he had to be urged to accept his. He unwrapped it ever so slowly, looking grateful yet ashamed. His attitude toward Christmas was decidedly negative. Years later, he told a friend that children should not be told Santa Claus exists.

Malcolm's reluctance to accept charity echoed his parents' reluctance. Like many people, his mother was apparently ashamed of her poverty and loath to acknowledge it. When friends or social workers asked if they could get her anything, her response was usually negative. She did, however, accept offers to repair and improve the house. But she insisted on giving what little she could in return—a freshly baked pie, if nothing else. And as badly as she and her children needed other peoples' castoff clothes, she gave them back if they had missing buttons. She proudly maintained that the meager public assistance she received was a loan, not a gift.

The charity issue was further aggravated by provincial relief workers who appeared to resent Louise's precise, impeccable English, which frequently put theirs to shame. One would-be benefactor gave her old, stale fig newtons containing worm holes; Malcolm fed them to the chickens. The county's "poor commissioner" was particularly disrespectful to Malcolm's mother, who was not the only welfare recipient he forced to grovel for assistance. But even the compassionate, well-meaning social workers became exasperated by Louise's insistence that money be spent on her broken-down car instead of on necessities. Her kitchen stove, for example, was in dangerous disrepair. A flat-topped, coal- and wood-burning affair, it had two doors—one for fuel, the other for ash-removal. The latter door was partly unhinged, and live coals could have easily fallen out and caused a fire.

The authorities offered to increase Louise's allotment if she would spend the extra funds to fix the stove. No one, however, could tell Louise Little how to run her home. "As long as my back and arms are strong enough," she replied, "I will drive that automobile." The vehicle—a real status symbol in those days—clearly meant a great deal to her, and Philbert labored valiantly to keep it running. The nearest bus stop was about three quarters of a mile away and the busses ran infrequently.

Louise's children could not understand their mother's reluctance to accept the free food the State of Michigan provided. She even refused a large quantity of pork that her next-door neighbor offered, for the church she had recently joined—an offshoot of the Seventh Day Adventist Church called the Seventh Day Church of God—did not permit its members to eat pork. As the economic crunch grew more severe and it became increasingly difficult to cope, she turned more and more to her Job-like religion of self-denial, which gave dignity and meaning to her privation. It was a religion that stressed fasting and cleanliness of mind and body. It discouraged "worldly" pleasures such as movie-going and dancing. In addition, it demanded total abstinence from tobacco, liquor, narcotic drugs, gambling, and, of course, extra-marital sex.

Outwardly, Malcolm did not blame his mother for being proud at her children's expense. He insisted he loved her. But his growing rebellion against her authority suggested otherwise. He ignored her demands for punctuality and became increasingly reluctant to perform his household chores. The part of the vegetable garden that he had once attended so diligently became weedy and unfit for cultivation. The older children tried in vain to get him to mend his ways. But he was not yet ready to assume the responsibility that had been prematurely forced on him by his father's death.

The economic and emotional pressure upon Louise, who had never fully recovered from her husband's death, kept intensifying. Her magnificent ebony hair began to gray. Her face grew expressionless. Neighbors and callers found her unapproachable. Her interest in her children ebbed. She devoted less and less time to them, and her ability to wield authority diminished. The county welfare authorities partly filled the vacuum; as a result, the children were unsure whom to obey. It was the same disconcerting, rudderless feeling they had experienced when their father had died.

Malcolm reacted to his mother's withdrawal by withdrawing himself. He began to steal, not only from his mother's purse but also from grocery stores. He freely acknowledged the latter offense yet concealed the former one. His stealing elicited maternal punishment. But the punishment failed to deter him, perhaps because the attention his thefts provoked was what he craved. Though he had grown big enough to think about resisting the beatings his mother gave him, he never once raised a hand against her. He was very proud of his self-restraint.

Crime and punishment would have additional implications. Every time Malcolm's mother whipped him, he yelled so loudly that the neighbors heard his cries, which, together with his stealing, provided the authorities with ammunition for their accusations that Louise was unfit to raise her children.

Throughout his teens Malcolm Little—or "Big Red" as he came to be known on the streets (for the color of his hair)—mixed odd jobs with petty crime in Detroit, Boston, New Haven, and New York until he was sentenced for larceny in 1946, at the age of nineteen, to an eight-year prison term in Massachusetts. In the Concord Reformatory, where he served part of his term, Malcolm was converted by an inmate to the Nation of Islam and introduced to the teachings of its leader, the Honorable Elijah Muhammad.

In the following excerpt from his autobiography Malcolm talks about the effects of that conversion and recounts how time passed for him in the Massachusetts state prison system.

from *The Autobiography of Malcolm X*
as told to Alex Haley
"Saved"

I did write to Elijah Muhammad. He lived in Chicago at that time, at 6116 South Michigan Avenue. At least twenty-five times I must have written that first one-page letter to him, over and over. I was trying to make it both legible and understandable. I practically couldn't read my handwriting myself; it shames even to remember it. My spelling and my grammar were as bad, if not worse. Anyway, as well as I could express it, I said I had been told about him by my brothers and sisters, and I apologized for my poor letter.

Mr. Muhammad sent me a typed reply. It had an all but electrical effect upon me to see the signature of the "Messenger of Allah." After he welcomed me into the "true knowledge," he gave me something to think about. The black prisoner, he said, symbolized white society's crime of keeping black men oppressed and deprived and ignorant, and unable to get decent jobs, turning them into criminals.

He told me to have courage. He even enclosed some money for me, a five-dollar bill. Mr. Muhammad sends money all over the country to prison inmates who write to him, probably to this day.

Regularly my family wrote to me, "Turn to Allah . . . pray to the east."

The hardest test I ever faced in my life was praying. You

understand. My comprehending, my believing the teachings of Mr. Muhammad had only required my mind's saying to me, "That's right!" or "I never thought of that."

But bending my knees to pray—that *act*—well, that took me a week.

You know what my life had been. Picking a lock to rob someone's house was the only way my knees had ever been bent before.

I had to force myself to bend my knees. And waves of shame and embarrassment would force me back up.

For evil to bend its knees, admitting its guilt, to implore the forgiveness of God, is the hardest thing in the world. It's easy for me to see and to say that now. But then, when I was the personificaiton of evil, I was going through it. Again, again, I would force myself back down into the praying-to-Allah posture. When finally I was able to make myself stay down—I didn't know what to say to Allah.

For the next years, I was the nearest thing to a hermit in the Norfolk Prison Colony. I never have been more busy in my life. I still marvel at how swiftly my previous life's thinking pattern slid away from me, like snow off a roof. It is as though someone else I knew of had lived by hustling and crime. I would be startled to catch myself thinking in a remote way of my earlier self as another person.

The things I felt, I was pitifully unable to express in the one-page letter that went every day to Mr. Elijah Muhammad. And I wrote at least one more daily letter, replying to one of my brothers and sisters. Every letter I received from them added something to my knowledge of the teachings of Mr. Muhammad. I would sit for long periods and study his photographs.

I've never been one for inaction. Everything I've ever felt strongly about, I've done something about. I guess that's why, unable to do anything else, I soon began writing to people I had known in the hustling world, such as Sammy the Pimp, John Hughes, the gambling house owner, the thief Jumpsteady, and several dope peddlers. I wrote them all about Allah and Islam and Mr. Elijah Muhammad. I had no idea where most of them lived. I addressed their letters in care of the Harlem or Roxbury bars and clubs where I'd known them.

I never got a single reply. The average hustler and criminal was too uneducated to write a letter. I have known many slick, sharp-looking hustlers, who would have you think they had an interest in Wall Street; privately, they would get someone else to read a letter if they received one. Besides, neither would I have replied to anyone writing me something as wild as "the white man is the devil."

What certainly went on the harlem and Roxbury wires was that Detroit Red was going crazy in stir, or else he was trying some hype to shake up the warden's office.

During the years that I stayed in the Norfolk Prison Colony, never did any official directly say anything to me about those letters, although, of course, they all passed through the prison censorship. I'm sure, however, they monitored what I wrote to add to the files which every state and federal prison keeps on the conversion of Negro inmates by the teachings of Mr. Elijah Muhammad.

But at that time, I felt that the real reason was that the white man knew that he was the devil.

Later on, I even wrote to the Mayor of Boston, to the Governor of Massachusetts, and to Harry S. Truman. They never answered; they probably never even saw my letters. I handscratched to them how the white man's society was responsible for the black man's condition in this wilderness of North America.

It was because of my letters that I happened to stumble upon starting to acquire some kind of a homemade education.

I became increasingly frustrated at not being able to express what I wanted to convey in letters that I wrote, especially those to. Mr. Elijah Muhammad. In the street, I had been the most articulate hustler out there—I had commanded attention when I said something. But now, trying to write simple English, I not only wasn't articulate, I wasn't even functional. How would I sound writing in slang, the way I would *say* it, something such as, "Look, daddy, let me pull your coat about a cat, Elijah Muhammad—"

Many who today hear me somewhere in person, or on television, or those who read something I've said, will think I went to school far beyond the eighth grade. This impression is due entirely to my prison studies.

It had really begun back in the Charlestown Prison, when Bimbi first made me feel envy of his stock of knowledge. Bimbi had always taken charge of any conversation he was in, and I had tried to emulate him. But every book I picked up had few sentences which didn't contain anywhere from one to nearly all of the words that might as well have been in Chinese. When I just skipped those words, of course, I really ended up with little idea of what the book said. So I had come to the Norfolk Prison Colony still going through only book-reading motions. Pretty soon, I would have quit even these motions, unless I had received the motivation that I did.

I saw that the best thing I could do was get hold of a dictionary—to study, to learn some words. I was lucky enough to reason also that I should try to improve my penmanship. It was sad. I couldn't even write in a straight line. It was both ideas together that moved me to request a dictionary along with some tablets and pencils from the Norfolk Prison Colony school.

I spent two days just riffling uncertainly through the dictionary's pages. I'd never realized so many words existed! I didn't know which words I needed to learn. Finally, just to start some kind of action, I began copying.

In my slow, painstaking, ragged handwriting, I copied into my tablet everything printed on that first page, down to the punctuation marks.

I believe it took me a day. Then, aloud, I read back, to myself, everything I'd written on the tablet. Over and over, aloud, to myself, I read my own handwriting.

I woke up the next morning, thinking about those words—immensely proud to realize that not only had I written so much at one time, but I'd written words that I never knew were in the world. Moreover, with a little effort, I also could remember what many of these words meant. I reviewed the words whose meanings I didn't remember. Funny thing, from the dictionary first page right now, that ''aardvark'' springs to my mind. The dictionary had a picture of it, a long-tailed, long-eared, bur-rowing African mammal, which lives off termites caught by sticking out its tongue as an anteater does for ants.

I was so fascinated that I went on—I copied the dictionary's next page. And the same experience came when I studied that. With every succeeding page, I also learned of people and places and events from history. Actually the dictionary is like a minia-ture encyclopedia. Finally the dictionary's A section had filled a whole tablet—and I went on into the B's. That was the way I started copying what eventually became the entire dictionary. It went a lot faster after so much practice helped me to pick up handwriting speed. Between what I wrote in my tablet, and writing letters, during the rest of my time in prison I would guess I wrote a million words.

I suppose it was inevitable that as my word-base broadened, I could for the first time pick up a book and read and now begin to understand what the book was saying. Anyone who has read a great deal can imagine the new world that opened. Let me tell you something: from then until I left that prison, in every free moment I had, if I was not reading in the library, I was reading on my bunk. You couldn't have gotten me out of books with a wedge. Between Mr. Muhammad's teachings, my correspondence, my visitors—usually Ella and Reginald—and my reading of books, months passed without my even thinking about being imprisoned. In fact, up to then, I never had been so truly free in my life.

The Norfolk Prison Colony's library was in the school build-ing. A variety of classes was taught there by instructors who came from such places as Harvard and Boston universities. The weekly debates between inmate teams were also held in the school building. You would be astonished to know how worked up convict debaters and audiences would get over subjects like "Should Babies Be Fed Milk?"

Available on the prison library's shelves were books on just about every general subject. Much of the big private collection that Parkhurst had willed to the prison was still in crates and boxes in the back of the library—thousands of old books. Some of them looked ancient: covers faded, old-time parchment-looking binding. Parkhurst, I've mentioned, seemed to have been principally interested in history and religion. He had the money and the special interest to have a lot of books that you wouldn't have in general circulation. Any college library would have been lucky to get that collection.

As you can imagine, especially in a prison where there was heavy emphasis on rehabilitation, an inmate was smiled upon if he demonstrated an unusually intense interest in books. There was a sizable number of well-read inmates, especially the popular debaters. Some were said by many to be practically walking encyclopedias. They were almost celebrities. No university would ask any student to devour literature as I did when this new world opened to me, of being able to read and *understand*.

I read more in my room than in the library itself. An inmate who was known to read a lot could check out more than the permitted maximum number of books. I preferred reading in the total isolation of my own room.

When I had progressed to really serious reading, every night at about ten P.M. I would be outraged with the "lights out." It always seemed to catch me right in the middle of something engrossing.

Fortunately, right outside my door was a corridor light that cast a glow into my room. The glow was enough to read by, once my eyes adjusted to it. So when "lights out" came, I would sit on the floor where I could continue reading in that glow.

At one-hour intervals the night guards paced past every room. Each time I heard the approaching footsteps, I jumped into bed and feigned sleep. And as soon as the guard passed, I got back out of bed onto the floor area of that light-glow, where I would read for another fifty-eight minutes—until the guard approached again. That went on until three or four every morning. Three or four hours of sleep a night was enough for me. Often in the years in the streets I had slept less than that.

The teachings of Mr. Muhammad stressed how history had been "whitened"—when white men had written history books, the black man simply had been left out. Mr. Muhammad couldn't have said anything that would have struck me much harder. I had never forgotten how when my class, me and all of those whites, had studied seventh-grade United States history back in Mason, the history of the Negro had been covered in one paragraph, and the teacher had gotten a big laugh with his joke, "Negroes' feet are so big that when they walk, they leave a hole in the ground."

This is one reason why Mr. Muhammad's teachings spread so swiftly all over the United States, among *all* Negroes, whether or not they became followers of Mr. Muhammad. The teachings ring true—to every Negro. You can hardly show me a black adult in America—or a white one, for that matter—who knows from the history books anything like the truth about the black man's role. In my own case, once I heard of the "glorious history of the black man," I took special pains to hunt in the library for books that would inform me on details about black history.

I can remember accurately the very first set of books that really impressed me. I have since bought that set of books and have it at home for my children to read as they grow up. It's called *Wonders of the World*. It's full of pictures of archeological finds, statues that depict, usually, non-European people.

I found books like Will Durant's *Story of Civilization*. I read H. G. Wells' *Outline of History*. *Souls of Black Folk* by W. E. B. Du Bois gave me a glimpse into the black people's history before they came to this country. Carter G. Woodson's *Negro History* opened my eyes about black empires before the black slave was brought to the United States, and the early Negro struggles for freedom.

J. A. Rogers' three volumes of *Sex and Race* told about race-mixing before Christ's time; about Aesop being a black man who told fables; about Egypt's Pharaohs; about the great Coptic Christian Empires; about Ethiopia, the earth's oldest continuous black civilization, as China is the oldest continuous civilization.

Mr. Muhammad's teaching about how the white man had been created led me to *Findings In Genetics* by Gregor Mendel. (The dictionary's G section was where I had learned what "genetics" meant.) I really studied this book by the Austrian monk.

Reading it over and over, especially certain sections, helped me to understand that if you started with a black man, a white man could be produced; but starting with a white man, you never could produce a black man—because the white chromosome is recessive. And since no one disputes that there was but one Original Man, the conclusion is clear.

During the last year or so, in the *New York Times*, Arnold Toynbee used the word "bleached" in describing the white man. (His words were: "White (i.e. bleached) human beings of North European origin. . . .") Toynbee also referred to the European geographic area as only a peninsula of Asia. He said there is no such thing as Europe. And if you look at the globe, you will see for yourself that America is only an extension of Asia. (But at the same time Toynbee is among those who have helped to bleach history. He has written that Africa was the only continent that produced no history. He won't write that again. Every day now, the truth is coming to light.)

I never will forget how shocked I was when I began reading about slavery's total horror. It made such an impact upon me that it later became one of my favorite subjects when I became a minister of Mr. Muhammad's. The world's most monsterous crime, the sin and the blood on the white man's hands, are almost impossible to believe. Books like the one by Frederick Olmstead opened my eyes to the horrors suffered when the slave was landed in the United States. The European woman, Fannie Kimball, who had married a Southern white slaveowner, described how human beings were degraded. Of course I read *Uncle Tom's Cabin*. In fact, I believe that's the only novel I have ever read since I started serious reading.

Parkhurst's collection also contained some bound pamphlets of the Abolitionist Anti-Slavery Society of New England. I read descriptions of atrocities, saw those illustrations of black slave women tied up and flogged with whips; of black mothers watching their babies being dragged off, never to be seen by their mothers again; of dogs after slaves, and of the fugitive slave catchers, evil white men with whips and clubs and chains and guns. I read about the slave preacher Nat Turner, who put the fear of God into the white slavemaster. Nat Turner wasn't going around preaching pie-in-the-sky and "non-violent" freedom for the black man. There in Virginia one night in 1831, Nat and seven other slaves started out at his master's home and through the night they went from one plantation "big house" to the next, killing, until by the next morning 57 white people were dead and Nat had about 70 slaves following him. White people, terrified for their lives, fled from their homes, locked themselves up in public buildings, hid in the woods, and some even left the state. A small army of soldiers took two months to catch and hang Nat Turner. Somewhere I have read where Nat Turner's example is said to have inspired John Brown to invade Virginia and attack Harper's Ferry nearly thirty years later, with thirteen white men and five Negroes.

I read Herodotus, "the father of History," or, rather, I read about him. And I read the histories of various nations, which opened my eyes gradually, then wider and wider, to how the whole world's white men had indeed acted like devils, pillaging and raping and bleeding and draining the whole world's non-white people. I remember, for instance, books such as Will Durant's story of Oriental civilization, and Mahatma Gandhi's accounts of the struggle to drive the British out of India.

Book after book showed me how the white man had brought upon the world's black, brown, red, and yellow peoples every variety of the sufferings of exploitation. I saw how since the sixteenth century, the so-called "Christian trader" white man began to ply the seas in his lust for Asian and African empires, and plunder, and power. I read, I saw, how the white man never has gone among the non-white peoples bearing the Cross in the true manner and spirit of Christ's teachings—meek, humble, and Christ-like.

I perceived, as I read, how the collective white man had been actually nothing but a piratical opportunist who used Faustian machinations to make his own Christianity his initial wedge in criminal conquests. First, always "religiously," he branded "heathen" and "pagan" labels upon ancient non-white cultures and civilizations. The stage thus set, he then turned upon his non-white victims his weapons of war.

I read how, entering India—half a *billion* deeply religious brown people—the British white man, by 1759, through promises, trickery and manipulations, controlled much of India through Great Britain's East India Company. The parasitical British administration kept tentacling out to half of the subcontinent. In 1857, some of the desperate people of India finally mutinied—and, excepting the African slave trade, nowhere has history recorded any more unnecessary bestial and ruthless human carnage than the British suppression of the non-white Indian people.

Over 115 million African blacks—close to the 1930's population of the United States—were murdered or enslaved during the slave trade. And I read how when the slave market was glutted, the cannibalistic white powers of Europe next carved up, as their colonies, the richest areas of the black continent. And Europe's chancelleries for the next century played a chess game of naked exploitation and power from Cape Horn to Cairo.

Ten guards and the warden couldn't have torn me out of those books. Not even Elijah Muhammad could have been more eloquent than those books were in providing indisputable proof that the collective white man had acted like a devil in virtually every contact he had with the world's collective non-white man. I listen today to the radio, and watch television, and read the headlines about the collective white man's fear and tension concerning China. When the white man professes ignorance about why the Chinese hate him so, my mind can't help flashing back to what I read, there in prison, about how the blood forebears of this same white man raped China at a time when China was trusting and helpless. Those original white "Christian traders" sent into China millions of pounds of opium. By 1839, so many of the Chinese were addicts that China's desperate government destroyed twenty thousand chests of opium. The first Opium War was promptly declared by the white man. Imagine! Declaring *war* upon someone who objects to being narcotized! The Chinese were severely beaten, with Chinese-invented gunpowder.

The Treaty of Nanking made China pay the British white man for the destroyed opium; forced open China's major ports to British trade; forced China to abandon Hong Kong; fixed China's import tariffs so low that cheap British articles soon flooded in, maiming China's industrial development.

After a second Opium War, the Tientsin Treaties legalized the ravaging opium trade, legalized a British-French-American control of China's customs. China tried delaying that Treaty's ratification; Peking was looted and burned.

"Kill the foreign white devils!" was the 1901 Chinese war cry in the Boxer Rebellion. Losing again, this time the Chinese were driven from Peking's choicest areas. The vicious, arrogant white man put up the famous signs, "Chinese and dogs not allowed."

Red China after World War II closed its doors to the Western white world. Massive Chinese agricultural, scientific, and industrial efforts are described in a book that *Life* magazine recently published. Some observers inside Red China have reported that the world never has known such a hate-white campaign as is now going on in this non-white country where, present birthrates continuing, in fifty more years Chinese will be half the earth's population. And it seems that some Chinese chickens will soon come home to roost, with China's recent successful nuclear tests.

Let us face reality. We can see in the United Nations a new world order being shaped, along color lines—an alliance among the non-white nations. America's U.N. Ambassador Adlai Stevenson complained not long ago that in the United Nations "a skin game" was being played. He was right. He was facing reality. A "skin game" *is* being played. But Ambassador Stevenson sounded like Jesse James accusing the marshal of carrying a gun. Because who in the world's history ever has played a worse "skin game" than the white man?

Mr. Muhammad, to whom I was writing daily, had no idea of what a new world had opened up to me through my efforts to document his teachings in books.

When I discovered philosophy, I tried to touch all the landmarks of philosophical development. Gradually, I read most of the old philosophers, Occidental and Oriental. The Oriental philosophers were the ones I came to prefer; finally, my impression was that most Occidental philosophy had largely been borrowed from the Oriental thinkers. Socrates, for instance, traveled in Egypt. Some sources even say that Socrates was initiated into some of the Egyptian mysteries. Obviously Socrates got some of his wisdom among the East's wise men.

I have often reflected upon the new vistas that reading opened to me. I knew right there in prison that reading had changed forever the course of my life. As I see it today, the ability to read awoke inside me some long dormant craving to be mentally alive. I certainly wasn't seeking any degree, the way a college confers a status symbol upon its students. My homemade education gave me, with every additional book that I read, a little bit more sensitivity to the deafness, dumbness, and blindness that was afflicting the black race in America. Not long ago, an English writer telephoned me from London, asking questions. One was, "What's your alma mater?" I told him, "Books." You will never catch me with a free fifteen minutes in which I'm not studying something I feel might be able to help the black man.

Yesterday I spoke in London, and both ways on the plane across the Atlantic I was studying a document about how the United Nations proposes to insure the human rights of the oppressed minorities of the world. The American black man is the world's most shameful case of minority oppression. What makes the black man think of himself as only an internal United States issue is just a catch-phrase, two words, "civil rights." How is the black man going to get "civil rights" before first he wins his *human* rights? If the American black man will start thinking about his *human* rights, and then start thinking of himself as part of one of the world's great peoples, he will see he has a case for the United Nations.

I can't think of a better case! Four hundred years of black blood and sweat invested here in America, and the white man still has the black man begging for what every immigrant fresh off the ship can take for granted the minute he walks down the gangplank.

But I'm digressing. I told the Englishman that my alma mater was books, a good library. Every time I catch a plane, I have with me a book that I want to read—and that's a lot of books these days. If I weren't out here every day battling the white man, I could spend the rest of my life reading, just satisfying my curiosity—because you can hardly mention anything I'm not curious about. I don't think anybody ever got more out of going to prison than I did. In fact, prison enabled me to study far more intensively than I would have if my life had gone differently and I had attended some college. I imagine that one of the biggest troubles with colleges is there are too many distractions, too much panty-raiding, fraternities, and boola-boola and all of that. Where else but in a prison could I have attacked my ignorance by being able to study intensely sometimes as much as fifteen hours a day?

Schopenhauer, Kant, Nietzsche, naturally, I read all of those. I don't respect them: I am just trying to remember some of those whose theories I soaked up in those years. These three, it's said, laid the groundwork on which the Facist and Nazi philosophy was built. I don't respect them because it seems to me that most of their time was spent arguing about things that are not really important. They remind me of so many of the Negro "intellectuals," so-called, with whom I have come in contact—they are always arguing about something useless.

Spinoza impressed me for a while when I found out that he was black. A black Spanish Jew. The Jews excommunicated him because he advocated a pantheistic doctrine, something like the "allness of God," or "God in everything." The Jews read their bural services for Spinoza, meaning that he was dead as far as they were concerned; his family was run out of Spain, they ended up in Holland, I think.

I'll tell you something. The whole stream of Western philosophy has now wound up in a cul-de-sac. The white man has perpetrated upon himself, as well as upon the black man, so gigantic a fraud that he has put himself into a crack. He did it through his elaborate, neurotic necessity to hide the black man's true role in history.

And today the white man is faced head on with what is happening on the Black Continent, Africa. Look at the artifacts being discovered there, that are proving over and over again, how the black man had great, fine, sensitive civilizations before the white man was out of the caves. Below the Sahara, in the places where most of America's Negroes' foreparents were kidnapped, there is being unearthed some of the finest crafts- manship, sculpture and other objects, that has ever been seen by modern man. Some of these things now are on view in such places as New York City's Museum of Modern Art. Gold work of such fine tolerance and workmanship that it has no rival. Ancient objects produced by black hands . . . refined by those black hands with results that no human hand today can equal.

History has been so "whitened" by the white man that even the black professors have known little more than the most igno- rant black man about the talents and rich civilizations and cul- tures of the black man of millenniums ago. I have lectured in Negro colleges and some of these brain-washed black Ph.D.'s, with their suspenders dragging the ground with degrees, have run to the white man's newspapers calling me a "black fa- natic." Why, a lot of them are fifty years behind the times. If I were president of one of these black colleges, I'd hock the campus if I had to, to send a bunch of black students off digging in Africa for more, more and more proof of the black race's historical greatness. The white man now is in Africa digging and searching. An African elephant can't stumble without fall- ing on some white man with a shovel. Practically every week, we read about some great new find from Africa's lost civiliza- tions. All that's new is white science's attitude. The ancient civilizations of the black man have been buried on the Black Continent all the time.

Here is an example: A British anthropologist named Dr. Louis S. B. Leakey is displaying some fossil bones—a foot, part of a hand, some jaws, and skull fragments. On the basis of these, Dr. Leakey has said it's time to rewrite completely the history of man's origin.

This species of man lived 1,818,036 years before Christ. And these bones were found in Tanganyika. In the Black Continent.

It's a crime, the lie that has been told to generations of black men and white men both. Little innocent black children, born of parents who believed that their race had no history. Little black children seeing, before they could talk, that their parents considered themselves inferior. Innocent black children growing up, living out their lives, dying of old age—and all of their lives ashamed of being black. But the truth is pouring out of the bag now.

Two other areas of experience which had been extremely formative in my life since prison were first opened to me in the Norfolk Prison Colony. For one thing, I had my first experiences in opening the eyes of my brainwashed black brethren to some truths about the black race. And, the other: when I had read enough to know something, I began to enter the Prison Colony's weekly debating program—my baptism into public speaking.

I have to admit a sad, shameful fact. I had so loved being around the white man that in prison I really disliked how Negro convicts stuck together so much. But when Mr. Muhammad's teachings reversed my attitude toward my black brothers, in my guilt and shame I began to catch every chance I could to recruit for Mr. Muhammad.

You have to be careful, very careful, introducing the truth to the black man who has never previously heard the truth about himself, his own kind, and the white man. My brother Reginald had told me that all Muslims experienced this in their recruiting for Mr. Muhammad. The black brother is so brainwashed that he may even be repelled when he first hears the truth. Reginald advised that the truth had to be dropped only a little bit at a time. And you had to wait a while to let it sink in before advancing the next step.

I began first telling my black brother inmates about the glorious history of the black man—things they never had dreamed. I told them the horrible slavery-trade truths that they never knew. I would watch their faces when I told them about that, because the white man had completely erased the slaves' past, a Negro in America can never know his true family name, or even what tribe he was descended from: the Mandingos, the Wolof, the Serer, the Fula, the Fanti, the Ashanti, or others. I told them that some slaves brought from Africa spoke Arabic, and were Islamic in their religion. A lot of these black convicts still wouldn't believe it unless they could see that a white man had said it. So, often, I would read to these brothers selected passages from white men's books. I'd explain to them that the real truth was known to some white men, the scholars; but there had been a conspiracy down through the generations to keep the truth from black men.

I would keep close watch on how each one reacted. I always had to be careful. I never knew when some brainwashed black imp, some dyed-in-the-wool Uncle Tom, would nod at me and then go running to tell the white man. When one was ripe— and I could tell—then away from the rest, I'd drop it on him, what Mr. Muhammad taught: "The white man is the devil."

That would shock many of them—until they started thinking about it.

This is probably as big a single worry as the American prison system has today—the way the Muslim teachings, circulated among all Negroes in the country, are converting new Muslims among black men in prison, and black men are in prison in far greater numbers than their proportion in the population.

The reason is that among all Negroes the black convict is the most perfectly preconditioned to hear the words, "the white man is the devil."

You tell that to any Negro. Except for those relatively few "integration"-mad so-called "intellectuals," and those black men who are otherwise fat, happy, and deaf, dumb, and blinded, with their crumbs from the white man's rich table, you have struck a nerve center in the American black man. He may take a day to react, a month, a year; he may never respond, openly; but of one thing you can be sure—when he thinks about his own life, he is going to see where, to him, personally, the white man sure has acted like a devil.

And, as I say, above all Negroes, the black prisoner. Here is a black man caged behind bars, probably for years, put there by the white man. Usually the convict comes from among those bottom-of-the-pile Negroes, the Negroes who through their entire lives have been kicked about, treated like children—Negroes who never have met one white man who didn't either take something from them or do something to them.

You let this caged-up black man start thinking, the same way I did when I first heard Elijah Muhammad's teachings: let him start thinking how, with better breaks when he was young and ambitious he might have been a lawyer, a doctor, a scientist, anything. You let this caged-up black man start realizing, as I did, how from the first landing of the first slave ship, the millions of black men in America have been like sheep in a den of wolves. That's why black prisoners become Muslims so fast when Elijah Muhammad's teachings filter into their cages by way of other Muslim convicts. "The white man is the devil" is a perfect echo of that black convict's lifelong experience.

I've told how debating was a weekly event there at the Norfolk Prison Colony. My reading had my mind like steam under pressure. Some way, I had to start telling the white man about himself to his face. I decided I could do this by putting my name down to debate.

Standing up and speaking before an audience was a thing that throughout my previous life never would have crossed my mind. Out there in the streets, hustling, pushing dope, and robbing, I could have had the dreams from a pound of hashish and I'd never have dreamed anything so wild as that one day I would speak in coliseums and arenas, at the greatest American universities, and on radio and television programs, not to mention speaking all over Egypt and Africa and in England.

But I will tell you that, right there, in the prison, debating, speaking to a crowd, was as exhilarating to me as the discovery of knowledge through reading had been. Standing up there, the faces looking up at me, the things in my head coming out of my mouth, while my brain searched for the next best thing to follow what I was saying, and if I could sway them to my side by handling it right, then I had won the debate—once my feet got wet, I was gone on debating. Whichever side of the selected subject was assigned to me, I'd track down and study everything I could find on it. I'd put myself in my opponent's place and decide how I'd try to win if I had the other side; and then I'd figure a way to knock down those points. And if there was any way in the world, I'd work into my speech the devilishness of the white man.

"Compulsory Military Training—Or None?" That's one good chance I got unexpectedly, I remember. My opponent flailed the air about the Ethiopians throwing rocks and spears at Italian airplanes, "proving" that compulsory military training was needed. I said the Ethiopians' black flesh had been spattered against trees by bombs the Pope in Rome had blessed, and the Ethiopians would have thrown even their bare bodies at the airplanes because they had seen that they were fighting the devil incarnate.

They yelled "foul," that I'd made the subject a race issue. I said it wasn't race, it was a historical fact, that they ought to go and read Pierre van Paassen's *Days of Our Years*, and something not surprising to me, that book, right after the debate, disappeared from the prison library. It was right there in prison that I made up my mind to devote the rest of my life to telling the white man about himself—or die. In a debate about whether or not Homer had ever existed, I threw into those white faces the theory that Homer only symbolized how white Europeans kidnapped black Africans, then blinded them so that they could never get back to their own people. (Homer and Omar and *Moor*, you see, are related terms; it's like saying Peter, Pedro, and *petra*, all three of which mean rock.) These blinded Moors the Europeans taught to sing about the Europeans' glorious accomplishments. I made it clear that was the devilish white man's idea of kicks. Aesop's *Fables*—another case in point. "Aesop" was only the Greek name for an Ethiopian.

Another hot debate I remember I was in had to do with the identity of Shakespeare. No color was involved there; I just got intrigued over the Shakespearean dilemma. The King James translation of the Bible is considered the greatest piece of literature in English. Its language supposedly represents the ultimate in using the King's English. Well, Shakespeare's language and the Bible's language are one and the same. They say that from 1604 to 1611, King James got poets to translate, to write the Bible. Well, if Shakespeare existed, he was then the top poet around. But Shakespeare is nowhere reported connected with the Bible. If he existed, why didn't King James use him? And if he did use him, why is it one of the world's best kept secrets?

I know that many say that Francis Bacon was Shakespeare. If that is true, why would Bacon have kept it secret? Bacon wasn't royalty, when royalty sometimes used the *nom de plume* because it was "improper" for royalty to be artistic or theatrical. What would Bacon have had to lose? Bacon, in fact, would have had everything to gain.

In the prison debates I argued for the theory that King James himself was the real poet who used the *nom de plume* Shakespeare. King James was brilliant. He was the greatest king who ever sat on the British throne. Who else among royalty, in his time, would have had the giant talent to write Shakespeare's works? It was he who poetically "fixed" the Bible—which in itself and its present King James version has enslaved the world.

When my brother Reginald visited, I would talk to him about new evidence I found to document the Muslim teachings. In either volume 43 or 44 of The Harvard Classics, I read Milton's *Paradise Lost*. The devil, kicked out of Paradise, was trying to regain possession. He was using the forces of Europe, personified by the Popes, Charlemagne, Richard the Lionhearted, and other knights. I interpreted this to show that the Europeans were motivated and led by the devil, or the personification of the devil. So Milton and Mr. Elijah Muhammad were actually saying the same thing.

I couldn't believe it when Reginald began to speak ill of Elijah Muhammad. I can't specify the exact things he said. They were more in the nature of implications against Mr. Muhammad—the pitch of Reginald's voice, or the way that Reginald looked, rather than what he said.

It caught me totally unprepared. It threw me into a state of confusion. My blood brother, Reginald, in whom I had so much confidence, for whom I had so much respect, the one who had introduced me to the nation of Islam. I couldn't believe it! And now Islam meant more to me than anything I ever had known in my life. Islam and Mr. Elijah Muhammad had changed my whole world.

Reginald, I learned, had been suspended from the Nation of Islam by Elijah Muhammad. He had not practiced moral restraint. After he had learned the truth, and had accepted the truth, and the Muslim laws, Reginald was still carrying on improper relations with the then secretary of the New York Temple. Some other Muslim who learned of it had made charges against Reginald to Mr. Muhammad in Chicago, and Mr. Muhammad had suspended Reginald.

When Reginald left, I was in torment. That night, finally, I wrote to Mr. Muhammad, trying to defend my brother, appealing for him. I told him what Reginald was to me, what my brother meant to me.

I put the letter into the box for the prison censor. Then all the rest of that night, I prayed to Allah. I don't think anyone ever prayed more sincerely to Allah. I prayed for some kind of relief from my confusion.

It was the next night, as I lay on my bed, I suddenly, with a start, became aware of a man sitting beside me in my chair. He had on a dark suit. I remember. I could see him as plainly as I see anyone I look at. He wasn't black, and he wasn't white. He was light-brown-skinned, an Asiatic cast of countenance, and he had oily black hair.

I looked right into his face.

I didn't get frightened. I knew I wasn't dreaming. I couldn't move, I didn't speak, and he didn't. I couldn't place him racially—other than that I knew he was a non-European. I had no idea whatsoever who he was. He just sat there. Then, suddenly as he had come, he was gone.

Soon, Mr. Muhammad sent me a reply about Reginald. He wrote, "If you once believed in the truth, and now you are beginning to doubt the truth, you didn't believe the truth in the first place. What could make you doubt the truth other than your own weak self?"

That struck me. Reginald was not leading the disciplined life of a Muslim. And I knew that Elijah Muhammad was right, and my blood brother was wrong. Because right is right, and wrong is wrong. Little did I then realize the day would come when Elijah Muhammad would be accused by his own sons as being guilty of the same acts of immorality that he judged Reginald and so many others for.

But at that time, all of the doubt and confusion in my mind was removed. All of the influence that my brother had wielded over me was broken. From that day on, as far as I am concerned, everything that my brother Reginald has done is wrong.

But Reginald kept visiting me. When he had been a Muslim, he had been immaculate in his attire. But now, he wore things like a T-shirt, shabby-looking trousers, and sneakers. I could see him on the way down. When he spoke, I heard him coldly. But I would listen. He was my blood brother.

Gradually, I saw the chastisement of Allah—what Christians would call "the curse"—come upon Reginald. Elijah Muhammad said that Allah was chastising Reginald—and that anyone who challenged Elijah Muhammad would be chastened by Allah. In Islam we were taught that as long as one didn't know the truth, he lived in darkness. But once the truth was accepted, and recognized, he lived in light, and whoever would then go against it would be punished by Allah.

Mr. Muhammad taught that the five-pointed star stands for justice, and also for the five senses of man. We were taught that Allah executes justice by working upon the five senses of those who rebel against His Messenger, or against His truth. We were taught that this was Allah's way of letting Muslims know His sufficiency to defend His Messenger against any and all opposition, as long as the Messenger himself didn't deviate from the path of truth. We were taught that Allah turned the minds of any defectors into a turmoil. I thought truly that it was Allah doing this to my brother.

One letter, I think from my brother Philbert, told me that Reginald was with them in Detroit. I heard no more about Reginald until one day, weeks later, Ella visited me; she told me that Reginald was at her home in Roxbury, sleeping. Ella said she had heard a knock, she had gone to the door, and there was Reginald, looking terrible. Ella said she had asked, "Where did you come from?" And Reginald had told her he came from Detroit. She said she asked him, "How did you get here?" And he had told her, "I walked."

I believed he *had* walked. I believed in Elijah Muhammad, and he had convinced us that Allah's chastisement upon Reginald's mind had taken away Reginald's ability to gauge distance and time. There is a dimension of time with which we are not familiar here in the West. Elijah Muhammad said that under Allah's chastisement, the five senses of a man can be so deranged by those whose mental powers are greater than his that in five minutes his hair can turn snow white. Or he will walk nine hundred miles as he might walk five blocks.

In prison, since I had become a Muslim, I had grown a beard. When Reginald visited me, he nervously moved about in his chair; he told me that each hair on my beard was a snake. Everywhere, he saw snakes.

He next began to believe that he was the "Messenger of Allah." Reginald went around in the streets of Roxbury, Ella reported to me, telling people that he had some divine power. He graduated from this to saying that he was Allah.

He finally began saying he was *greater* than Allah.

Authorities picked up Reginald, and he was put into an institution. They couldn't find what was wrong. They had no way to understand Allah's chastisement. Reginald was released. Then he was picked up again, and was put into another institution.

Reginald is in an institution now. I know where, but I won't say. I would not want to cause him any more trouble than he has already had.

I believe, today, that it was written, it was meant, for Reginald to be used for one purpose only: as a bait, as a minnow to reach into the ocean of blackness where I was, to save me.

I cannot understand it any other way.

After Elijah Muhammad himself was later accused as a very immoral man, I came to believe that it wasn't a divine chastisement upon Reginald, but the pain he felt when his own family totally rejected him for Elijah Muhammad, and this hurt made Reginald turn insanely upon Elijah Muhammad.

It's impossible to dream, or to see, or to have a vision of someone whom you never have seen before—and to see him exactly as he is. To see someone, and to see him exactly as he looks, is to have a pre-vision.

I would later come to believe that my pre-vision was of Master W. D. Fard, the Messiah, the one whom Elijah Muhammad said had appointed him—Elijah Muhammad—as His Last Messenger to the black people of North America.

My last year in prison was spent back in the Charlestown Prison. Even among the white inmates, the word had filtered around. Some of those brainwashed black convicts talked too much. And I know that the censors had reported on my mail. The Norfolk Prison Colony officials had become upset. They used as a reason for my transfer that I refused to take some kind of shots, an inoculation or something.

The only thing that worried me was that I hadn't much time left before I would be eligible for parole-board consideration. But I reasoned that they might look at my representing and spreading Islam in another way: instead of keeping me in they might want to get me out.

I had come to prison with 20/20 vision. But when I got sent back to Charlestown, I had read so much by the lights-out glow in my room at the Norfolk Prison Colony that I had astigmatism and the first pair of the eyeglasses that I have worn ever since.

I had less maneuverability back in the much stricter Charlestown Prison. But I found that a lot of Negroes attended a Bible class, and I went there.

Conducting the class was a tall, blond, blue-eyed (a perfect "devil") Harvard Seminary student. He lectured, and then he started in a question-and-answer session. I don't know which of us had read the Bible more, he or I, but I had to give him credit; he really was heavy on his religion. I puzzled and puzzled for a way to upset him, and to give those Negroes present something to think and talk about and circulate.

Finally, I put up my hand; he nodded. He had talked about Paul.

I stood up and asked, "What color was Paul?" And I kept talking, with pauses, "He had to be black . . . because he was a Hebrew ... and the original Hebrews were black ... weren't they?''

He had started flushing red. You know the way white people do. He said "Yes."

I wasn't through yet. "What color was Jesus ... he was Hebrew, too ... wasn't he?"

Both the Negro and the white convicts had sat bolt upright. I don't care how tough the convict, be he brainwashed black Christian, or a ''devil'' white Christian, neither of them is ready to hear anybody saying Jesus wasn't white. The instructor walked around. He shouldn't have felt bad. In all of the years since, I never have met any intelligent white man who would try to insist that Jesus was white. How could they? He said, ''Jesus was brown.''

I let him get away with that compromise.

Exactly as I had known it would, almost overnight the Charlestown convicts, black and white, began buzzing with the story. Wherever I went, I could feel the nodding. And anytime I got a chance to exchange words with a black brother in stripes, I'd say, ''My man! You ever heard about somebody named Mr. Elijah Muhammad?''

Upon his release from prison in 1952, like all the brothers in the Nation of Islam, Malcolm K. Little renounced forever his family's slave name and became Malcolm X. He rose quickly in the Black Muslim ranks. In 1954 he assumed the ministry of the New York mosque, Temple No. 7, and by the end of the decade he was second only to the NOI's national leader, Elijah Muhammad himself. He debated at Oxford, he lectured at universities, he traveled in Africa, he spellbound huge outdoor rallies. His popularity continued to grow, and then—in apparent defiance of an NOI directive not to discuss the assassination of President Kennedy—he spoke out of turn. On December 4, 1963, Malcolm X was suspended by the NOI leadership for ninety days. In March 1964 he left the NOI forever. In June he founded the Organization of Afro-American Unity to forward the cause of human rights for African Americans.

From the outset of his public career in 1953 up to his untimely death in 1965, at the age of thirty-nine, Malcolm X continually addressed the plight of his people; he spoke, as he repeatedly said, for twenty-two million black Americans. He spoke with sincerity, he spoke with passion. And sometimes he spoke, it seemed, with the voice of a prophet. In the selection that follows, some of the people whose lives were dramatically touched or radically altered by Malcolm X speak in their own words about their brother, minister, teacher, champion.

from *Malcolm X: As They Knew Him*
"As They Knew Him
Oral Remembrances of Malcolm X"
by David Gallen and Peter Skutches

In Ghana, at Temple No. 7 or the Audubon in Harlem, at the Oxford Union, at Harvard and Howard, at outdoor rallies and in the streets—like Robert Haggins, they were ready for him.

Robert Haggins, in 1960 a staff photographer and reporter for the New York *Citizen-Call*, arrived early at the restaurant on 116th Street and Lenox Avenue for his interview with Malcolm X. He had been sitting there maybe five minutes when, as Haggins tells it, "this tall gentleman with a briefcase came in. His entourage following him, he came over to my table and said, 'Are you Mr. Haggins? I'm Malcolm X.' I said, 'Fine,' and pulled out my pad. 'What is your last name?' I said. And he said, 'That's it, X.' And I said, 'How did you get a name like X? X must be an initial. What is the whole name, what is the rest?' He said, 'You want me to give you my slave name?' 'Slave name?' I said. And he said, 'Yes. I dropped my slave name. That name was Malcolm Little, but I don't carry a slave name anymore. I carry X. I carry X because I don't know my real last name.' Then we got into an exchange, one that was going to change my life forever. We started talking about how we got our names and how ridiculous it was for me to carry the name of Haggins or any other English or Irish name when I was not ethnically either and how people were bought and slaved like cattle and their names changed to reflect who owned them. I had never had anybody awaken me like that before in my life. . . . Malcolm X was, I think, the realization of everything that was recessed in my mind. I was ready for Malcolm. I didn't know it at first, but I was."

Malcolm too was ready. In the restaurant, mosque, ballroom, street, or lecture hall, he rarely missed the opportunity to teach. And like the best teachers he was equally willing and always eager to learn. "He was the fastest learner of anybody I've ever known," states John Henrik Clarke, who was "his history man—if you want something on history, you turn to me—and once he had read it and analyzed it, he knew more than I knew about it." Malcolm's passion for learning is reflected in what Benjamin Karim perceives as three of the things Malcolm loved most: "truth, knowledge, I mean knowledge just for its own sake, and teaching"—and according to Karim, "the thing that he hated most was ignorance."

Ignorance, certainly, was not tolerated by Malcolm at Temple No. 7. Karim, like all the assistant ministers, soon found himself attending a public speaking class in which "he gave us assignments that, believe it or not, would make a Harvard student put his books down and leave. We had to read *The New York Times* daily or the old *Tribune*, either one of those papers, and the London *Times* and *The Peking Review*, which was published in China; then there was a newspaper out of Indonesia and many papers from other countries. We would read them along with our *Time* magazine and *Newsweek*, and we watched the news, and with all this we studied geography too. And history, the history of the events in the news and how it led to a particular thing that was going on at the moment. Malcolm was more of a teacher than he was the man the public thought he was."

"He was always very witty," says Karim, "and he always had an answer for questions; it may not have been the answer that you were looking for, but most times he would answer, and sometimes he would answer in a way that you would have to figure out what he meant by that." For an instance Karim offers Malcolm's answer to a question a Muslim brother once asked Karim. " 'What is the strongest urge in a human being?'

he asked me. So I thought a minute and I said perhaps the urge to reproduce himself, the sex urge; but I also said that I would ask Brother Minister—we never called him Malcolm, we always called him Brother Minister or Brother Minister Malcolm—and when I asked him, do you know what he told me? He said the strongest urge in a human being is the urge to eat. He said to take a man's food from him for a week, then bring in the most beautiful woman you can find and strip her, and then bring in a plate of lamb chops and peas and mashed potatoes and set it in front of him—and then see which one he takes a piece of first. I soon saw the picture.''

Any occasion or encounter might prompt a lesson from Malcolm. "We were going to Bridgeport one night," Karim recalls, "and this man came up, obviously a person who begs for money to buy something to drink, you know, wine or something—I think we were on St. Nichols Avenue or Seventh Avenue—and he said, 'Mr. X, could you give me fifty cents so I could get a bowl of bean soup?' Because at that time fifty cents could buy a big bowl of bean soup and a big piece of corn bread, and that's a meal, or an even bigger bottle of wine. So he gave the guy fifty cents, right? So we were sitting in the car—we don't support wine habits, we don't give people money to buy alcohol, wine, or drugs and all that—and everybody was quiet, and Brother Minister gave a smile 'cause he knew this man didn't want anything to eat. So we're driving down Seventh Avenue, and nobody's talking, nobody's saying, 'Brother Minister, why did you give the man the fifty cents? You know the man is not going to buy any food with that money.' Nobody said anything. Then all of a sudden he said, after about twenty blocks on our way to Bridgeport, 'I know what you're thinking,' and he said, 'No, Brother Minister, no, we're not thinking anything,' and he said, 'Yes, you are.' He said, 'I don't know if that man is really hungry, if he really wants something to eat or something to drink, but had I not given him the fifty cents, it would have been on my conscience that perhaps the man was hungry, and I couldn't allow a person to be hungry if I could afford to feed that person.' And he started teaching us about charity, and he went right on down to nature, about the ants and how the female ant will regurgitate her food just to feed another ant. He taught us about charity all the way to Bridgeport, Connecticut.''

In the black youth of America—in their freshness of thought, in their energy and anger, in new ideas unencumbered by an old slave mentality—Malcolm saw hope for all black Americans. "The black college student," Malcolm told Benjamin Karim, "will be very instrumental in the liberation of black people in this country." Psychologist Kenneth B. Clark remembers a meeting he had arranged with Malcolm for students at the Lincoln School, and "when we got there he had the reporters and interviewers put aside. He spoke with the young students, and he said, 'You know I put students ahead of everything and everybody.' And he did."

Education, in Malcolm's view, bridged the river to liberation, and he urged young African-Americans to learn. Although he had no "formal Ph.D.," notes Sonia Sanchez, "he had a Ph.D. in Malcolmism, and he had a Ph.D. in Americanism, in what had gone wrong with this country, and he brought it to you. And for the first time many of us began to look at ourselves again, and to say hold it, it's possible to get an education and not sell your soul. It's possible to work at a job and not demean yourself, it's possible to walk upright like a human being. And, you see, what people don't really understand about what Malcolm taught me—I don't really know what he taught other people—he taught me that I could really be human myself and I didn't have to hate anyone to do that. He touched the core so thoroughly that you could walk upright, and therefore, you knew who you were and you just said to people, 'I'm coming among you as an equal,' with no need to put anyone down. And that is probably the most important lesson to be learned from his life. He taught me, and I'm sure a number of others, that you are indeed worthy of being on this planet earth.''

Malcolm X had no Ph.D.; nonetheless, he readily matched, and often trammeled, the wits of students and professors alike on numerous American college campuses, for the most part in the South and Northeast, in the early 1960s. Malcolm's addresses to college audiences aroused indignation, hostility, enthusiasm, rage; his debates stirred controversy. Indifference fled. From the outset, at Boston University in 1960, to Malcolm's memorable defense of extremism in the pursuit of human freedoms four years later, in December 1964, at Oxford University, an appearance by Malcolm X on any campus became an event.

In 1960 C. Eric Lincoln was working on a graduate degree in theology and preparing to research his dissertation on the black Muslims; he was also enrolled in a human relations seminar that included both students and faculty not only from Boston University but also from Harvard and MIT. Some of the participants in the seminar, aware that black Islam forebade its ministers to speak before any audience in which whites were present, challenged Lincoln to contact Malcolm and convince him to attend a meeting of the seminar as a guest lecturer. To everyone's surprise, the national leader of the NOI, the Honorable Elijah Muhammad, granted Malcolm the permission he needed.

Malcolm arrived at Boston University on a Thursday afternoon. Lincoln describes the occasion: "The place was packed with as many professors as graduate students from all three institutions [Boston University, Harvard, and MIT]. Malcolm arrived with an autoguard headed by Louis Farrakhan, who was then minister of Elijah Muhammad's Temple No. 11 in Boston and a protégé of Malcolm X. There were also perhaps fifteen members of the FOI [Fruit of Islam, the paramilitary arm of the NOI] from the local temple. Malcolm X showed up on schedule, and there was a very audible gasp from the people who were waiting to hear him; to the best of my knowledge, I was the only black person present. Once all these men had come in and taken their positions around the room to guard the speaker, I introduced Malcolm X. I believe he introduced Minister Farrakhan as the head of Temple No. 11 and then began to lecture on black Islam. It was an extremely interesting lecture. Malcolm talked the party line and did it with verve. He spoke part of the time in Arabic and showed that he had a good command of French, and the people were all sort of flabbergasted. There was also the whole physical presence of the Fruit; I recall that when the group walked in the professor next to me—he was from MIT—said to me, 'My god, Eric, every one of them has on a Brooks Brothers suit!' So Malcolm made a great impression on the crowd that day. The next week I got a call from a professor at Harvard asking if I could get Malcolm X to come and speak over there. He went to Harvard and afterwards said to me, 'Thank you for giving me the opportunity to speak to all those blue-eyed Willies. Now you can give me the opportunity to speak to some black people?' So I sent him to Clark College in Atlanta, my home base; he lectured at Clark and then went on to lecture at Morehouse, and that is what launched Malcolm lecturing on the college scene.''

Robert Haggins, who had recently become Malcolm's official photographer, accompanied him on his first trip to Harvard in 1961. He rode to Cambridge with Malcolm in the blue Oldsmobile. The FOI followed, conspicuously. So as not to ''attract too much attention—thirty cars, one behind the other, going through the streets—or to cause alarm,'' as Haggins tells it, ''we split up into smaller groups, like five cars, and let other cars go between so we would be staggered, so we wouldn't look like a parade. And we arrived at Harvard. They were very courteous, very polite. They had prepared a huge dinner for Malcolm, but Muslims only eat one meal a day, and Malcolm told them, 'I've eaten for the day; I only eat one meal a day, so I can't have anything to eat, but I will have ice cream and coffee.' And they said, 'Would you like some milk in your coffee?' And he said, 'Yes, that's the only thing I like integrated.' ''

Haggins also describes some of Malcolm's dinner table conversation with various Harvard University department heads. The head of the biology department, for instance, asked Malcolm, '' 'Mr. X, tell me, you don't really believe that one race of people is superior to another race of people, do you?' And Malcolm said, 'Of course not, but you teach that all the time.' And he said, 'No, I don't.' And Malcolm said, 'You do. You teach that, your books teach that. All of the biology books that I have looked at break people down into classifications; either they are dominant or recessive. Now, if you look at the dominant characteristics, you will find brown eyes, black hair, dark

skin; those are dominant characteristics. You look at the recessive side and you'll see blue eyes, blond hair, fair skin. So what
you are teaching black children is that they are superior human
beings. You've been telling them that for years, but they don't
believe you. All I've done is come and point out to them, if
they don't believe what I'm saying, to believe what you white
professors are saying. I just want black people to know where
we come from and we shouldn't be ashamed of how we look.
We are the dominant race of people.'

"Then he talked about history," Haggins continues, "and he
said, 'You've lied about history. You've lied to us, and one of
the biggest lies that you've told us is about all those white
discoverers, like Christopher Columbus.' " Haggins vigorously
espouses Malcolm's view of Columbus as a man lost both actually and morally. No brave voyager who discovered a new
world, Columbus, Haggins points out, never even landed on
American soil; he did, however, murder more than half the
populations of both Puerto Rico and Trinidad, says Haggins,
and then brought slavery to the islands from Africa. Haggins
recalls Malcolm saying, " 'Take Christopher Columbus: here's
a man who discovered absolutely nothing. He got lost, he didn't
know where he was. He was floundering around in a boat and
he didn't know where the boat was going. He was looking for
India and made a mistake. He thought that he had discovered
India and called those people Indians, after the word *indigo*, a
Latin word which means blue-black. The original Indians were
blue-black, the blackest people on earth, Indians. Then Columbus landed on this island, San Salvador, and told the people,
"I have discovered you in the name of the Queen of Spain,"
which is the most ridiculous thing I've ever heard. How can
you discover a human being? Somebody's about to have dinner
and you intrude, and he says to you—he's polite enough to
say—"Look, come in and partake of my meal. Sit down and
share what we have; it's not much, but we'll share it with you."
And then you stand up and say, "I discover you! You are now
discovered, you are Indian." They must have looked at each
other wondering, like, where did this fool come from.' Malcolm

told that story at Harvard, and they laughed. Then they looked at each other and said, 'He's right. That makes sense.' "

In 1962, at the invitation of the civil rights group Project Awareness, Malcolm visited Howard University in Washington D.C. to debate the future of the black community in America with integrationist Bayard Rustin. Malcolm at that time stood firmly in the forefront of Elijah Muhammad's black Muslim nationalist, separatist ranks. Media coverage of the upcoming debate, especially of Malcolm's appearance, had generated considerable excitement on the campus; it had also aroused a lot of curiosity, and some disdain. Michael Thelwell, then a student at Howard and a participant in Project Awareness, recalls that "a number of not particularly distinguished faculty who were approached to moderate the debate and invited to have dinner with the speakers had declined because they wouldn't 'dignify' Malcolm with their presence. Which we found to be extremely odd. At that time the attitude among my friends who organized the event was one of curiosity about Malcolm; we only knew what the media was reporting about him. But in terms of an intellectual commitment, a political commitment, we were all convinced that the only practical solution, the only alternative, for black people was integration—changing the country's situation so as to include black people on all levels of society: political, cultural, and above all, economic—and that anything else couldn't work. And that Bayard Rustin was the most articulate and militant spokesman for this position."

Whoever may have declined their invitations to that dinner had little effect on its success. At Howard as at Harvard Malcolm politely refused his meal. "He didn't eat anything; he just sat there really kind of alert and drank endless cups of coffee," recalls Thelwell. "But the thing is, even though there were about twenty-five people gathered in this little dining room to have dinner with him and Bayard Rustin, who was an eminent national figure, it was Malcolm's extraordinary charisma, the magnetism of the guy—or perhaps it was because the press had created such a demagogue out of this guy—that kept everybody's eyes turning to him every time he very graciously answered any question directed to him or very graciously avoided any question he didn't feel like answering, but in a very skillful and disarming manner. He completely dominated the occasion; he had a way of looking at people very calmly before he'd answer a question, and you'd see the person who'd raised the question look back at him and be mesmerized as he smiled . . . I mean, people had a very strange response. He was simply one of the most impressive presences and naturally charismatic figures I'd ever seen. There was a certain kind of integrity, his presence suggested a certain kind of control, and intense purposefulness a dignity, and an independence of mind that was quite unusual in black men then. A pride.''

Later that evening, at the debate, the twenty-five hundred people who packed the Crampton Auditorium at Howard University responded thunderously to that presence. The stature of ''a very tall, wiry, handsome guy'' stands out in Thelwell's memory of that night. ''When Malcolm strolled to the microphone for the first time there was a radiant intensity—he may have stood in a spotlight, I don't know, but radiant was certainly the impression I got—and then he started his delivery. He spoke of our origins and then said that he came to us in the name of all that is eternal, the black man—that before you are an American you're black, before you were a Republican you were black, before you were a Democrat you were black—and it was just extraordinary. The audience just erupted, and it continued through the whole course of that debate. Whether or not Malcolm won that debate doesn't matter, the fact is that emotionally and intellectually he was in total control. It wasn't necessarily just the function of rhetoric or the elegance of poetry in the delivery, it was the message. And you have to understand that here's an audience at Howard University—at that time, as it is perhaps now, an institution that saw itself as a means of ascension for young black people into the American dream, the mainstream, a school that prepared southern black students to be what the school imagined was acceptable to white America. That integration, as I now reflect on it, was the aim of the vast majority of the upwardly mobile Howard University students, and yet that whole place erupted viscerally, powerfully, with a shout. It wasn't an intellectual experience purely; it was a very primal, emotional thing. I've never really seen a crowd respond quite that way, especially a crowd I'd have predicted to respond just the opposite way.''

As Thelwell reflects further upon that evening at Howard, he attempts to identify what qualities other than Malcolm's "incredible magnetism" might account for the astounding effect he had on his audience. Thelwell believes that, for one thing, Malcolm "was able to be totally and fearlessly honest because, unlike Bayard Rustin and other civil rights leaders, he had no intellectual and political obligations to a set of allies or to any constituency in the liberal establishment. Rustin had to constrain his remarks, had to couch them in terms that were acceptable to his white allies—I mean, it was a kind of self-censorship; it limited what he said, limited his analysis of the black situation to a certain mainstream, orthodox, accepted version of reality. Malcolm didn't have to do that. Malcolm had no obligation to any liberal orthodoxy. His constituency was black, the Nation of Islam, so he could speak the truth in terms as blunt as possible or necessary and not worry about anybody being offended, not worry about support, and this made him extraordinarily attractive to young black people because finally here was somebody who didn't have to kowtow to anybody. He spoke exactly what the goddamn truth was as he saw it. And that is very different from somebody appealing for tolerance, somebody appealing for acceptance. Malcolm said, 'What the hell are you talking about? The American white man is the worst killer the world has ever seen. Who brought the Africans here? Who killed the red man? Who dropped the bomb on Hiroshima? What are you talking about?' The other thing he had which most people don't know about is a remarkable gentleness and tenderness for black people—a real compassion. Not compassion, but a real love and a real solidarity, a real sensitivity to black people. He held a genuine concern for us, and people recognized it immediately. When Malcolm X said brother or sister, or any of those terms of kinship and mutual responsibility, he meant it.''

In any debate Malcolm X was a formidable opponent, as James Farmer, the founding director of the Congress of Racial

Equality (CORE), well knows. In his autobiography, *Lay Bare the Heart*, Farmer recounts one of Malcolm's most memorable single blows in a public debate. In response to Malcolm's insistent demand that blacks call themselves blacks because they were blacks before they were Americans, Malcolm's adversary—a black but not, in this instance, Farmer—repeatedly stated that he called himself first of all an American. When Malcolm then asked why, his adversary, now shouting, replied that he had been born here, in America. "Malcolm smiled," writes Farmer, "and spoke softly: 'Now, brother, if a cat has kittens in the oven, does that make them biscuits?'"

With some circumspection, then, Farmer agreed to debate Malcolm at Cornell University in 1962 on the condition, as he relates it, "that Malcolm speak first and I speak second so that Malcolm would rebut first and I would rebut last. I didn't want him to blow me away with one of his great one-liners, as he did Rustin. Malcolm accepted that until almost the last minute when he wired the people at Cornell and said that 'the Honorable Elijah Muhammad teaches us only to attack when attacked; so I must speak last or no debate!' So they asked me if I would debate him speaking last. I told them yes, provided that Malcolm agreed to an open-ended cross discussion between the two of us, after his rebuttal, with the moderator staying out of it; and he agreed to that."

Farmer, of course, had devised a strategy, which was "to make Malcolm's speech for him." Stealing Malcolm's fire, Farmer enumerated in his opening speech the many crimes against them that blacks had endured throughout history. After vividly presenting the plight of twenty-two million black Americans, he offered CORE's nonviolent direct action solution. Before turning the platform over to Malcolm, however, Farmer asked that Malcolm speak no further of the disease—its symptoms were clear, the diagnosis certain—but to put forward his solution, his cure. "That's where he was very weak," Farmer points out. "When he was called upon to give a program or plan, he began to quote the dogma of Elijah Muhammad, calling for land or a black state or demanding the government give us money which it owed us for reparations to purchase an island someplace. He was very weak on that, so I wanted him to spend his time wandering around in that jungle. He didn't want to do that because he knew that was his weak point and I was going to eat him alive on it. So when he stood up he was at first thrown off balance because he couldn't give his usual speech, because I had given it already. He fumbled with the microphone, with the gooseneck; there was nothing wrong with it. Then he began, saying, 'I have a lot of respect for Brother James; he's the only top leader of so-called Negroes who has the guts to face me in a debate on a public platform, and I respect him for that,' and he talked in that vein for two or three minutes, and obviously he was fishing around for a speech, and he was flustered, and then the speech came together and it was vintage Malcolm. The ideas came together in his mind and he roared, not attacking me but attacking this idiocy of nonviolence, 'Someone slaps you on one cheek and you're going to turn the other? What kind of nonsense is that?' He said, 'You've seen it on TV! You've seen those firehoses rolling black women down the street! The skirts flying! You've seen the police dogs turned loose on little black children, biting their flesh and tearing their clothes!' And then he roared again, 'Don't let those dogs bite those children! Kill the damn dogs!' Everybody in the audience rose to their feet in applause. He had the audience then, and most of them were white. Not many speakers could throw a speech out a window like that and start from scratch and come through the way he did. He came through like a champion, which he was.''

A young, blond coed from a college in New England boarded a plane to New York; she was obviously upset. Just a few hours earlier Malcolm X had spoken at the college. He had drawn parallels between the racism of white slavemasters, the ''white devils'' who so cruelly victimized blacks in the South before the Civil War, and their sexism in the treatment of women— white women, their wives, mothers, sisters, daughters—whose gentility, it was purported, divorced them from their female sexuality and therefore justified the sexual use, and abuse, of black women by the white male oppressor. The plantation had thus bred in white America a deplorable moral history that included the hatred, rejection, and denial not only of the African slave but also of white southern womanhood. After the lecture Malcolm had flown back to New York.

The coed must have boarded the first flight that followed Malcolm's to New York. On her arrival she took a cab to Harlem. She found the Muslim restaurant on Lenox Avenue, where, as it happened, Malcolm was sitting with Benjamin Karim and some other members of his staff. Still noticeably disturbed, the young woman approached Malcolm. She spoke with a white southern accent; her clothes spoke money, and her demeanor shouted white breeding, privilege, background. Confronting Malcolm, she demanded to know if he truly believed there were no good white people. When Malcolm replied by telling her he believed only in people's deeds, not their words, she asked him what then she could do. "Nothing," he informed her.

"Nothing." Of any of the statements Malcolm may have made to his own regret, this one comes first to Alex Haley's mind. "All he had said was 'nothing,' " says Haley, "but he worried about it; he played it back and wished it had been played differently."

According to Benjamin Karim, it would have been played differently, had Malcolm been alone when the young, blond, white college student approached him. Karim feels that Malcolm had to answer as he did because he had to "satisfy us wicked people around him who at that time didn't believe there were any white people anywhere that were any good. I think that he would have been more amiable if we hadn't been there; he had a softness that could be touched." Karim had, after all, witnessed Malcolm's amiability with college students, both white and black. He remembers how, when Malcolm had finished one of his lectures, the students, mostly white, "just crowded around him, I mean just like bees around honey in August. Malcolm was a very amiable person, he was really a very likable person. He had a very sincere admiration for college students, whether they were white or black—I could see that in him—I guess, because of his respect for knowledge and the fact that he believed that the younger students wouldn't grow up as racist as their parents. We grew up in a society as racist as its law, but Malcolm had some faith that the younger white college students would grow up different.''

Malcolm's rebuff of the white college coed who sought him out in a Harlem restaurant reached the pages of *Life* magazine. Political activist Yuri Kuchiama had read the article in *Life*; she remembers it on September 16, 1963, the day she spotted Malcolm X at the center of a crowd of black people in the Brooklyn criminal courthouse. ''I had thought, gee, that takes a lot of nerve,'' says Kuchiama about the coed, ''and I could see why Malcolm was upset and said there's nothing you can do for me, you should just work in your own community. I didn't want to make the same mistake,'' she continues, ''but I did want to meet him. I stood on the outer rim of the group around him, and I kept moving in closer, and I could see that he was looking and noticed this Asian woman was coming in closer and closer, and then I went right up to him and said—I know it sounds so stupid—'Can I shake your hand?' He looked at me very quizzically and sternly, then he showed that fantastic smile of his and put out his hand, and asked, 'For what?' I got a little bit scared and just sort of blurted out, 'I just wanted to congratulate you on all you're doing for your people.' He looked at me distrustingly. 'I don't know what you mean,' he said, and I said, 'I admire all you do, but I don't agree with everything you say.' Malcolm asked, 'What don't you agree with?' I said, 'Your feelings about integration,' and he said, 'I can't give you a two-minute dissertation on my feelings toward integration. Why don't you come to my office and we'll discuss it.' I couldn't believe it. 'Make an appointment with my secretary,' he said.''

As it turned out, Yuri Kuchiama did not see Malcolm again until the following year, on June 4, when Malcolm attended a reception at her apartment in Harlem for the Hiroshima-Nagasaki Peace Study Mission. Malcolm also spoke on that occasion, and ''the one person in the United States the Mission most wanted to meet'' that day disappointed no one—neither the Mission nor Kuchiama herself. Prior to that Kuchiama had been personally ''sort of disappointed,'' because Malcolm had not replied to several letters she had written him, but "when he came to my apartment that day," she recalls, "the first thing he said was that he knew I had written to him several times, and although he hadn't responded to my letters, he did appreciate them, but he had lost my address and he had been traveling. He then promised that 'from here onward, if I ever go anywhere again, I'll write to you.' And I couldn't believe it! He kept his word. He knew thousands of people, and I got twelve postcards from eleven countries from him. I hope I never lose them; I hope to pass them on to my kids. I will always treasure them."

A white college coed followed Malcolm to Harlem. He offered her only nothing. He did not allow her to see the Malcolm who surprised Yuri Kuchiama, the Malcolm who, to her, was "very warm, very sincere, and genuine and humble."

The coed burst into tears She ran out of the Muslim restaurant, out onto Lenox Avenue, and disappeared in a taxicab. Malcolm X may have convinced her that he indeed believed there were no good white people, that he viewed her as useless and held her at best in contempt. Chances are, he had. To his own regret.

"Blue-eyed Willies" he called them, the students at Harvard University. Malcolm nevertheless returned to Harvard several times and each time found his audience receptive, stimulating, eager—and even, Benjamin Karim tells us, a reason for hope.

Too, white men were denounced by Malcolm as "white devils." He fervently preached that all white peoples, Jews and Gentiles alike, their babies and women and children, would be struck down by the almighty hand of Allah. The time of Armageddon had begun, Malcolm declaimed, and his pulpit rhetoric spared only the faithful among the black Muslims. Still, blue-eyed sportscaster Dick Schaap particularly remembers an afternoon he spent with Malcolm. "Malcolm was looking to move out of the Hotel Theresa," Schaap recalls. "He had his offices, I think, on the mezzanine or the second floor, and he was looking to move, and I went with him, looking at various places where he enjoyed the game of haggling with all the Jewish merchants as to what rent he would pay. It was a game; he knew it was a game and he was enjoying it—he was having fun doing it."

Apparently, Malcolm did not always conform to his pulpit image. Schaap observes that, as with "many activists of the time, Malcolm's rhetoric and his personal beliefs were not exactly the same thing. He preached one way and he preached hatred, but one-to-one he did not hate people until they showed whether they deserved to be hated or not. I found the same thing true of Harry Edwards, who was a leader of the revolt of black athletes against the white establishment. Harry's rhetoric was all 'kill whitey' and 'burn the stadiums' and all that, and then he'd say, 'Let's go have a drink.' And I think Malcolm was similar. Malcolm didn't hate people because of their color, Malcolm hated the injustices he had seen."

Journalist Claude Lewis was introduced to the minister of Muslim Mosque No. 7 at a New York radio station in 1962. Malcolm's public image had not led Lewis to expect the man he met. "Malcolm was the first to offer his seat to a white woman who came into the studio," Lewis recalls, "which surprised me, because that wasn't his image. He was so polite and friendly and warm and kind of engaging; that's what stood out, and it made me want to know the real Malcolm X as opposed to his image."

By 1962 the image was fierce, and the black nationalist rhetoric inflammatory. It augured violence, it advertised intolerance, it mongered racist hatred. Malcolm's words were quoted in the daily press and broadcast on the radio. His image was repeatedly being cast on television screens across America. Malcolm X was news.

The media lent Malcolm's compelling voice further force. "It's 1991, and we've now heard all the shocking rhetoric it's possible to hear," notes author and journalist Peter Goldman, but "in Malcolm's day a guy standing up on television saying white folks are the devil and are going to suffer the wrath of Allah, and it's going to be bad; saying that your cities will burn, and that black people do not or may not want the company of white people and that we reject you, that we want power over our own communities and we don't want integration or, as Malcolm put it, 'coffee with a cracker'; saying that black people have a worth and pride and history of their own—I mean, that was radical stuff then. It was revolutionary.''

The fact that Malcolm failed to ''produce a twelve-point program for the salvation of black America'' Goldman finds far less significant than Malcolm's ''great force as a teacher, as a consciousness-raiser, at a time when that was a very critical role.'' Not only television but also radio and the press helped Malcolm realize more fully the power of that role. ''He was very public relations conscious, very sophisticated about the modern media and how to use it,'' says Goldman, who is currently working on a book about political consultants, and adds, ''They could learn a few things from Malcolm about creating media events.''

Schaap too comments on Malcolm's skill at ''manipulating the press. He charmed the press and provided it with material; he was exciting. He probably never had the following that he liked to imply he had, but most political leaders don't have the following they imply they have. He was good at dealing with the press and good at using the press.'' Although ''Malcolm tried to call it as hard and as straight as he could with the press in terms of his philosophy and outlook,'' says former newspaperman James Booker, ''he did know how to play his loaded words and get in his emotional comments so they would get good mileage in the right places.''

Malcolm clearly recognized the power of the press, television, and radio. Indeed, Robert Haggins recalls a conversation in which Malcolm identified the news media as ''the most powerful entity on earth. And I asked him how,'' says Haggins, ''and he answered that the media has the power to make the innocent guilty and to make the guilty innocent; and that's power. Because they control the minds of the masses. And it's easy to do, once you understand how the media works, he said. You see, with the media you are very selective about what information you give people—you don't have to lie to them, you just have to be selective about what you tell them—because human beings gather information and they form opinions based on the information you have given them.''

However masterfully Malcolm may have used the news media, he was, Haggins believes, at the same time misused— or misrepresented—by them. Referring to a photograph in a German publication, Haggins says, "That's Malcolm, with his family; it's a side of Malcolm that most people never saw. Let me tell you a story about that. You know Malcolm sometimes, during his deliveries, would get so worked up and get so emotionally charged and angry—I think it's normal for any human being in the position of being black in white America to be angry—and he would be so angry that sometimes he would ball his fists and do like that [Haggins raises a clenched fist]; and the press would wait for that and take those pictures, and they would be the only pictures that would get published. I did the same thing, and Malcolm called me aside and said, 'I can get those pictures any day of the week, a dime a dozen. I don't like those pictures. I am not a monster, and I want you to show me as a human being.' That is why now, after twenty-five years, everybody wants to see my photographs; newspapers and magazines, everybody."

The balled fist or pointed finger, the raised arm; the indignation and the anger; the rhetoric; the fire, irony, and conviction; the grimace, the snarl: the image. The media collaborated with Malcolm in making that image, and the image in turn made news. According to Alex Haley, it also made Malcolm uneasy. Haley explains: "I think that Malcolm was embarrassed, genuinely embarrassed, by a lot of his prominence in the media. I know he was discomfited by it, because—I didn't know this until later—his prominence in the media was what some others in the movement were using to undermine him with Mr. Elijah Muhammad." . . .

Malcolm twice appeared with PBS newsman Joe Durso on the WNDT-TV interview program *The World at Ten*, which in the 1960s often featured significant figures in the civil rights movement. Already familiar with Malcolm's public image, Durso had expected "somebody who was more—I'm not sure what word to use—not more active, not more dynamic. Perhaps more extreme, but that's not the right word either. More militant, I guess, or more flamboyant. And I think the name added a mystique, it had a certain impact: Malcolm X. It was a very memorable name, so I expected someone with a little more fire perhaps.'' Instead, Durso was struck by Malcolm's conservative manner and appearance: ''He was dressed in a business suit—as I remember, a pinstripe suit—and he looked for all the world like a businessman or a person who might make news behind the scenes but not like somebody who was out front and visible and fiery. He was much more low-key than I had expected.'' For Duros, ''low-key'' also describes Malcolm's style in the PBS interviews: ''He was very forthright. He didn't make fiery speeches; he responded to questions and he made his points compellingly, in a dialogue. I guess I expected more of a platform speaker, somebody who was very militant. He was more cerebral than physical. He reasoned. He was almost like a college professor.'' Malcolm may have adopted this style, Durso suggests, because PBS was ''considered the home of intellectual programming in those days'' and Malcolm probably ''understood the audience that he was reaching was more interested in dialogue than in his more flamboyant theatrics.'' Durso's suggestion that Malcolm understood his audiences, their predispositions as well as their expectations, was in general true, so it would appear; he also evidently understood the effect and value of inconsistency. Malcolm's behavior often failed to conform to his image, and often confounded his observers.

Attorney William Kunstler first interviewed Malcolm on WMCA radio in 1960. Before that, though, they had ''met on a number of occasions and got to be, relatively speaking, friends.'' Kunstler speaks relatively because ''at the time Malcolm was talking a lot about white devils—this was before he came back from Mecca—and it would have been impossible, I think, for any white person to get too close to him during that period of his life.'' One interview with Malcolm that Kunstler will never forget, however, was neither broadcast on the radio nor conducted by him. Kunstler tells the story: ''My first wife had become quite friendly with Malcolm and he did many favors for her, including one which I've always remembered. He agreed to sit for an interview by a paraplegic reporter from *The Patent Trader*, which is an up-country Westchester newspaper with probably no black readers at all, and he sat for four hours doing an interview with a man who could only take down what Malcolm said by typing with the big toe of one foot on a typewriter. It was apparently an excruciating ordeal for Malcolm, but he sat for this white reporter, whose constituency could be only all white, and was as kind and considerate as anyone could be in such an interview, and I've always remembered that. It was a side of Malcolm that no one really knows about, and it was indicative that the man really had enormous compassion and was willing to give up four hours to a reporter whose column really meant nothing to him one way or the other."

Malcolm's image did not capture many sides of the man. It simplified the man; it could not contain him.

The NOI could not contain Malcolm either. On March 8, 1964, *The New York Times* ran an article announcing "Malcolm X Splits With Muhammad," and reporting Malcolm's plans to establish a black nationalist party and to cooperate with other local civil rights actions in order to heighten the political consciousness of African Americans. The announcement cannot have come entirely to the NOI leader's surprise. Three months later, on December 4, 1963, Elijah Muhammad had suspended Malcolm from his ministry, supposedly for ninety days, because at an NOI rally on December 1, contrary to a directive from Muhammad that no Muslim minister discuss the recent assassination of President Kennedy, Malcolm had replied to a question from the floor that Kennedy "never foresaw that the chickens would come home to roost so soon."

Benjamin Karim remembers it this way: "Mr. Muhammad had issued an edict, I guess you could say, that no minister should speak out against the dead president, because black people loved President Kennedy so much and it could turn the black community against the Muslims. Mr. Muhammad was supposed to speak in New York City on December 1, 1963, at Manhattan Center. He canceled it, perhaps because of Kennedy's assassination, and Malcolm asked him if he could speak in his place, which he allowed him to do. The title of his speech, which was the only written speech I've ever known

Malcolm to speak from—I had the written speech at one time and I let somebody have it, but hopefully I can get it back— was 'God's Judgment on America.' It wasn't 'The Chickens Coming Home to Roost.' But a lady stood up in the audience and asked Malcolm what did he think of Kennedy's assassination, and he made that statement that it was a sign of its chickens coming home to roost."

Malcolm's statement was of course widely reported in the press, and to many Americans, both black and white, it seemed exultant. The statement is ambiguous, but in Dick Schaap's opinion, "it was not a very smart thing to say. Only I don't think he meant it in the way people interpreted it, I don't think he was exactly gloating over it. I think he was being realistic— that the atmosphere of violence had produced more violence." What Malcolm meant, according to Karim, was that "the chickens coming home to roost was simply the culmination of American history; it had culminated in the act of a citizen of this country assassinating his own president."

After the rally "John Ali went back to Chicago," says Karim, "and told Mr. Muhammad that Malcolm had spoken out against the dead president, and they suspended him. I was in the temple when this happened. We were told that if Malcolm comes back to give him a job in the restaurant washing dishes, and I went and told him what had taken place. Plus," Karim adds, "he knew that he wasn't going to be able to get back in. I think that's the point at which he actually made up his mind to leave."

Although dedicated to his ministry and to the leadership of Elijah Muhammad, Malcolm had been frustrated by the apolitical stance of the NOI for some time prior to the suspension, according to Benjamin Karim. Karim cites the Ronald Stokes incident as a case in point. Stokes died of gunshot wounds on April 27, 1962, when the Muslim mosque in Los Angeles was fired upon by police; six other Muslims were also wounded. The next day Malcolm was dispatched to California by Elijah Muhammad. "When he went out there," says Karim, "he told these Muslims that they should retaliate in kind. The police commissioner in L.A. called Mr. Muhammad and told him to bring Malcolm out of California because he was about to cause some bloodshed. That's what it really got down to; he had actually gone out there to have the Muslims retaliate against the police for that incident. Mr. Muhammad went along with the police commissioner. Malcolm became very disillusioned, but he never went against Mr. Muhammad or did an opposite thing from what he was told to do. That was just one of the things.''

Karim mentions two other things that thwarted Malcolm's emerging political consciousness. ''We were never active in any kind of civil rights movement. And we didn't even vote. As Malcolm became more worldly he saw that we were becoming smaller and smaller and not moving in the direction that the whole world was moving. And I believe that all these negatives that were happening within the Nation of Islam—always very vocal, but no movement—had much to do with him leaving.''

In Karim's view, then, Malcolm's eventual split with Muhammad was effected by his own ambitions as well as by pressures from within the ranks of the NOI. Karim offers the following analogy: ''It's like a baby, like when a baby outgrows his mother's womb and forces push him into a higher world. I think there were forces, so to speak, that were pushing Malcolm on, along with the exterior forces of those corrupt [NOI] officials.''

That forces inside the NOI conspired to oust Malcolm from his ministry, and indeed from the Nation of Islam itself, is echoed by other voices. Malcolm had begun his career as a Muslim minister in 1953. ''Until Malcolm came on the scene,'' Charles Kenyatta says of the Nation of Islam, ''you could have put all their following in a station wagon and still have some room left. The teaching of Islam was never geared to reach from the back streets to the universities. It was strictly what we could call a back street religion.''

In 1963 the back street religion was a national phenomenon; so was Malcolm X. In eleven years he had risen through the ranks of the NOI to become by far the most dynamic of the Muslim ministers and certainly the most visible both in the Nation and in the national media. Malcolm's popularity easily rivaled Elijah Muhammad's own. As Claude Lewis sees him, "Malcolm had developed into such a dominant figure in the eyes of the blacks that he had superseded Elijah Muhammad. People liked Elijah Muhammad because he brought us Malcolm X. But when Malcolm spoke, people really listened, and I think that disturbed people in the Nation at that time and it certainly pushed Elijah Muhammad into the background."

Malcolm's prominence in the media and his high regard among American blacks outside the Nation as well as in it increasingly irritated the NOI officials in Elijah Muhammad's Chicago headquarters, in the opinion of Benjamin Karim. They had more than face to lose. Karim explains: "Mr. Muhammad had an illness—bronchitis—and many of the officials around him thought that he was going to die; and if he had died, Malcolm would have inherited that position as the leader of the Nation of Islam. At that time Muslims had built quite a few businesses—very lucrative ones—and had even bought a jet, a jet plane. There was a lot of money floating around and a lot of people were spending money in areas where it shouldn't have been spent, and Malcolm spoke out against it. And they knew that if Mr. Muhammad had passed on, they would not have their positions anymore, because they were the first people that Malcolm would have gotten rid of. I think that had more to do with it—economics—and they had gotten greedy. They were living a lifestyle they had never lived before and had money, the kind of money they'd never dreamed that they would have had before."

Nor did Elijah Muhammad himself escape Malcolm's moral scrutiny. Malcolm was visiting the NOI headquarters in Chicago, according to Karim, when "one of Mr. Muhammad's sons, W. D. Muhammad, who is well known today, Wallace D. Muhammad, had taken Malcolm aside and told him—matter of fact, Dick Gregory did too, in Chicago; he and Dick Gregory were very close, they had a very close friendship—but W. D. Muhammad had told Malcolm that these secretaries had these children, had been pregnant. He said they were children of Mr. Muhammad and that they were afraid that the newspaper would get a hold of it and in so doing they could almost destroy the

Nation of Islam, because we thought that Mr. Muhammad was infallible. Really, seriously, you can't imagine; you know, like Hirohito—the same as the Japanese thought of Hirohito is how we thought of Mr. Muhammad. So what Malcolm did was to call a gathering of all the ministers, and he told them what had happened and that they should take stories out of the Bible that showed an imperfection in a holy men—like Noah, you know, after the flood, he got drunk. . . . So you're planting these seeds of imperfection about these holy man [in the minds of the Muslim brothers and sisters, Malcolm told us], so when the paper hits, the imperfections of the prophets that have already been implanted in their minds will absorb the shock that the newspapers come out with. It would have caused shock waves throughout the Nation of Islam.''

By December 1963 Malcolm was uncomfortably enmeshed in the internal politics of the NOI. He had his enemies inside the NOI ranks, and his ill-timed comment on Kennedy may indeed, as some believe, have provided them with the very pretext they needed to suspend, and in effect disempower, Malcolm X. Elombe Braath describes a cartoon he himself drew around that time. It shows ''Malcolm, who has written on the blackboard, like a hundred times, 'JFK was not a devil.' He is holding his wrist, wringing it, and Elijah Muhammad is sitting at a table with his son-in-law Raymond leaning over and whispering in his ear. It was sort of a conspiracy. And Malcolm had got suspended.''

And silenced. For ninety days. ''One thing I used to remind him of,'' says Charles Kenyatta, ''is that for twelve years you have been teaching these men how to love Elijah Muhammad and I said in ninety days they haven't changed their mind that easy, and I was right, because they too were part of the plot.''

About two weeks before the official announcement in *The New York Times* of Malcolm's break with Elijah Muhammad, the *Amsterdam News* printed an article by James Booker that suggested tensions inside the NOI might be widening the rift between the suspended minister of Mosque No. 7 and the leader of the black Muslims. The article did not please Malcolm or the NOI. Booker recounts that ''Malcolm had told me or implied there was friction between him and Elijah Muhammad, and I had heard from others close to him about the nature of the problems, and no one had told me this was off the record. After I wrote an item which hinted at these problems, this friction, Malcolm caught a lot of flak from within the [black Muslim] movement and he came up to the office to deny that he had said it, and he came up with about five of his guys. And while he was going into the editor's office, which was on the same floor as mine, five of his guys just stood around me. They shook up the office, they were like storm troopers. Malcolm just stormed past me. Everybody on the staff knew what it was about. I was a little nervous, but I knew that what I had written I had gotten directly. And for Malcolm to now deny it because of internal problems, that was not my concern. My editor did not make me retract it, and in fact, as conditions developed, two weeks later he had his official split with the movement. The next time he saw me he just gave me this wry smile.''

After ninety days of silence Malcolm announced his split with Elijah Muhammad; from the outset it was probably inevitable. Like Benjamin Karim, Peter Goldman thinks that when Malcolm was first informed of his suspension from the NOI, ''he knew that he would not be going back. I think he had sources, and he had an understanding of the way their procedures worked. I was working for *Newsweek*,'' Goldman continues, ''and it was right in the thick of the massive Kennedy coverage. We were doing a short item on Malcolm's remark about the chickens coming home to roost and his suspension, and I called him—in this case not for an extended interview but just for, in effect, one quote—and I thought we'd be on the phone for a couple of minutes. He understood that kind of thing; he was used to TV guys wanting sound bytes, so normally it would have been a quick, businesslike phone call—in effect, him saying here's your quote, and I would say thanks and then good luck, and good-bye. In this case he kept the conversation going and asked me what I thought, which he had never done before, and he never did it afterwards; so that's not a bad indicator. I'm not sure that vulnerability is the word, but he seemed to have a contingent sense of his own life at that moment, I think.''

For three months Malcolm stood outside the Nation of Islam. His suspension stripped him of his ministry. It shut him out of the Muslim community in Harlem that he had led and cut him off from the brothers and sisters whose lives he had touched and changed, like that of Benjamin Karim. ''We ate only once a day,'' Karim relates, ''and believe it or not, a lot of people don't bathe every day, but that was insisted upon. Our diet changed; where we ate white bread we were told to eat wheat bread, what a lot of people now call health food. Movies were cut out. Parties were cut out. We had a juke box that only played jazz and Middle Eastern music or music from Africa— no blues, perhaps because a lot of blues is sad and a lot is talking about my woman left me or I caught somebody with her, or something like that.'' According to Karim, suspension meant for Malcolm, as for any member of the mosque, that ''you are not supposed to speak to any Muslim, in fact. If you were suspended, say, for instance, for taking someone's watch, you would probably be given a year out. That's really like a year in prison, because not many people speak your language now that you have learned to live a certain lifestyle, and to take you out of that lifestyle and put you back in the public so you can no longer associate with Muslims is hell. And it's hard for somebody outside the community to really understand that that was a punishment.'' Nonetheless, whatever pain the suspension may have caused Malcolm, ''when he first left, split, he didn't,'' Karim points out, ''say anything against Mr. Muhammad.''

Robert Haggins emphasizes too that Malcolm ''never really attacked Elijah Muhammad as such; he always respected him because he was his first real teacher. And he taught Malcolm that he was a black man, that he was an African and had every right to be proud of his heritage and every right to understand and to learn the truth and to look at the truth of religion and to look at the truth of history.'' What Malcolm was taught as Muslim doctrine, according to C. Eric Lincoln, ''could be summed up and often was summed up by Elijah as, quote, 'to tell you the truth about the white man and to tell you the truth about yourself. Only when you know these two truths can you ever be free and can you ever obtain justice or equality.' "

C. Eric Lincoln also recalls an exchange between Malcolm and the late journalist Louis Lomax at the Muslim restaurant in Harlem. "In the course of this conversation Lomax, who wrote the book on the Muslims called *When the Word Is Given*, said to Malcolm, he said, 'Look, Malcolm, why don't you stop all that Mr. Muhammad shit? Why don't you start your own movement and lead your own movement? You got the brains,' and so on and so forth. And Malcolm leaped up from the table as if he had been stuck with a hat pin—I had never seen a man so furious—as if he was going to attack Lomax on the spot, but we were all friends, and he said, 'Lou Lomax, don't you *ever* say that to me again. Mr. Muhammad is responsible for everything that I am today. He brought me from nowhere to where I am and as long as I live I will be loyal to him, and I don't want to hear that anymore!' "

On March 11, 1964, three days after Malcolm severed his ties with the NOI, he issued a public telegram in which he acknowledged Elijah Muhammad as his "leader and teacher" and gave him "full credit for what I know and who I am."

Then he continued.

Peter Goldman views Malcolm's departure from the NOI as part of a continuum, a process of politicization, that had started years before. "The Nation of Islam is a very cloistered group," explains Goldman, "or was, as Malcolm found it and as he left it, and to a great degree still is. Its politics was a kind of anti-politics, a psychic withdrawal from the white world. Its metaphor was 'give us four or five stars, give us some land of our own,' but its reality was a kind of psychic withdrawal from the community. Meanwhile, the civil rights movement was coming to life in the South and Malcolm was viewing it from the North with a kind of split vision. It was irresistible in terms of black people fighting for justice in society. On the other hand, it did not relate to the lives of black people in the northern ghetto, and he realized both these things. He wanted to be, as I said before, part of his time. And to be part of his time, he was going through a process of politicization, taking the Nation public, putting on these great rallies, being on the air a lot, being in the papers a lot—I think, not for self-aggrandizement; I'm sure he enjoyed the attention, but I don't think that that was his motive. I think his motive was to make the Nation relevant to the world. So I think a metamorphosis had begun. He got involved too in the internal politics of the Nation, which led to his exile. At that point, though, I think he was probably ready to be exiled. I think it was a continuum that started years before. It wasn't simply breaking with Elijah Muhammad; it was a process.''

In the process Malcolm lost one of his most valued friends.

According to Alex Haley, between 1962 and 1964, when he and Malcolm were working together on the autobiography, besides "Mr. Muhammad, whom Malcolm revered, absolutely adulated,'' there were "two other people he highly respected. One of them was a young fellow who . . . Malcolm called 'my little brother,' and they were most fond of each other. And this young man was Louis Farrakhan, as he is known today. . . . And similarly, there was another young fellow who got to know Malcolm and vice versa, and they just had a marvelous attachment to each other, and that was the young Cassius Clay.''

"It was Malcolm,'' as Charles Kenyatta tells it, "who was most responsible for him [Clay] wanting to become a member of the NOI. He had a brother in there by the name of Rudy. Rudy had been a member, but Muhammad Ali had not been. So Muhammad Ali—I mean Cassius, as he was called at that time—used to come to the mosques at different places, whatever city he would be in, and Malcolm might be there too, and like many others, he was so attracted to Malcolm's teaching that when he would come to the mosque, he would always sit up front.''

In January 1964, six weeks into his suspension, Malcolm spent some time with Cassius Clay at his training camp in Miami, Florida, where Clay was preparing for the world heavyweight boxing championship match with Sonny Liston the next month. Malcolm was there again in February, when Clay won the title. Despite the silence imposed upon him by the NOI,

Malcolm had continued to serve Clay as his spiritual advisor, and Haley remembers that "Cassius wasn't going to have it without Malcolm being there, and Malcolm was there. Malcolm called me before the fight and said it was sure to be one of the greatest upsets in modern times. . . . And then they fell out. When Malcolm was ejected from the Nation of Islam, Cassius Clay stayed with the Messenger, Mr. Muhammad."

Clay's friend James Brown, then the star running back for the Cleveland Browns, was also in Florida that February. Because Malcolm had been suspended by the NOI for his statement regarding the Kennedy assassination, James Brown believes, "Malcolm decided, I guess, that he was going to form his own group. And he was there, in Miami, basically to see if Ali would be a part of his group. Everybody was avoiding Malcolm at the time, because he wasn't in good standing with the Nation, and of course he wasn't in good standing with America, so he was more or less by himself, and I used to go visit with him and we used to talk. Then, the night of the fight, the night he won, after Ali won, we all went to this little black motel. Ali went with me into the back room; he left Malcolm and the other people in the front room, and Ali talked for about two hours about Elijah Muhammad and the powers of Elijah Muhammad, and that he wasn't going to go with Malcolm because the power was with the little man—a man of little physical stature, but he was a brilliant man, and he, Ali, was his follower and from that night on he would not really deal with Malcolm.

"When he came out of the room, Malcolm said to me, 'Jim, don't you think that now that Ali is the heavyweight champion of the world, he should stop bragging as much as he used to?' I agreed with him, because I felt that now Ali was in the driver's seat and he did not have to talk the way he did before. So that was the only conversation that Malcolm, Ali, and I had after Ali had come out of the back room and joined everybody else. The essence of the situation was that Ali said that he would no longer deal with Malcolm. That part of it bothered me, because I knew Malcolm had been the one who recruited him into the Nation of Islam."

It was soon after the Liston fight that Cassius Clay changed his name to Muhammad Ali. He remained loyal to the NOI and the leadership of the little man with the powers, Elijah Muhammad. On March 12, 1964, at a press conference in New York, Malcolm announced the formation of the Muslim Mosque, Incorporated. If he was upset or hurt by the disaffection of Ali, "this is something I never heard him say," says Charles Kenyatta, "but I know that it affected him to a degree, because, at the time, and as a matter of fact, Ali was supposed to go with us when the split came."

On May 17, 1964, in Accra, near the end of an exhilarating African tour, Malcolm by chance encountered Muhammad Ali, who was also touring Africa; accompanying Ali was Herbert Muhammad, Elijah's son. Malcolm shared some of the pain in that moment with Alex Haley: "He was walking through the airport; he turned left, and then saw that there was Muhammad Ali—he had changed his name now—and they came towards each other and their eyes met, and Malcolm saw Muhammad Ali look away from him and walk past him without speaking, and that just ripped Malcolm up and down. I don't think he ever got over the hurt of that."

In the spring of 1964, from April 13 to May 21, Malcolm toured the Middle East and Africa. He flew first to Cairo, then to Jedda, and made a pilgrimage to Mecca. He sent Dick Schaap a postcard. "It said, 'Greetings from Mecca,' " and described the holy city as " 'the fountain of truth, love, peace, and brotherhood.' " (Schaap mentions by the way that the *Herald-Tribune* printed Malcolm's message "the day after he was shot, and unfortunately, the original of the postcard vanished in the composing room that day; so all I've got is a photostat.")

Alex Haley also received a postcard from Mecca. In "fine handwriting," says Haley, Malcolm wrote that he had " 'eaten from the same plate with fellow Muslims whose eyes were bluer than blue, whose hair was blond, blonder than blond, whose skin was whiter than white.' " Malcolm then added, " 'And we were all the same.' " Haley finds in this message from Mecca a sign of profound change in Malcolm: "I don't think anything I ever saw or heard connected with him gave me the feeling or impact that that did of how much he had changed, because that would not have been the Malcolm I had known earlier . . .''

"I had gotten two postcards from him," recounts James Farmer, "from Mecca, on his two separate trips there. He went to Mecca and then left Mecca and went elsewhere, the Third World, and then returned to Mecca. At a later date I asked him if those postcards had indicated a change in his thinking, and he asked if I could refresh his memory as to what he had said in the cards. I told him the first card had said: 'Dear Brother James, I am now in Mecca, the most beautiful and sacred city in the world, where I have witnessed pilgrims of all colors'— and he had underscored all colors—'worshipping Allah in perfect peace and harmony and brotherhood such as I have never seen in the States.' Second card, and it was signed with his new name, the name he had accepted over there—Malik El-Shabazz: 'Here I am, back in Mecca. I am still traveling, trying to broaden my mind, for I've seen too much of the damage narrow-mindedness can make of things, and when I return home to America, I will devote what energies I have to repairing the damage.' When I asked him if that indicated a change in his thinking, he said that yes, as a matter of fact, it did. 'I have some explaining to do,' he said, 'I was not so lucky as you were. I have very little formal education, eight grades. I am self-educated. I read for myself; mostly in prison I read the dictionary backwards,' and he said, 'consequently I believed everything the Honorable Elijah Muhammad told us, and the Honorable Elijah Muhammad told us that Islam was a black man's religion—exclusively—and that the blue-eyed devils could not get close to Mecca, that they would be killed if they tried to enter that sacred city. In Mecca I saw blue-eyed blonds worshipping Allah just as I was, kneeling right beside me, so obviously the Honorable Elijah Muhammad had lied.'

"Malcolm had to do a lot of rethinking then," Farmer continues. "He was an honest man. He didn't try to adjust the facts to fit what he had been saying, he tried to adjust what he had been saying to fit the facts. He said then, 'When I was in Accra, Ghana, I met with the Algerian ambassador to Ghana, and he asked me what my program was, and I proceeded to tell him my plan and programs for my black brothers and sisters. He said, "Well, Brother Malcolm, that leaves me out, doesn't it?" I asked what he meant; he said, "I'm your Mohammedan brother, but I'm not your black brother. Racially, I'm Caucasian." ' And Malcolm said that shook him up even more for some reason and he really had to sit down and do some thinking. And reexamine, search his soul, ask himself where the process had led him. He said, 'Well, I have come to the conclusion, Brother James, that anybody who will fight along with us—not for us, but with us—is my bother and that goes for your three guys, too'—Schwerner, Goodman, and Chaney; those were the three who were killed in Mississippi, and he knew very well that two of those were my staff members and that two of them, Schwerner and Goodman, were Jewish. So this was quite a concession for Malcolm X to be making. I asked him why his speeches at Harlem Square Saturday afternoons had not reflected that so far, that change in direction, and he said, 'Brother James, you must be enough of a politician to understand that if a leader makes a sudden right angle turn, he turns alone.' "

Benjamin Karim too was struck by the change in Malcolm, because, like Malcolm, he had been "taught there were no white people who were Muslims, no Caucasians. We were also taught that Caucasians could not enter the city of Mecca. So we really had something unique, just unique for black people. Not only that, but our Islam was different than that the rest of the Muslims had in the world. But when Malcolm made the pilgrimage to Mecca—the hajj—when the hajj is made, there are millions of people from all over the world, every color, every shade in the world—and during that pilgrimage he did not see any signs of any kind of racism, any kind of color prejudice, or any notion of it, or any consciousness of anybody conscious of his or her own color. The Mufti—the Grand Mufti, I believe, of Jordan—with blond hair and blue eyes! So he was really shocked into reality, and that shock woke Malcolm up that humanity is one." Karim does note, however, that "everybody is not ready for the same truth."

Perhaps Malcolm himself was not ready for that truth five years before, in July 1959, when he visited Mecca for the first time, or perhaps he was in no position to acknowledge it. He was traveling then as Elijah Muhammad's ambassador. "He had been to the Middle East before," Peter Goldman points out. "He had gone over there for Elijah Muhammad. He was quite aware that there were white Muslims. He would deny it, I mean, he would flat out deny it, as a matter of politics, when he was in the NOI." C. Eric Lincoln also remarks that when Malcolm had traveled to the Middle East before, he had gone "as the emissary for Elijah Muhammad, and he always wore the blinders of being the most faithful follower of Elijah Muhammad, so what he saw he saw through those eyes. But it is possible that on that last trip the blinders were off, or at least partially." Change has its degrees. "I do not believe," Lincoln states further, "that Malcolm was suddenly and completely metamorphosed with his break with Elijah Muhammad; I think that would have taken time."

Lincoln observes too that "people who look for changes see them." They also interpret them. John Henrik Clarke views Malcolm as a man who had been constantly undergoing change long before the events in "the last few years of his life. People think," says Clarke, perhaps referring to a letter from Malcolm about his experience in Mecca that was printed in *The New York Times*, "that when Malcolm went to Mecca and wrote that card back saying he observed whites and browns and all different colors praying together, they think that meant his change toward integration, but that was an observation and not an analysis, and people have done Malcolm a terrible injustice by misinterpreting that." What may have seemed like a very abrupt change was, Clarke repeats, "not a change at all, it was an observation."

Or it may have been an ambiguity. Malcolm was quite familiar with ambiguities, according to Peter Goldman: "Probably as long as I had known him, he was feeling ambiguities. He just couldn't admit them, ambiguities about the world. It was not quite so—no pun intended—it was not so black and white as the doctrines of the Lost-Found Nation of Islam made it seem. I think he had already come to understand that whites were not literally the devil. I think he continued to believe, probably till the day he died, that you can search the history of white people for angelic deeds and not find a whole lot of them. I think in his sort of mercurial last year—*mercurial*'s the wrong word, *protean* is probably better—he was going through changes at great velocity, and I think as he was learning more about the world he was, I think, growing himself. I mean, I think his move toward 'orthodox' Islam—I'm not sure there is such a thing as orthodox in Islam, but I mean the way Islam is practiced in the Middle East—I think it deepened his religious understanding and also deepened his human understanding. He was no longer a man of certainties, and I think that once that falls away, a guy of his intelligence flowers.''

A month after his pilgrimage to Mecca Malcolm visited Ghana. Among the African-American expatriates in residence there Malcolm again met Maya Angelou. She recalls that ''the trip was a real eye-opener for Malcolm on so many levels.'' Angelou had always respected and appreciated Malcolm, ''but my appreciation increased really noticeably after he said, 'I have always said whites were blue-eyed devils, but I have been to Mecca and I have seen whites with blue eyes with whom I felt a brotherhood, and so I can no longer say this—that all whites are evil.' It took a lot of courage to say that—an amazing amount of courage. It took an incredible amount of insight, first to give up what one had said for years and years and say, 'Just wait a minute, let me relook at this, let me rethink, respeak this,' but he had the courage to do so and the insight to do so, and then the courage to say so, which just humbled me. He had no loyalty to misconceptions. He was intelligent and courageous enough to admit when a position no longer held true, and that's amazing. Very few people have that; most people would rather like to say what they say they believe in and then repeat themselves instead of saying, 'I'm not in love with the position, I'm in love with the search for truth'—and that was Malcolm.''

Alice Windom had been living in Ghana since the autumn of 1962. She had met Malcolm only once before, in 1960 or 1961, in Chicago, at the NOI temple, where he had spoken and demonstrated his "spectacular and spellbinding" oratorical skills. In Africa Malcolm was equally exciting with a crowd, but Windom and other of the African-American residents in Accra also had the opportunity to see him and speak with him in more leisurely circumstances. "He seemed very relaxed," says Windom, and "we felt we got to know him there. He was a very sensitive and very wise person."

Windom reflects upon that spring when Malcolm was in Africa. "He had been in Ghana for a week, May 10 to 17. That week was just filled with high points, everything was a highlight—the speeches, the time we would sit in the hotel talking, when Malcolm wasn't too tired. Usually, we were all smoking, and he wasn't, and he would talk about the bad effect of smoking on your health and advise us that we ought to stop, not in any holier-than-thou way, but just to say that if you were going to be around for the struggle, you needed to take care of your health and smoking was bad for you. Those were the quiet times, and also when we would be in a restaurant or hotel, chatting. . . .

"We talked about what was going on in the States, what his plans for political activity were when he returned to the U.S., what those of us who were African residents could do to cooperate with his new organization—the OAAU [Organization of Afro-American Unity]. He said that when he got back to the U.S., he intended to organize people to work on racial problems in the U.S., and we would be his cooperating or coordinating agency in Africa. One of the things he was doing in Africa was eliciting support to bring charges against the U.S. for racism with the United Nations. Malcolm had been chafing to get into the political life of the U.S.; that was one of the differences he had with the NOI. The prohibition that the NOI had placed on Malcolm's political involvement was the only specific aspect he mentioned about being happy that he was no longer a member of the NOI. I didn't get the impression he was glad to be out of the Nation. I doubt that he was, because it meant he had to go out and build a new organization."

In July 1964 Malcolm returned to Africa as the representative of the OAAU for the African Summit Conference in Cairo, at which he appealed to the delegates of the thirty-four African nations to bring the cause of the twenty-two million African Americans in the United States before the United Nations. After the second summit conference in August Malcolm extended his stay in Africa well into November; he visited a third of its countries, talked with their heads of state, addressed their parliaments. In Ethiopia he ran into Alice Windom.

"The only time I saw Malcolm after he left Accra [In May]," Windom recalls, "was in Ethiopia later on that same year. I had gone with Julian [Mayfield] and Maya [Angelou] to Cairo, hoping to meet Malcolm there, and I had found him gone. I went on to Ethiopia to work for the United Nations, and the second or third day I was there he walked into the hotel dining room. He was traveling in East Africa. He was interested in seeing Emperor Haile Selassie and he was not successful in doing that; the Emperor was a client of the U.S. and really did not want to meet with Malcolm for that reason. He told me about the other heads of state that he had met in East Africa and he felt he had had a successful trip there, but again Ghana probably was the high point because of the presence of the large African-American community there. The Ghanaians were also progressive politically because of Kwame Nkrumah's leadership and the groundwork he had laid to educate people about the whole racial situation everywhere in the world; everybody was ready for Malcolm there."

More than Malcolm's understanding of Islam had changed when he returned to New York that May from his tour of the Middle East and Africa, although his experience in Mecca was of course, in Charles Kenyatta's words, "the big story, and the reporters kept asking, 'Did you see them?' And Malcolm said, 'Yes, I saw them. They had blond hair and blue eyes,' and it developed that their religion was different. So this is what caused a big stir." Another change—less dramatic perhaps, but one noticed immediately by Kenyatta—was that "he and I were the first to start growing beards. He had started when he was over there, and he came back and I had a beard, so we were both laughing about it. In Islam, at that time, black Muslims had skinny heads, clean faces, and they started to say he and I were losing our minds.'' What the black Muslims were saying had more to do with hope than hyperbole: "Because,'' says Kenyatta, "that was one of the things that Elijah Muhammad— due to the fact that Malcolm had a number of mental break- downs in his family, that was one of the things that they were relying upon, that Malcolm would eventually go crazy.''

There was also another story that May, according to Ken- yatta. "I think I'm one of the only ones—in fact, I know I'm one of the only ones—that detected his hurt. And he was going to be, if you could understand how the Nation of Islam was when a member was put out of the mosque. Oh, I've seen older men cry and weep, because they didn't want to go back into what they called the grave; and Malcolm was no different. And the whole crux of the story, I believe, is that ten or fifteen minutes before he was assassinated, if Elijah Muhammad had asked him to come back, he would have come back.'' Rather than working through the recently formed MMI or founding the OAAU, Malcolm, Kenyatta says, "would have preferred to stay [with the NOI]. No question about it, that I do know.''

Malcolm's independence from the NOI meant, as Alice Win- dom has observed, "he had to go out and build a new organiza- tion.'' Similarly, Alex Haley notes that "he had to create some organization of his own because the power base was gone. His power base had been the Nation of Islam.'' To use television journalist Mike Wallace's terms, he had lost his constituency. Wallace remembers "feeling at the time that this is a man in transition, this is a man who is evolving, this is a man who deserves a wider constituency. And I remember feeling how sad it was that he was unable to find that constituency and the money and whatever else is needed to get launched. As a re- porter—obviously, I'm just a reporter—but in my heart I felt that he had a great deal to offer and I was sad that he wasn't finding the support in the community.''

The black community, however, was already divided. "Deter- mined [as Malcolm was] to start his own organization,'' in Claude Lewis's opinion, for him or "for anybody to step away from the original leader and come up with his own program, and to offer a new ideal, a new playing ground" required more than intelligence, will, charisma, or rhetoric. It required staff, financing, strategy, community support. Malcolm had entered a field already crowded with players—among them his one friend in the civil rights leadership, James Farmer, director of CORE. The public, Lewis continues, "had grown used to people like Roy Wilkins [of the NAACP] and like the head of the Urban League, Whitney Young, whom Malcolm referred to as 'Whitey' Young—he would pretend to slip in his language." And, of course, like the eloquent president of the Southern Christian Leadership Conference, Dr. Martin Luther King, Jr. (After the split with Elijah Muhammad, Lewis notes, Malcolm "began to say kinder things about Martin Luther King, Jr., because he used to laugh at King. King got the peace prize, but we've got the problem, he would say." The sally James Farmer particularly remembers come "after King's speech in the March on Washington, which I missed—I was in jail at the time—and Malcolm said [of King's dream] that it was a nightmare, only he's too dumb to know it.") As Mike Wallace points out: "There were so many leaders, there were so many voices. I mean, think back to that time. I mean, there were so many black voices out there and talking and established and it was a very jealous group, one vying with the other for attention, constituency, support, money."

On March 12, 1964, when Malcolm had announced at a press conference the formation of his militant black nationalist organization, the Muslim Mosque, Incorporated, he had stated emphatically that he would use his personal resources not "to fight other Negro leaders or organizations" but to "find a common approach, a common solution, to a common problem." Malcolm had spoken earlier that day with C. Eric Lincoln, who recounts the conversation. "Malcolm was [going to be] on the news at about 11:00 that morning and I asked him what he was going to do, and he said, 'I really don't know, Professor; I haven't made up my mind, but I'll tell you what I am not going to do: I am not going to start a movement in the competition of the Honorable Elijah Muhammad. I could never do that.' He said he might start some kind of school for black people to learn how to become Muslims, and I guess what he meant by that, although he didn't say so, was orthodox Muslims. He made it clear to me that he wasn't going to start a community movement and that he hadn't thought through what he was going to do."

Up to that time Malcolm had needed neither his own organization nor a plan. Professor Lincoln thinks it a "truthful hypothesis to conclude that because Malcolm was so completely reliant on Muhammad, it was never necessary to work out a plan for the future." He also suspects that "when Malcolm and Elijah came to a parting of ways, it was a sudden, cataclysmic event in the lives of both people. If Malcolm had had any intention of leading a group from that point on, he was caught without having had a chance to give it any kind of thought. One would suppose that had Malcolm survived he would have had the time to do that because he had spent all of his time, as [Louis] Lomax correctly said, telling us what Mr. Muhammad had said." Mike Wallace has a similar thought: "I felt that Malcolm had yet to realize himself on his own. I used to say back then in discussing him that he was playing Bishop Fulton Sheen to Elijah's pope."

"A new Malcolm," though, was in the making; so Peter Goldman feels. Struggling to define both a new role and a new politics for himself, he was, Goldman asserts, "in effect recreating himself yet again, not for the first time in his life, and he didn't have long enough to do it. He was like a guy suddenly out there in the sunlight and blinking in the bright sun and sort of sorting out ideas in literal and psychic motion for the rest of his life, and there wasn't time to make it whole. When he did come out, he was sort of arguing a very conventional line— I hate to say conventional; it was probably akin to the early black power ideology. It was black control of the politics and the economy of the ghetto, blacks controlling places where they were. That was probably routine stuff even then, but it flowered with the black power movement a couple years after Malcolm's death. But as he traveled abroad other elements came into his thinking, both religious and political, and I think he was still trying to sort all of them out. And he had a lot of contending

voices at home, a lot of factions within his group and a lot of
outside people all wanting a piece of him, essentially. So would
he have ever found what he was looking for? I'm not sure, but
he sure didn't have a chance to try.''

On June 28, 1964, six weeks after Malcolm's return to New
York from Africa, he announced the formation of the Organization of Afro-American Unity. "It was formed in my living
room," remembers John Henrik Clarke. "I was the one who
got the constitution from the Organization of African Unity in
order to model our constitution after it. Malcolm's joy was that
we could match up [our constitution with the African one]; we
could find parallels between the African situation and the African-American situation—that plus a whole lot of other things
we agreed with that had nothing to do with religion, because
we agreed with the basic struggle. We agreed on self-reliance,
about what people would have to do, and that an ethnic community was really a small nation and that you need everything
within that community that goes into a small nation, including
a person who would take care of the labor, the defense, employment, morality, spirituality—no matter what religion you follow,
you need one person whose main concern is the spirituality of
the community." In essence, though, thc OAAU was designed
to alter the perception of the African-American struggle for
freedom as a domestic issue by placing it on the international
level of human rights. "Malcolm saw the African-American
situation," Clarke says, "and he saw civil rights really as a
part of human rights, and he wanted to internationalize it." It
was a program, if not a plan.

Although Malcolm may have not yet formulated a concrete
plan, a pursuable strategy, for the struggle of blacks in America,
he was nevertheless, Peter Goldman thinks, "trying a number
of things. He was trying to make a human case against the
United States at the U.N., charging systematic violation of
human rights. That was getting nowhere; there were too many
U.S. client states who gave him attention but not much more.
He had committees of well-meaning people working on various
aspects of various programs; none of it ever happened. That
was not his thing, and I don't think it's important to, not quite

relevant to, judge him solely by that measure.'' For Goldman, the measure of Malcolm's greatness lies in his power as a teacher, in his ability to raise the consciousness of his people to their race and to history. Goldman sees Malcolm ''moving beyond a kind of victim psychology. The Nation of Islam was a kind of codification of a victim psychology, and I think Malcolm was trying to move beyond that—and in very different ways from what Martin Luther King was doing. For all the vast differences between them, they had a similar objective, which was to get people in motion to seize history so as not to be its objects but to be its subjects, to grab control of history.''

Malcolm strove to change history. ''He was the cutting edge of the black struggle,'' in William Kunstler's view, and he was fighting a war. ''There really is no concrete plan,'' says Kunstler. ''This is a civil war, essentially, waged in many corners of this country, and it's a war that is in many ways a highly psychological one. It is a war that changed black people's awareness of themselves—the terribly low self-image, which was created by whites in a racist attempt to keep blacks in a subservient slave or neo-slave capacity, and a corollary feeling of white superiority over blacks.'' Attitudes have changed, but ''until those things are eradicated—which will take generations, or even centuries,'' Kunstler thinks—Malcolm's war goes on.

Another generation is hearing Malcolm's words. ''Because he spoke to separatism,'' Mike Wallace concludes, ''because he spoke to nationalism, because he spoke to black pride. Because he was a superb speaker and in the national media capital . . . But the fact is,'' Wallace adds, ''he was on his uppers, wasn't he? I mean, he didn't have money, he didn't have funds. He didn't have a big following. He had a devoted but small following.''

Small though Malcolm's following was, Claude Lewis indicates that ''a lot of blacks—Negroes, in those days—identified with Malcolm, but they were afraid to come out in the open. I suggested that I would like to sign up with him, and he said that you don't have to come out in the open, because the roots are the strongest part of the tree—only you don't see them.'' Malcolm's appeal, and contribution to the black movement in the 1960s, for Lewis, ''was that he made blacks feel good about themselves and to feel more confidence; to appreciate their physical characteristics. I remember clearly in those days people trying to bleach their skin and straighten their hair. Malcolm said that was wrong, [that we should] love Mother Africa. Here was a guy who made black people feel good about their thick lips and their hair, which used to be called nappy, and he allowed them to have self-esteem and convinced them that they had power, they had authority, and that they were not minorities if you looked at it from a world perspective.''

Malcolm was "dangerous," says Sonia Sanchez. He indeed roused the pride of black Americans, but he also stirred their minds and imaginations, and after his return from Mecca, Sanchez explains, we felt "his impact on the black intellectual class—the black middle class, the class of people who had other influences too—as he was in New York, which was the center of the new Black Renaissance. In the same fashion that [Marcus] Garvey finally guided some of the intellectuals to deal with him on some levels, [so] Malcolm did with us. Our poetry [echoed] this man, resounded with what he was saying. The point is, most of the intellectuals I knew at that time were followers of Malcolm, although they had not announced it (that's the key)—even the so-called middle-class blacks. He stirred their imaginations through his words to remove the restraints and constraints that they found themselves in; they were beginning to give money to him. Malcolm stirred the imaginations of all blacks, whether they admitted it or not. He stirred them to go back to their yearning of 'I want to be a lawyer, a doctor, an Indian chief—but I also want to have my dignity,' and he was saying it's possible. You had to have the experience after coming through this educational system that hounded you, that said, 'Yes, you have a degree, but you're inferior. Yes, you're a doctor, but you're still a nigger,' [and Malcolm said,] 'I can tell you how not to be a nigger in this country.' ''

The messages of Malcolm X had always reached the streets, and the urban reality warranted his cries for freedom and dignity and justice. The northern ghettos echoed his calls for unity, for racial solidarity. In Harlem they rallied and demanded the human right to be "by any means necessary." Malcolm's people were city people. "The line that he adopted," notes Elombe Braath, was "more militant ... more African nationalist and more revolutionary—you know, really more germane to black people in this country, particularly those in the urban areas. Malcolm, his people, the people who supported him, were in the cities. . . . And people took up that line, and all in the spirit of Malcolm X. And all through the years the more they've professed it, the more people have been out here [in the streets]. That goes for myself. I see Malcolm as representative of an era. . . .

"Malcolm represented that era."

In July 1959 the news show "News Beat" aired "The Hate That Hate Produced," a five-part report by Mike Wallace on the Black Muslim movement that featured, among others, Malcolm X and journalist Louis Lomax. Besides bringing the Nation of Islam to the attention of the general American public for the first time, that telecast also established Malcolm X as its most stirring and articulate spokesman.

Malcolm X became news. In the months that followed and throughout the early sixties the national media followed his career, as did Louis Lomax. Malcolm X was telling America that white people were the devil, that their racist sins were soon to be punished by the wrath of Allah, that their cities would burn, that their children were cursed. White America was also learning that for Malcolm X "coffee with a [Georgia] cracker" in no way compensated for the oppression blacks had been suffering for four hundred years.

In 1963, for his book When the Word Is Given, Louis Lomax interviewed a candid Malcolm X about the Black Muslim movement and his role in it.

from *When the Word Is Given*
by Louis Lomax
"A Summing-Up
Louis Lomax Interviews Malcolm X"

LOMAX: Minister Malcolm, we are all by now familiar with your basic philosophy; we have heard you speak, seen you on television, and read your remarks in magazines and newspapers. By now, I think, everybody knows your position that the white man is a devil, a man incapable of doing right; you hold that the black man is of God's divine nature, that he fell from power because of weakness; you hold further that the white man's rule over the earth was scheduled to end in 1914, but that his end has been delayed because of the need to get the American Negro into the fold of black brotherhood.

MALCOLM X: Yes, sir, that is what The Honorable Elijah Muhammad teaches us. The white devil's time is up; it has been up for almost fifty years now. It has taken us that long to get the deaf, dumb, and blind black men in the wilderness of North America to wake up and understand who they are. You see, sir, when a man understands who he is, who God is, who the devil is . . . then he can pick himself up out of the gutter; he can clean himself up and stand up like a man should before his God. This is why we teach that in order for a man to really understand himself he must be part of a nation; he must have some land of his own, a God of his own, a language of his own. Most of all he must have love and devotion for his own kind.

LOMAX: Wouldn't you say the Negro has a nation—America?

MALCOLM X: Sir, how can a Negro say American is *his* nation? He was brought here in chains; he was put in slavery and worked like a mule for three hundred years; he was separated from his land, his culture, his God, his language!

The Negro was taught to speak the white man's tongue, worship the white God, and accept the white man as his superior.

This is a white man's country, and the Negro is nothing but an ex-slave who is now trying to get himself integrated into the slave master's house.

And the slave master doesn't want you! You fought and bled and died in every war the white man waged, and he still won't give you justice. You nursed his baby and cleaned behind his wife, and he still won't give you freedom; you turned the other cheek while he lynched you and raped your women, but he still won't give you equality. Now, you integration-minded Negroes are trying to force yourselves on your former slave master, trying to make him accept you in his drawing room; you want to hang out with his women rather than with women of your own kind.

LOMAX: Are you suggesting that all of us who fight for integration are after a white woman?

MALCOLM X: I wouldn't say *all* of you, but let the evidence speak for itself. Check up on these integration leaders, and you will find that most of them are either married to or hooked up with some white woman. Take that meeting between James Baldwin and Robert Kennedy; practically everybody there was interracially married. Harry Belafonte is married to a white woman; Lorraine Hansberry is married to a white man; Lena Horne is married to a white man.

Now how can any Negro, man or woman, who sleeps with a white person speak for me? No black person married to a white person can speak for me!

LOMAX: Why?

MALCOLM X: Why? Because only a man who is ashamed of what he is will marry out of his race. There has to be something wrong when a man or a woman leaves his own people and marries somebody of another kind. Men who are proud of being black marry black women; women who are proud of being black marry black men.

This is particularly true when you realize that these Negroes who go for integration and intermarriage are linking up with the very people who lynched their fathers, raped their mothers, and put their kid sisters in the kitchen to scrub floors. Why would any black man in his right mind want to marry a lyncher, a murderer, a rapist, a dope peddler, a gambler, a hog eater . . . Why would any black man want to marry a *devil* . . . for that's just what the white man is.

LOMAX: I have heard you say that a thousand times, but it always jolts me. Why do you call the white man a devil?

MALCOLM X: Because that's what he is. What do you want me to call him, a saint? Anybody who rapes, and plunders, and enslaves, and steals, and drops hell bombs on people . . .anybody who does these things is nothing but a devil.

Look, Lomax, history rewards all research. And history fails to record one single instance in which the white man—as a people—did good. They have always been devils; they always will be devils, and they are about to be destroyed. The final proof that they are devils lies in the fact that they are about to destroy themselves. Only a devil—and a stupid devil at that— would destroy himself!

Now why would I want to integrate with somebody marked for destruction?

The Honorable Elijah Muhammad teaches us to get away from the devil as soon and as fast as we can. This is why we are demanding a separate state. Tell the slave master we will no longer beg for crumbs from his table; let him give us some land of our own so we can go for ourselves. If he doesn't give us some land, there is going to be hell to pay. As I said at Howard University and Queens College, once the white man let the Negro get an education, the Negro began to want what the white man has. But he let Negroes get education and now they are demanding integration; they want to have exactly what he has. And the white man is not going to give it to them!

LOMAX: But we have made some gains. . . .

MALCOLM X: What gains? All you have gotten is tokenism—

one or two Negroes in a job or at a lunch counter so the rest of you will be quiet. It took the United States Army to get one Negro in the University of Mississippi; it took troops to get a few Negroes in white schools at Little Rock and another dozen places in the South. It has been nine years since the Supreme Court decision outlawing segregated schools, yet less than ten per cent of the Negro students in the South are in integrated schools. That isn't integration, that's tokenism! In spite of all the dogs, and fire hoses, and club-swinging policemen, I have yet to read of anybody eating an integrated hamburger in Birmingham.

You Negroes are not willing to admit it yet, but integration will not work. Why, it is against the white man's nature to integrate you into his house. Even if he wanted to, he could no more do it than a Model T can sprout wings and fly. It isn't in him.

Now The Honorable Elijah Muhammad says it would be the easiest thing in the world for the white man to destroy the Black Muslims. We contend that the white man is a devil. If he is not a devil, let him prove it!

He can't do it, Lomax; it isn't in him; it is against his nature.

He'll keep on granting tokenism; a few big Negroes will get big jobs, but the black masses will catch hell as long as they stay in the white man's house.

The only possible way out for the white man is to give us some land of our own; let us get out, get away from his wicked reign and go for ourselves.

But the white man will not do that, either. He is going to keep you integration-minded Negroes cooped up here in this country, and when you discover that the white man is a trickster, a devil, that he has no intentions of integrating, then you Negroes will run wild. That will be the time . . .

LOMAX: The time for what?

MALCOLM X: Only The Honorable Elijah Muhammad can answer that!

LOMAX: This is strong gospel, Minister Malcolm; many people, Negro and white, say what you preach amounts to hate, that your theology is actually anti-Semitic. What is your comment to that?

MALCOLM X: The white people who are guilty of white supremacy are trying to hide their own guilt by accusing The Honorable Elijah Muhammad of teaching black supremacy when he tries to uplift the mentality, the social, mental, and economic condition of the black people in this country. Jews who have been guilty of exploiting the black people in this country, economically, civically, and otherwise, hide behind— hide their guilt by accusing The Honorable Elijah Muhammad of being anti-Semitic, simply because he teaches our people to go into business for ourselves and try and take over the economic leadership in our own community.

And since the white people collectively have practiced the worst form of hatred against Negroes in this country and they know that they are guilty of it, now when The Honorable Elijah Muhammad comes along and begins to list the historic deed— the historic attitude, the historic behavior of the white man in this country toward the black people in this country, again, the white people are so guilty, and they can't stop doing these things to make Mr. Muhammad appear wrong, so they hide their wrong by saying "he is teaching hatred." History is not hatred. Actually we are Muslims because we believe in the religion of Islam. We believe in one God. We believe in Muhammad as the Apostle of God. We practice the principles of the religion of Islam, which mean prayer, charity, fasting, brotherhood, and The Honorable Elijah Muhammad teaches us that since the Western society is deteriorating, it has become overrun with immorality, that God is going to judge it and destroy it, and the only way the black people who are in this society can be saved is not to integrate into this corrupt society but separate ourselves from it, reform ourselves, lift up our moral standards and try and be godly—try to integrate with God—instead of trying to integrate with the white man, or try and imitate God instead of trying to imitate the white man.

LOMAX: It is suggested also that your movement preaches violence.

MALCOLM X: No, sir. The black people of this country have

been victims of violence at the hands of the white men for four hundred years, and following the ignorant Negro preachers, we have thought that it was godlike to turn the other cheek to the brute that was brutalizing us. Today The Honorable Elijah Muhammad is showing black people in this country that, just as the white man and every other person on this earth has God-given rights, natural rights, civil rights, any kind of right that you can think of, when it comes to defending himself, black people—we should have the right to defend ourselves also. And, because The Honorable Elijah Muhammad makes black people brave enough, men enough to defend ourselves no matter what the odds are, the white man runs around here with a doctrine that Mr. Muhammad is advocating violence when he is actually telling Negroes to defend themselves against violent people.

LOMAX: Reverend Martin Luther King teaches a doctrine of nonviolence. What is your attitude toward this philosophy?

MALCOLM X: The white man supports Reverend Martin Luther King, subsidizes Reverend Martin Luther King, so that Reverend Martin Luther King can continue to teach the Negroes to be defenseless—that's what you mean by nonviolent—be defenseless in the face of one of the most cruel beasts that has ever taken people into captivity—that's this American white man, and they have proved it throughout the country by the police dogs and the police clubs. A hundred years ago they used to put on a white sheet and use a bloodhound against Negroes. Today they have taken off the white sheet and put on police uniforms and traded the bloodhounds for police dogs, and they're still doing the same thing. Just as Uncle Tom, back during slavery, used to keep the Negroes from resisting the bloodhound or resisting the Ku Klux Klan by teaching them to love their enemies or pray for those who use them despitefully, today, Martin Luther King is just a twentieth-century or modern Uncle Tom or religious Uncle Tom, who is doing the same thing today to keep Negroes defenseless in the face of attack that Uncle Tom did on the plantation to keep *those* Negroes defenseless in the face of the attack of the Klan in that day.

Now, the goal of Dr. Martin Luther King is to give Negroes a chance to sit in a segregated restaurant beside the same white man who has brutalized them for four hundred years. The goal of Martin Luther King is to get Negroes to forgive the people, the people who have brutalized them for four hundred years, by lulling them to sleep and making them forget what those whites have done to them, but the masses of black people today don't go for what Martin Luther King is putting down.

LOMAX: Minister Malcolm, you often speak of unity among our people. Unity for what?

MALCOLM X: The Honorable Elijah Muhammad teaches us that God now is about to establish a kingdom on this earth based upon brotherhood and peace, and the white man is against brotherhood and the white man is against peace. His history on this earth has proved that. Nowhere in history has he been brotherly toward anyone. The only time he is brotherly toward you is when he can use you, when he can exploit you, when he will oppress you, when you will submit to him, and since his own history makes him unqualified to be an inhabitant or a citizen in the kingdom of brotherhood, The Honorable Elijah Muhammad teaches us that God is about to eliminate that particular race from this earth. Since they are due for elimination, we don't want to be with them. We are not trying to integrate with that which we know has come to the end of its rope. We are trying to separate from it and get with something that is more lasting, and we think that God is more lasting than the white man.

LOMAX: Then your movement does not share the integration goals of the NAACP, CORE, Martin Luther King's movement, and the Student Nonviolent movement.

MALCOLM X: You don't integrate with a sinking ship. You don't do anything to further your stay aboard a ship that you see is going to go down to the bottom of the ocean. Moses tried to separate his people from Pharaoh, and when he tried, the magicians tried to fool the people into staying with Pharaoh, and we look upon these other organizations that are trying to get Negroes to integrate with this doomed white man as nothing but modern-day magicians, and The Honorable Elijah Muhammad is a modern-day Moses trying to separate us from the modern-day Pharaoh. Until the white man in America sits down and talks with The Honorable Elijah Muhammad, he won't even known what the race problem—what makes the race problem what it is. Just like Pharaoh couldn't get a solution to his problem until he talked to Moses, or Nebuchadnezzar or Belshazzar couldn't get a solution to his problem until he talked to Daniel, the white man in America today will never understand the race problem or come anywhere near getting a solution to the race problem until he talks to The Honorable Elijah Muhammad. Mr. Muhammad will give him God's analysis, not some kind of political analysis or psychologist's analysis, or some kind of clergyman's analysis, but God's analysis. That's the analysis that Moses gave Pharaoh; that's the analysis that Daniel gave Belshazzar. Today we have a modern Belshazzar and a modern Pharaoh sitting in Washington, D.C.

LOMAX: I am struck by the fact that each of the biblical figures you mentioned—Pharaoh, Nebuchadnezzar, and Belshazzar— came to a rather sorry end. Are you willing to complete the analogy and say the American white establishment will come to a bitter end, perhaps be destroyed?

MALCOLM X: I have spoken on this many times, and I am sure you know what The Honorable Elijah Muhammad teaches on this. But since we are on record I will—as they sometimes say in Harlem—make it plain.

Now, sir, God is going to punish this wicked devil for his misdeeds toward black people. Just as plagues were visited on Pharaoh so will pestilences and disasters be visited on the white man. Why, it has already started: God has begun to send them heat when they expect cold; he sends them cold when they expect heat. Their crops are dying, their children are being born with all kinds of deformities, the rivers and the lakes are coming out of the belly of the earth to wash them away.

Not only that, but God has started slapping their planes down from the sky. Last year [1962] God brought down one of their planes loaded with crackers whose fathers had lynched your and my brothers and sister. They were from your state, Lomax, down there in Georgia where both you and Mr. Muhammad come from. Now, long before that plane crash I predicted [in Los Angeles] that God was going to strike back at the devil for the way white cops brutalized our brothers in Los Angeles. When the plane fell, I said this was God's way of letting his wrath be known. Now for that I was called names—some of these Uncle Tom Negroes rushed into print to condemn me for what I said. But what was wrong with what I said? Everybody has a God and believes that his God will deliver him and protect him from his enemies! Why can't the black man have a God? What's so wrong when a black man says his God will protect him from his white foe? If Jehovah can slay Philistines for the Jews, why can't Allah slay crackers for the so-called Negro.

I said much the same thing when that submarine—the *Thresher*—went down to the bottom of the sea. I realize that there were some originals [Negroes] on board, but that simply underlines my point that the so-called Negro should not integrate with white people. He should stay as far as possible from them at all times.

LOMAX: Just a moment, if I may, Minister Malcolm. Now, you talk about separation from the white man.

MALCOLM X: Yes, sir.

LOMAX: You even take it so far as to suggest that we shouldn't even get on airplanes and ships with white people. Am I correct in that?

MALCOLM X: Yes, sir, on the whole. Yes.

LOMAX: But Minister Malcolm, few people, Negro or white, travel as much as you and I do. You spend much of your life getting on and off aircraft. Don't you fear that you just might be aboard when God sees fit to slap down a jet and kill a few score white people?

MALCOLM X: Sir, my faith in God is such that I am not afraid. I know that I will not die until my time comes. But if I am aboard one of these vessels, I will be happy to give my life to see some of these white devils die. Like Samson, I am ready to pull down the white man's temple, knowing full well that I will be destroyed by the falling rubble.

LOMAX: But Minister Malcolm, you make no accommodation for the changes that have come about as a result of the Negro Revolt. What do you think will be the results of the current demonstrations against segregation?

MALCOLM X: Lomax, as you know, these Negro leaders have been telling the white man everything is all right, everything is under control, and they have been telling the white man that Mr. Muhammad is wrong, don't listen to him. But everything that Mr. Muhammad has been saying is going to come to pass, is now coming to pass. Now the Negro leaders are standing up saying that we are about to have a racial explosion. You're going to have a racial explosion, and a racial explosion is more dangerous than an atomic explosion. It's going to explode because black people are dissatisfied; they're dissatisfied not only with the white man, but they're dissatisfied with these Negroes who have been sitting around here posing as leaders and spokesmen for black people and actually making the problem worse instead of making the problem better.

LOMAX: Do you deny that Negroes are now getting the protection of the Federal Government; after all, both the President and the Attorney General have come to our aid.

MALCOLM X: You never will get protection from the Federal Government. Just like King is asking Kennedy to go to Alabama to stand in a doorway—to put his body in a doorway. That's like asking the fox to protect you from the wolf! The masses of black people can see this, and it is only the Negro leadership, the bourgeois, hand-picked, handful of Negroes who think that they're going to get some kind of respect, recognition, or protection from the Government. The Government is responsible for what is happening to black people in this country. The President has power. You notice he didn't send any troops into Birmingham to protect the Negroes when the dogs were biting the Negroes. The only time he sent troops into Birmingham was when the Negroes erupted, and then the president sent the troops in there, not to protect the Negroes, but to protect them white people down there from those erupting Negroes.

LOMAX: Are not Negroes American citizens?

MALCOLM X: If they were citizens, you wouldn't have a race problem. If the Emancipation Proclamation was authentic, you wouldn't have a race problem. If the 13th, 14th, and 15th Amendments to the Constitution were authentic, you wouldn't have a race problem. If the Supreme Court desegregation decision was authentic, you wouldn't have a race problem. All of this is hypocrisy that has been practiced by the so-called white so-called liberal for the past four hundred years that compounds the problem, makes it more complicated, instead of eliminating the problem.

LOMAX: What, then, do you see as the final result of all these demonstrations?

MALCOLM X: Any time you put too many sparks around a powder keg, the thing is going to explode, and if the thing that explodes is still inside the house, then the house will be destroyed. So The Honorable Elijah Muhammad is telling the white man, "Get this powder keg out of your house—let the black people in this country separate from you, while there's still time." If the black man is allowed to separate and go into some land of his own where he can solve his own problems, there won't be any explosion, and the Negroes who want to stay with the white man, let them stay with the white man— but those who want to leave, let them go with The Honorable Elijah Muhammad.

LOMAX: Now that you have mentioned the Messenger, I would like to ask you about this article in the [New York] *Amsterdam News.* . . .

MALCOLM X: It's a lie. Any article that says there is a "minor" difference between Mr. Muhammad and me is a lie. There is no such thing as a "minor" difference with the Messenger. Any difference with him is *major.* It is a lie, a lie, a lie somebody paid [the author] to write. I was up there in his office yesterday and I was ready to waste [harm, or kill] him for that. He planted a false seed, and it could start trouble. He [the author] knows my telephone number. If he ran on talk of a difference between me and the Messenger, he could have called me. No, he went ahead and printed this lie.

He was not there, but I told the editor of the paper that I was out to find him; I told him to call the police then, because as soon as I found the man who wrote this I was going to do him in.

How could there be any difference between the Messenger

and me? I am his slave, his servant, his son. He is the leader, the only spokesman for the Black Muslims.

But I will tell you this: The Messenger has seen God. He was with Allah and was given divine patience with the devil. He is willing to wait for Allah to deal with this devil. Well, sir, the rest of us Black Muslims have not seen God, we don't have this gift of divine patience with the devil. The younger Black Muslims want to see some action.

LOMAX: What kind of action?

MALCOLM X: Some things are better done than said.

LOMAX: According to your own newspaper, one of the things you Muslims may *do* in the near future is vote.

MALCOLM X: Yes. After long and prayerful consideration, The Honorable Elijah Muhammad allowed us to announce the possibility of Muslims voting. The announcement came at our annual Saviour's Day convention in Chicago.

LOMAX: What does it mean?

MALCOLM X: Mr. Muhammad is the only one who can explain that fully. However, I can say that we may register and be ready to vote. Then we will seek out candidates who represent our interests and support them. They need not be Muslims; what we want are race men who will speak out for our people.

LOMAX: There are rumors that you may run against Adam Clayton Powell.

MALCOLM X: Why must I run against a Negro? We have had enough of Negroes running against and fighting each other. The better bet is that we would put a Muslim candidate in the field against a devil, somebody who is against all we stand for.

LOMAX: What are the chances of the Black Muslims joining us in picket lines for better jobs? . . .

MALCOLM X: As I told you, only Mr. Muhammad can answer that. But let me tell you something: Better jobs and housing are only temporary solutions. They are aspects of tokenism and don't go to the heart of the problem.

This is why integration will not work. It assumes that the two races, black and white, are equal and can be made to live as one. This is not true.

The white man is by nature a devil and must be destroyed.

The black man will inherit the earth; he will resume control, taking back the position he held centuries ago when the white devil was crawling around the caves of Europe on his all fours. Before the white devil came into our lives we had a civilization, we had a culture, we were living in silks and satins. Then he put us in chains and placed us aboard the "Good Ship Jesus," and we have lived in hell ever since.

Now the white man's time is over. Tokenism will not help him, and it will doom us. Complete separation will save us—and who knows, it might make God decide to give the white devil a few more years.

Of the thousands upon thousands who heard Malcolm X speak, few would disagree with Benjamin Karim: There was fire in his words.

Words were his weapon, and life, as Malcolm saw it, according to Peter Goldman, was combat. In the study of Malcolm's character that follows, Goldman explores the political battlegrounds, moral lines and ideological fronts on which Malcolm so brilliantly waged his verbal warfare. He discerns, too, beyond the metaphor and the rhetoric, some of the fire in Malcolm's soul.

from *The Death and Life of Malcolm X*
by Peter Goldman
"Malcolm"

He saw his life as combat, and words as his weapon. It has been said of him that he brought no pursuable strategy, no concrete program, to the struggle of the blacks in white America—that he stood talking on the sidelines through the most momentous years in our race relations since the Civil War. He was denouncing intermarriage on a radio talk show the night James Meredith and five thousand soldiers "integrated" the University of Mississippi; he watched the police dogs and fire hoses of Birmingham on television in New York; he was off in Cairo pursuing a dream alliance with black Africa when the first of the big-city ghetto insurrections exploded out of the alleys of Harlem. He was always somewhere else, it was said, with a lavaliere mike or a little knot of reporters, hooting, heckling, scolding, accusing, but never participating. He never got anybody a job or decent housing, Whitney Young once complained in a moment of private bitterness, but you could find his name in the *TV Guide* program listings more times than Johnny Carson's.

All of it was true, and probably beside the point. Malcolm's life was itself an accusation—a passage to the ninth circle of that black man's hell and back—and the real meaning of his ministry, in and out of the Nation of Islam, was to deliver that accusation to us. If he lived at the margins of our national life, he was rarely out of sight. He was a dark presence, angry, cynical, implacable; a man whose good will or forgiveness or even pity we could neither earn nor buy. He meant to haunt us—to play on our fears and quicken our guilts and deflate our dreams that everything was getting better—and he did. "America's problem is *us*," he said. Others had been telling us that politely for years, and now we have the judgment of a Presidential commission that we are a society decisively shaped by our racism. The difference was that most of the others offered us the hope that matters could be put right with application and conscience and money. Malcolm did not. He did not believe that America had a conscience; he offered as proof the tragic past of the blacks beginning the day the first trader took the first slave out of Africa. He therefore did not accept the formulation that there is an American Dilemma—a constant tension between the ideals of the American Creed and the realities of caste and color. Our Creed and our Constitution were never meant to include black people, Malcolm told us, and if we argued that the sins of the past ought not to be visited on us, he replied: "Your father isn't here to pay his debts. My father isn't here to collect. But I'm here to collect, and you're here to pay."

Malcolm may never really have hated all white people with that pure wrath he preached during his dozen years in the service of Elijah Muhammad, the Last Messenger of Allah, and his little Lost-Found Nation in the Wilderness. Whites who encountered Malcolm even in those days and who could see past his press reputation as a hatemonger found him unfailingly civil and occasionally friendly, in a distant way. Later, during the year between his break with Muhammad and his death, he absolved us of the blanket judgment that we were all devils and announced that he would thereafter hold us accountable only for our behavior, not for our color or our genes. Whereupon we missed the point again and made too much of our absolution; it seemed somehow terribly important to us, as Ivanhoe Donaldson of the old Student Nonviolent Coordinating Committee put it sourly, "that this man shouldn't have the audacity to go to his grave saying that all white folks are full of shit."

He didn't—but neither did he alter the fundamental terms of the indictment: that American whites collectively remain the enemy of the blacks collectively until their behavior proves otherwise. "He was always challenging the white man, always debunking the white man," said his friend C. Eric Lincoln, whose book *The Black Muslims in America* helped bring Malcolm and the Nation to public light. "I don't think he was ever under any illusion that a powerless black minority could mount a physical challenge to a powerful white majority and survive. But they could mount a psychological challenge, and if they were persistent, they might at least produce some erosion in the attitudes and the strategies by which the white man has always protected himself and his interests. His challenge was to prove that you are as great as you say you are, that you are as moral as you say you are, that you are as kind as you say you are, that you are as loving as you say you are, that you are as altruistic as you say you are, that you are as *superior* as you say you are." One after another of Malcolm's friends, Lincoln among them, felt obliged to assure me that this never really changed—that Malcolm never softened on whitey. Maybe they were afraid I would try to make him an integrationist; maybe they were suspicious of a white writer even raising the question. I remember meeting John Oliver Killens, the novelist, one afternoon in a midtown Manhattan bar, an overwhelmingly white place with twittering birds and syrupy violins. Killens, who had befriended Malcolm before it was fashionable or even respectable to do so, was particularly insistent: sure, Malcolm saw some White Muslims on his pilgrimage to Mecca, but he knew when he came home that America was still the same white-supremacist society he had left. We had two or three rounds, and then Killens got up to leave. "Malcolm," he said, "knew what color he was."

Malcolm did reach some whites, probably more than he imagined, and far more after his death and the publication of his posthumous *Autobiography* than during his lifetime. But the redemption of whites was of secondary interest to him, and then only because we had the power, not because he thought we deserved redeeming. "His main message," said Killens, "was to the black grass roots. If white folks dug what he was saying, fine. If not, shame *on* them.'' His more urgent business was the retrieval of black people from what he saw as the worst crime white America had done them: we had taught them to hate themselves.

Malcolm himself had been dragged low by self-hatred; had pimped and hustled and sniffed coke and flashed his white women and had finally done time for burglary; had even in the Black Muslim days occasionally tripped over one of his stock formulations and said he hated every drop of black blood—uh, *white* blood—in his body. His self-esteem was purchased first at the cost of indenturing his mind and soul to Mr. Muhammad and the mysteries of the Lost-Found Nation; only later did he find it in his own manhood. He achieved it, out of the ashes of his old life, by creating a totally new one. He determined that his past was ours, a part of our landscape of ruins, and he declared his independence of it, and of us. He became in his own eyes neither a Negro nor an American—''I'm not going to sit at your table,'' he told us, ''and watch you eat, with nothing on my plate, and call myself a diner''—but a spiritual DP, an African Muslim in forced exile in the mother country. Melvin Van Peebles, now a successful moviemaker, once trailed Malcolm around Paris for a free-lance French newspaper piece and asked him routinely what he thought had been the most significant event of the year just passing. That was November 1964; Khrushchev had fallen; Lyndon Johnson had delivered the Republic from a Goldwater Presidency and, so we thought, a widening Vietnam war; the Civil Rights Bill had passed; the first of the riot summers was just behind us. But Malcolm without hesitation chose the successful detonation of China's first primitive nuclear bomb. Van Peebles was surprised, and impressed. ''The cat,'' he said, ''had a decolonized mind.''

Malcolm understood decolonization to be his work in black America. Whatever one made of the particulars of his argument, he delivered it with a personal authority that few other pretenders to leadership could claim, since he had lived so much of the black experience himself. ''Malcolm,'' said Killens, ''was all of us.'' Having experienced the degradation of the blacks, he was appalled by it, and even more by their acquiescence in it. He understood what Charles Silberman, a white writer he respected, has called "the black man's Negro problem"—the demoralization and the anomie of the ghetto. The original sin in his eyes was the white man's—he had severed the blacks from their past and reduced them to property—but the responsibility for the salvation of the blacks, Malcolm always insisted, was their own. This meant getting up out of the mud, out from under the white man's charity as well as his tyranny. It meant forgetting about integration, which was only a further denial of the worth of black people, and about nonviolence, which was only a newer, subtler form of humiliation before the slavemaster. It meant embracing the African past, till then a source of shame; it meant identifying not with the white majority in America and the West but with the dark majority of the world. It meant the discovery of what Eric Lincoln terms "a negotiable identity" as black men and women, deserving of the world's respect and their own.

And it meant standing up to The Man. One of the worst humiliations of all, in Malcolm's eyes, was that paralytic silence, that head-bobbing surrender, that seemed to him to afflict so many blacks in the presence of white people. The ghetto had been cursing whitey for years, in its own parlors and chicken shacks and street-corner rallies, but seldom to his face; so seldom, indeed, that a black man who did so seemed to whites presumptively insane—a crazy nigger—and so was accorded a kind of gingerly safe-conduct against reprisal. Malcolm was the crazy nigger gone public: he undertook to carry Harlem's fury downtown, to tell white people to their faces, in their own mass media, what ordinary blacks had been saying about them backstairs for all those years. Malcolm didn't teach hate, or need to; he exploited a vein of hate that was there already and to which few black Americans were totally immune. "Malcolm was saying what people wanted to say themselves and couldn't," said Charles Kenyatta, who followed him in the Nation of Islam and beyond. "He relieved them. They have to walk around all the time with everything stored up inside. Malcolm was the beginning of putting some backbone into this black child.'' Malcolm believed that their rage, once surfaced, could be a liberating force for black people—could disabuse them of that stifling terror and move them to action. He saw the equal possibility that it might explode, at catastrophic cost, and he was prepared to run the risk. "Like Samson," he once said, "I am ready to pull down the white man's temple, knowing full well that I will be destroyed by the falling rubble."

He meant it. He was, as he saw himself, waging war—a war of words, maybe, but a war nevertheless—and in war anything goes. "There were two Malcolms, really," said M. S. Handler of the *New York Times,* one of the very few white journalists Malcolm allowed closer than arm's length. "There was the private Malcolm, a man of ineffable charm and courtesy; a born aristocrat. And there was the public Malcolm, Malcolm in combat, whose job it was to frighten the white man out of his shoes." He was a generously gifted leader, but his talents lay not nearly so much in organizing or programming as in that pitiless vision and that flailing tongue. His genius was attack. He often rationalized that you had to waken people first—that you couldn't give them a program until they knew they needed one. But the fact was that he loved the war; loved hearing the quick, sharp bursts of applause and seeing the white faces flush pink when he scored a point; loved outraging an enemy to whom black people could not otherwise cause pain.

Malcolm, as a consequence, could not resist a platform, or an interview, or even an audience of two or three in a hotel lobby in Jedda or on a street corner in Harlem. In his war, improvisation became a strategy. He discovered his art in a prison debating society and never lost the debater's faith in the quickness of his tongue and his mother wit; he did his cerebrating on his feet, in the heat of battle. Combat excited him, quickened his pulse, set his long fingers flying and jabbing the air, brought a red glow rising in his own face. Some of the brothers despaired of the time he gave the media, knowing as he did that the stories would usually come out Malcolm-the-man-of-hate. "It really destroyed him," one of them said. "He got drunk off it. He used to sit by the TV set and watch himself, and you could see how much he liked it." He could rarely bring himself to say so. His intuitive public-relations sense told him that the message, however badly refracted by the medium, would reach some black people who would listen—who would in fact be the more receptive precisely because the press put him down. There was thus a dividend in Malcolm's extempore war. He probably would have fought it anyway. Combat made him reckless of his time, his agenda and his reputation. It was at once his vice and his soul.

He could be quite conscienceless in a fight. He believed (and once defended in a debate at Oxford) the Goldwater homily that moderation in the pursuit of justice is no virtue, and, because he believed it, he quite literally didn't care what he said. "This is the thing—whatever I say, I'm justified," he ventured once, late in his life. "If I say that Negroes should get out here right tomorrow and go to war, I'm justified. Really. I may sound extreme, but you can't say that they wouldn't be justified." He saw nothing but the comfort of white people to be served by lowering one's voice and being "responsible." Once, in a debate at New York's Community Church, Bayard Rustin accused him of engaging in emotionalism. It stung. "When a man is hanging on a tree and he cries out," Malcolm retorted, his voice rising, "should he cry out unemotionally? When a man is sitting on a hot stove and he tells you how it feels to be there, is he supposed to speak without emotion? This is what you tell black people in this country when they begin to cry out against the injustices that they're suffering. As long as they describe these injustices in a way that makes you believe you have another hundred years to rectify the situation, then you don't call that emotion. But when a man is on a hot stove, he says, 'I'm coming up. I'm getting up. Violently or nonviolently doesn't even enter into the picture—I'm coming up, do you understand?' "

The end justified anything, even transient cruelties. Once, at a Harlem rally just after his break with Muhammad, someone in the question-and-answer period mentioned the six million Jews sent to the ovens in the Third Reich. "Everybody talks about the six million Jews," Malcolm said. "But I was reading a book the other day that showed that one hundred million of us were kidnaped and brought to this country—*one hundred million.* Now everybody's wet-eyed over a handful of Jews who brought it on themselves. What about our one hundred million?'' The line got a good hand; the Jews Harlem sees tend to be landlords, storekeepers and welfare workers, and nobody gets wet-eyed about them. Waiting for the applause to quiet, Malcolm glanced down at the row of reporters up front—the only whites in the house—and noticed one of them, Al Ellenberg of the New York *Post,* noting down his words. ''Now there's a reporter who hasn't taken a note in half an hour,'' he said, ''but as soon as I start talking about the Jews, he's busy taking notes to prove that I'm anti-Semitic.''

''Kill the bastard,'' a voice behind the reporters growled. ''Kill them all.''

Ellenberg, who actually had been taking notes throughout the speech, smiled unhappily. ''Look at him laugh,'' Malcolm gibed. ''He's not really laughing. He's just laughing with his teeth''—Malcolm grimaced in imitation of a laugh—''but look at his eyes and you'll see he's not laughing.'' The mood started turning palpably nasty—whereupon, as expertly as he had started it, Malcolm ended the game. ''The white man doesn't know how to laugh,'' he said. ''He just shows his teeth. But we know how to laugh—we laugh deep down, from the bottom up.'' He laughed; so did the crowd, and the tension wound down. It was a graceless performance, and Malcolm knew it. When Ellenberg chanced to call him a few days later for an interview, Malcolm half-apologized for having tormented him. ''When I'm talking, I use everything that's around,'' he said. ''It doesn't mean anything.''

In debate, Malcolm could cut (he addressed any well-spoken black opponent as ''doctor'' to set him apart as an accredited and therefore co-opted Negro) and he could bludgeon: once, on the mildest provocation, he called a luckless NAACP spokesman a ''well-dressed, fat, pompous Negro ... satisfied to get crumbs from the master's table'' and then charged *him* with getting personal. Malcolm nearly always won these encounters, or at least the crowds who attended them, partly because he was so brilliant at it, partly because he pre-empted a kind of moral high ground for himself. It was Malcolm who carried the indictment against white America for the historic wrong done the blacks, and he prosecuted it with a bleak moral fury. To answer that he overstated the case was to quibble with details; the condition of the blacks in America was proof enough of his basic claims. To oppose him by arguing the necessity of alliances and programs was to throw in with the enemy, since programs and alliances implied the good will or at least the tractability of whites. And to contend that there had after all been some progress was to deny the continuing pain of the great masses of blacks. "You don't stick a knife in a man's back nine inches and then pull it out six inches and say you're making progress," Malcolm said. "It's dangerous to even make the white man *think* we're making progress while the knife is still in our backs, or while the wound is still there, or while even the intention that he had is still there."

Malcolm's war challenged the leaders and the orthodoxies of the civil-rights movement in the midst of its glory days, and he paid for it; the cost was a kind of quarantine that lifted only with his death. Alive, he made the elders of the movement uncomfortable. They thought him a genuine danger to the cause of racial comity; they resented his running attacks on them; they envied his easy access to radio and television; they were embarrassed by his claim to the allegiance of a ghetto lumpenproletariat they had talked about but never reached. A few were willing to debate him—Rustin, for one, and the late writer Louis Lomax, for another; and James Farmer of CORE, until he and Malcolm finally agreed between themselves to quit putting on black family quarrels for the amusement of white people. But King wouldn't meet him (he once threatened to cancel out of a David Susskind television panel if Malcolm was invited), and neither would Roy Wilkins or Whitney Young. The two of them tried unsuccessfully to talk Farmer out of one TV confrontation with Malcolm; Young argued that the only black he had ever seen hold his own against Malcolm was the ultraconservative columnist George Schuyler, which proved that you couldn't be moderate or liberal or even conventionally militant and hope to win.

So Malcolm found himself in isolation from the front-line
struggle, even after he had broken with Mr. Muhammad and
wanted to join it. He was isolated from respect as well. Now
that he is dead and buried and beatified, a saint whom all must
praise, one easily forgets how little the recognized Negro leadership of the day—even the militant leadership—wantd to have
to do with him, at least in public. His commitment to the liberation of the blacks from bondage, body and soul, was total and
consuming. "My hobby is stirring up Negroes," He liked to
say, and he gave it eighteen or twenty hours a day every day.
Yet for the mainstream leaders, he was never a comrade-in-
arms, only a hobgoblin they could hold up to whites for a
certain scare effect: look who's waiting in the wings if you
don't deal with us. They placed him in moral Coventry, and it
wounded Malcolm; something in him wanted acceptance,
though never at the price he would have had to pay. "He really
hungered to be recognized as a national leader," one friend
said. "It hurt him when first Kennedy and then Johnson would
call King, Wilkins, Young and Farmer to the White House. He
wanted it to be a fivesome instead of a foursome." King's
celebrity particularly rankled him, built as it was on a philosophy and a style of action Malcolm found degrading. Harlem
put on a rally for King in late 1964, to celebrate his Nobel
Peace Prize. It wasn't Malcolm's party, but he and a few followers showed up anyway and watched in heavy silence from
a back row. "He got the peace prize, we got the problem," he
told a black writer bitterly a few days later. "I don't want the
white man giving me medals. If I'm following a general, and
he's leading me into battle, and the enemy tends to give him
rewards, or awards, I get suspicious of him. Especially if he
gets a peace award before the war is over."

His bad press ultimately wounded him, too, particularly after
he left the Nation of Islam with its iron black-and-white certitude and entered on the extraordinary personal transformations
of the last months of his life. He couldn't make us see those
changes; he remained, in print, a cartoon Black Muslim urging
our otherwise affectionate black masses to hatred and violence
against whites. Malcolm came to understand that he shared the

blame for this with the media—that he had after all been too obliging with his time and his hot rhetoric. He had been our Frantz Fanon; the natives in America have neither the numbers nor the guns to do whites that gratifying violence that Fanon identified at the heart of the Algerian terror, but, at least for a time in the 1960s, they could make whites jump when they said *Woof!* and that was something. It was Malcolm, really, who discovered this—discovered how close the specter of the black revenge lies to the surface of the white American conscious-ness—and, having discovered it, he could rarely resist its pleasures.

At his press conference formally declaring his independence of Mr. Muhammad, he argued that black people ought to get guns and organize to use them in their own defense wherever the government failed in its duty to protect them. It was not an unreasonable position, given the run of unpunished and unre-quited acts of violence against blacks in the South, and it was in any case only one of several themes Malcolm struck that morning. But the call to arms produced more questions at the news conference than any other point, and Malcolm responded with what seemed to me at the time an almost palpable relish. I saw him that afternoon in Harlem; I remember suggesting that he had anticipated the response to the business about guns and had actually enjoyed it. He grinned widely. "I bet they pass a bill to outlaw the sale of rifles," he said, "and it won't be filibustered either." But in his last days he began to have second thoughts—to wonder whether that kick-ass audacity that had made his reputation hadn't been a trap for him as well. His press image, he said, "was created by them and by me. . . . They were looking for sensationalism, for something that would sell papers, and I gave it to them."

People who met him privately—particularly black people—were baffled by the caricature; the Malcolm they knew was too complicated a man to fit the labels the rest of us attached to him. He had, given his feral reputation, a surprisingly formal look—a look of reserve heightened by his half-rimmed glasses, his high-polished shoes and his three-button, three-piece suits. The style went with an inner austerity, a final distance imposed by his role as a leader and his sense of what a leader ought to be. Malcolm achieved, by will and later by habit, a sort of contained calm that was part of his mastery of people and situations. Benjamin Goodman, who as Benjamin 2X was Malcolm's assistant minister in the Nation of Islam and a trusted deputy afterward, remembered that extraordinary discipline: "He was the kind of man that, if you came up and said there's a bomb in here, he'd say, 'Now sit down, brother, let's be cool, let's figure this out.' " Goodman remembered the distance as well. "Nobody was close to him—nobody. Some of these brothers now saying they were close to him—no, they weren't close. He used to send me out of town, and I'd come back and go to his house maybe at one in the morning and we'd talk. But we didn't get close. Not in the buddy sense. He was always in *command*. You didn't get close, that wasn't his way."

Malcolm was an ascetic man as well. The Nation of Islam holds its true believers to a very nearly monkish code of conduct: no drinking, no smoking, no drugs, no sexual license or even dating, no dances or ballgames or movies, no sleeping late, no more than one meal a day. Malcolm practiced it all scrupulously in the Nation; he wouldn't even go to his friend Ossie Davis's Broadway play, *Purlie Victorious,* without a dispensation from Mr. Muhammad. When he left, he brought the Muslims' morality with him, exacting it of himself even after he quit asking it of his followers. The code was particularly severe about sex. Malcolm was developing a considerable reputation in the Nation as a misogynist until he finally married Betty Shabazz in 1958, when he was nearly thirty-three. There were, particularly after the break with Mr. Muhammad, the usual rumors of dalliances that attach to public people—particularly to public men as masculine and as attractive as Malcolm. Some of the tales were promoted by the Nation once Malcolm began publicly to question Mr. Muhammad's own moral behavior. Most of his acquaintances simply refused to believe the talk. "It doesn't fit," one woman friend told me. "Anything amoral or immoral from Malcolm just would not follow. He loved Betty and he loved those children. And women never threw themselves at him. There was something about him that forbade—what's the word—vulgarity? Or intimacy?'' I offered "intrusion." "Intrusion. Exactly.''

Yet the distance was never forbidding, the morality never chilling. Malcolm could be a man of contagious warmth, which whites infrequently saw because he rarely squandered it on them. Black people, by contrast, found his presence transforming. "He could make you see things," his lawyer, Percy Sutton, recalled. "Malcolm undressed you, put you in front of the mirror and let you smile at yourself and say, 'I've got to change that.' '' He loved gossip and celebrities and parties, though his drink was usually orange juice or coffee, or tea late at night, and his small talk was almost all about The Problem. He commanded any room he was in. "You'd walk in and look around and see a crowd," Killens said, "and there'd be that tall man standing in the middle of it. When he would come over to my house, there would be people there whom other people ask for autographs. And they would ask for *his.*" Malcolm was oddly shy about his own celebrity, almost as if it so defied credibility that he couldn't quite believe it himself, and his diffidence made him the more attractive. "He didn't reach for power," Mike Handler said. "Power came to him.''

Away from the crowds and the microphones, Malcolm was rather a gentle man. His purposefulness never quit, but the jugular impulse did, and instead of the chance cruelties of the platform, there were the small kindnesses that people remembered. James Farmer's white wife went to the March on Washington alone—Farmer was in jail for demonstrating in Louisiana—and she happened into a hotel lobby where Malcolm was declaiming to a little clump of marchers about, among other things, his theory that most prominent black integrationists liked integration mainly because they had married white. Mrs. Farmer edged close and introduced herself. "That's exactly what I was talking about—" Malcolm started, turning back to his audience. But something checked him; he missed a beat, then went on: "Farmer's in jail and Kennedy isn't doing anything about it." Everyone sensed what he had begun to say, and was grateful that he hadn't.

Men with power over people are not always afflicted by conscience, but Malcolm was, much as his public role prevented him from displaying it. Some of his conversions to Black Islam caused him pain later; there were others he couldn't even bring himself to attempt. Kenneth Clark, the black psychologist, has never forgotten the days in the early 1960s when his son Hilton, then a freshman at Columbia, became "very taken with Malcolm. . . . He saw us on TV together, and I suppose he always felt that Malcolm came out on top. He began spending some time around the Muslim mosque in Harlem. He was *fascinated*. I suspected this, but I didn't know it, until one day I was down there and Malcolm took me aside."

"You know," said Malcolm, "Hilton has been around here rather frequently."

"Really?" Clark answered guardedly.

"Don't worry," Malcolm said.

"I won't," Clark replied. He understood Malcolm to be saying he wouldn't proselytize Hilton; Malcolm didn't, and, though they crossed paths often, they never discussed the subject again.

Malcolm was a man of rich, bubbling humor. Offstage, in the family, it was race humor, dependent not so much on word-play or memorable laugh-lines as on styles of speech—he could do wicked imitations of the national civil-rights leaders—and shadings of voice. "A lot of black American humor is based on tonal inflection," Maya Angelou, the novelist and poet, remarked. "Malcolm could talk for an hour and a half at a meeting, and then on the way to the car, he'd say something like 'Was I *bad*' "—her voice tripped high—" 'or was I *baaad?*' "—this time drawly and low. "Not those words exactly, but something like it, and he'd break you up. A minute before, he was showing you the pits of hell and the possible pinnacles of heaven, and then, between leaving the meeting and getting into the car, you'd be laughing."

On the platform, particularly before black audiences, Malcolm's bantery streak turned into authentic black comedy, all parody and self-deprecation. In a black crowd, the inflection would broaden, the correct mixed-company English would go slurred and slangy and the smiles would turn inward, lancing at black fears and black vanities. "And you gonna get nonviolent with this man—why, you out of your mind." It was a humor that could dissipate tensions. At street-corner rallies in Harlem, Malcolm would harangue the police unmercifully for their brutalities and corruptions, but never the particular police-man assigned to stand guard. "Maybe some of these blue-eyed devils in blue uniforms here are really black," he would say. "If any of them smiles, it's 'cause he knows he's a brother." Some cops would invariably grin, the crowd would laugh, and nobody would get hurt, which was precisely the object.

Comedy, for Malcolm, served the ends of war; his speeches mixed wit with a high, deadly seriousness. "During slavery," he would say in one of his set routines, "there were two kinds of Negroes—the field Negro and the house Negro. The house Negro was near Boss. He had Boss's ear. His job was to tell Boss what was going on in the field, among the field Negroes. He ate better. He dressed better. He had better housing. If you went to Uncle Tom and said, 'Let's go' "—this was during the Black Muslim days when Malcolm was still arguing for the separation of the races—"he said, 'Where'm I goin'? I'm livin' good. I've got a good house. I'm near my boss.' And when he would be talking to his master, he'd say, '*We* have good food. *We* have a fine home. *We* have fine clothes. Every time the master would say 'we,' the house Negro would say 'we'—he identified himself with his master. When his master got sick, he'd say, 'What's the matter, Boss? We sick?' If the master's house caught fire, he would fight even harder to put out the flames than the master himself.

"There were also the field Negroes. They were in the major-ity. They were the masses. If you went to them and said, 'Let's separate,' they wouldn't ask, 'Where we goin'?' They wouldn't even be interested. They were suffering. They were the down-trodden. They were the oppressed. If the master got sick, the field Negro would pray that he died. If the house caught on fire, the field Negro would pray that a heavy wind would come along and burn the house down."

"I am a field Negro," he would always wind up. That finally was the source of his authority. The recognized civil-rights lead-ers of his day were preoccupied with the desegregation of the

South and were not in any case at home in the ghetto; Malcolm never left it, not during working hours. "He spoke like a poor man," Dick Gregory observed, "and walked like a king." He liked to move on the back streets and talk with the bloods on the corners, the nodding kids, the maids waiting at the bus stops, the winos bibbing muscat out of bottles wrapped in brown paper bags. He spoke to them in their language; Malcolm, one friend told me dryly, was condescending only to white people.

Harlem is a cynical, street-wise place, and it had its quarrels with Malcolm from time to time, mainly over its brooding suspicion that he liked going on television too well and that he was all talk and no action. But Harlem knew, long before Malcolm died broke, that he couldn't be bought. One Harlem civic figure told me how, in the days before the poverty program regularized the practice of purchasing the good will of militants, you could go around doling out $100 or so to this or that black nationalist to guarantee peace at some public occasion. "But not Malcolm," he said. "You never approached him with money. You made it a matter of community pride." Nor could Harlem, even when it questioned his wisdom, doubt Malcolm's love. It was a passion that left neither time nor energy for any of the ordinary pleasures. Nobody remembers Malcolm watching a television show other than the news, going to a play other than *Purlie Victorious,* seeing a movie other than *Nothing But a Man*—the story of a young black couple fighting for air in Alabama. He read greedily but never as an escape; *Uncle Tom's Cabin* was the only novel he permitted himself after taking the vows as a Muslim. He plowed through books with a single utilitarian purpose. One of his favorites—one he quoted constantly—was Dwight Lowell Dumond's *Antislavery.* Dumond, a white scholar, saw his materials as the record of the heroism of the largely white abolition movement, achieving, in his words, "this country's greatest victory for democracy." But Malcolm read it not for its heroics, only for its proofs of the savagery of the slavemasters, and, by implication, their children. Being from America, he was indeed intensely sensitive to matters of color, and the victories of our democracy didn't impress him. "When I speak," he said, "I speak as a *victim* of America's so-called democracy."

"Malcolm," Charles Kenyatta thinks, "was the reincarnation of Nat Turner, Denmark Vesey and Gabriel Prosser. Lot of people don't know that, but he was. Stokely Carmichael, Rap Brown, LeRoi Jones—they can't identify with the masses. They went to the best schools. Came from middle-class homes. They can't talk about hardship and really know what it is. Me, I lived my life; I didn't get as good an education as Malcolm, even. But we lived in the streets and we knew the streets. Like Nat Turner, Denmark Vesey and Gabriel Prosser. They were field Negroes. They all identified with the masses." A moment slid by. Kenyatta looked wanly out the window of his uptown housing project, down into the streets he and Malcolm knew. "Course," he added softly, "they was destroyed by the masses, too."

So it was with Malcolm; the cruelest irony of the doom-haunted last months of his life was that he no longer felt he could walk the streets of Harlem safely after dark. People who knew him find it painful remembering the Malcolm of those days, his certainties shattered, his attention fragmented, his days a paranoid nightmare come to life. Even his rippling humor took on a corrosive bitterness. He talked about it one day with Claude Lewis, a black journalist, over coffee at 22 West, a little Harlem luncheonette he favored. "Anything that's paradoxical has to have some humor in it," he said, "or it'll crack you up. You know that? You put hot water in a cold glass, it'll crack. Because it's a contrast, a paradox. And America is such a paradoxical society, hypocritically paradoxical, that if you don't have some humor, you'll crack up. If you can't turn it into a joke, why, you'll crack up." He laughed, shortly and joylessly. "Imagine Adlai Stevenson standing up in the UN and saying, 'America needs no credentials for freedom'—I said, why, good God, this man is a joke, you know; and they had just turned loose twenty-one assassins in the South that had murdered three civil-rights workers. They didn't murder three criminals—they murdered three civil-rights workers. Naw. So that's a joke. And you have to laugh at it. You have to be able to laugh to stand up and sing, 'My country 'tis of thee, sweet land of liberty.' *That's* a joke. And if you don't laugh at it, it'll crack you up. I mean it's a *joke.* 'Sweet land of liberty'—that's a *joke."* The short laugh again. "If you don't laugh at it, you'll crack up."

Years later, I met Benjamin Goodman at 22 West; we sat near the back, at a table Malcolm had liked because you could watch for your friends—or, in the last days, your enemies—coming in from 135th Street. Those days had been difficult ones for Benjamin, a time of estrangement from Malcolm after years at his side, and he spoke carefully about them. Black people, he said, sing in the churches about a wall so high you can't get over it, so low you can't get under it, so wide you can't get around it—you've got to go in at the door. Black leaders come up against a wall like that, Benjamin said, and when they get to the door, they see death. He thought it had been that way with Malcolm; he had come to the wall, had been to the door, they see death. He thought it had been that way with Malcolm; he had come to the wall, had been to the door and had seen death. His own.

Yet, having seen death, Malcolm didn't run; he stood there and met it, with that certain audacity of bearing, that certain icy clarity of vision that are his enduring legacies today. We found that audacity frightening, that vision canted and unreasonable; we were innocent then, and he was the one who brought us the bad news. "The servant sees the master," he told us, "but the master doesn't see the servant. The servant sees the master eat, but the master doesn't see the servant eat. The servant sees the master sleep, but the master doesn't see the servant sleep. The servant sees the master angry, but the master never sees the servant angry. The master doesn't really see the servant at all." Malcolm was persuaded that that had to change—that we had not only to see the servant but to see him as potentially our enemy, aggressive, demanding, dangerous and quite beyond our logic, our reason and our compromises. We did glimpse him in Malcolm X, many of us for the first time.

Near the end of his personal journey, Malcolm did arrive at a wall he couldn't get over, under or around—not in the time he had left. At moments he himself began to wonder whether his real contribution to the struggle of the blacks wasn't in his role as bogeyman after all. It was sad that he should have thought so, even fleetingly. Malcolm helped to alter the style and the thought of the black revolt of the 1960s, even when it denied him a place in its certified leadership. He left another, more lasting bequest as well—the example of that unchained, unbowed black manhood. "Like somebody said," one of Malcolm's movement friends told me, "I never heard nobody call Malcolm X 'nigger.' " That was a considerable bequest to servant and master alike, and neither has been quite the same since.

An outraged Malcolm X flew to Los Angeles in the wake of the bloody events that left one Muslim brother dead and six others wounded on the night of April 27, 1962, after a meeting at their mosque.

At 11:15 that Friday night two Muslim brothers were accosted by two white policemen. The brothers were unloading suits from the back of an automobile parked about a block away from the mosque; they worked for a drycleaning establishment. The policemen, however, suspected them of burglary or theft. There was a scuffle. A shot was fired, and an alarm went off. A police squad converged not at the scene of the incident but at the mosque. In the ensuing gunfire the seven Muslim brothers, not one of them armed or even trying to defend himself, were shot. One of them was left completely paralyzed. Another, Ronald Stokes, the secretary of the mosque, died. He had been shot through the heart and then beaten repeatedly on the head with nightsticks. The next day Elijah Muhammad dispatched Malcolm to Los Angeles to prevent further violence. A week later Malcolm himself conducting the funeral services for Stokes.

from *Malcolm X: The FBI File*
by Clayborne Carson

SECTION 8

November 16, 1962–March 13, 1963

REPORTS: 1. November 16, 1962. New York
2. February 4, 1963. SAC, Washington Field Office to Director. Airtel
3. February 4, 1963. Report of W.C. Sullivan
4. March 13, 1963. SAC, Charlotte, North Carolina, to Director

Section 8 outlines the events surrounding the shooting death of NOI member Ronald Stokes by Los Angeles policemen and sketches the growing tension between Malcolm and Elijah Muhammad's family. Malcolm's role in the aftermath of the shooting was highly visible, and Los Angeles Mayor Samuel Yorty increased that visibility on June 6 by playing a tape in which Malcolm publicly referred to a French airline crash as Allah's divine revenge against the white race for the travesty in California. Yorty recommended wide publication of the statement "so the public could understand the threats of this philosophy."

The FBI soon decided that Yorty's methods were impractical because they tended to create interest in the NOI, even though they were designed to create the opposite effect. Assistant Director W.C. Sullivan here divulges an important policy decision, which is the policy of "taking no steps which would give them (NOI) additional publicity." This is one of the few examples of policy analysis which occurs in this edition of the file. An FBI agent offers his analysis of Malcolm's appeal in a memo relating a Charlotte speech of January 30. The agent discusses in depth how Malcolm "unites the individuals into an emotional entity, how he achieves rapport, reaches common understanding and responsiveness as he fuses individuals into a unit."

UNITED STATES DEPARTMENT OF JUSTICE
FEDERAL BUREAU OF INVESTIGATION

Report of: [BUREAU OF DELETION] b7C   Office: New York, New York
Date: 11/16/62
Field Office File No: 105–8999   Bureau file No.: 100–399321
Title: MALCOLM K. LITTLE
Character: INTERNAL SECURITY-NATION OF ISLAM

Synopsis:

Subject continues to reside at 23–11 97th Street, East Elmhurst, Queens, NY, and is Minister of NOI Temple No. 7, NYC and also considered a National NOI official, and the right hand man of ELIJAH MUHAMMAD. Subject's NOI activities and speeches at NYC and around the U.S. set out. Subject attempted to rally other Negroes in Los Angeles, California, to protest against the killing of a NOI member during a shooting incident between NOI members and the Los Angeles Police Department (LAPD). Subject's public appearances set out and he apparently has canceled all future college appearances. Subject invited to integration rally, Englewood, NJ, but did not attend when opposition developed among Negro leaders. Subject's association with Communist movement set out.

Subject's Activities Following the
Los Angeles Shooting Incident

Outlined below are the activities of the subject on behalf of the NOI following a shooting incident on April 27, 1962, between Los Angeles NOI members and the LAPD in Los Angeles, California, at which one NOI member was killed, several wounded and a number arrested. Also set forth are activities by the subject as a result of this incident in concert with various Los Angeles groups who protested alleged brutality against the Negro population there.

Subject attended and conducted funeral services held at 5606 South Broadway, Los Angeles, California, on May 5, 1962, for NOI member RONALD STOKES who was killed on April 27, 1962, in a shooting incident between Los Angeles NOI members and the LAPD.

[BUREAU DELETION]

The May 10, 1962 edition of the *Los Angeles Herald Dispatch,* a weekly Negro newspaper published in Los Angeles, California, contained an article which reflected that a crowd of over two thousand attended the funeral of RONALD STOKES, a Muslim, who was shot own by local police, which services were held at 5606 South Broadway, Los Angeles, California, on May 5, 1962, and conducted by the subject.

The May 10, 1962 edition of the *Los Angeles Herald Dispatch* also contained an article which reflected that on May 4, 1962, in the Statler-Hilton Hotel, Los Angeles, California, subject had held a press conference relative to the shooting on April 27, 1962, of seven Los Angeles NOI members, one of whom (RONALD STOKES) died.

The article reflected that subject's opening statement was that "... Seven innocent unarmed black men were shot down in cold blood by Police Chief WILLIAM J. PARKER's Los Angeles City Police." The article continued that subject referred to the incident as "one of the most ferocious, inhuman atrocities ever inflicted in a so-called 'democratic' and 'civilized' soci-

ety," and subject referred to the death of STOKES as a "brutal
and cold blooded murder by PARKER's well-armed storm
troopers.'

This article went on to say that according to the subject, the
official version of the incident which was related in the "white
press" was that the Muslims were engaged in a gun battle with
police provoked by the Muslims. Subject ridiculed this article
saying that the Muslims obey the law religiously and he further
ridiculed the "white press" for helping Chief PARKER "sup-
press the facts."

Also during this conference, the subject refused to clarify
how one of the white policemen was shot, stating that he was
acting on the advice of the attorneys of the Muslims who were
accused and arrested for assault.

The May 17, 1962 edition of the *Los Angeles Herald Dispatch* contained an article which reflected that a Los Angeles
Coroner's Jury inquiring into the death of RONALD STOKES
on April 27, 1962, at the hands of the LAPD, ruled that it was
"justifiable homicide under lawful performance of duty and in
self defense." The article further indicated that only the police
officers testified and that the nine Muslims who were arrested
at the scene refused to testify and left the hearing after being
advised that they were not required to testify if they thought
their testimony might incriminate them.

This same article quoted the subject as saying after hearing
the above verdict that STOKES's death was "a murder in cold
blood" and that the Muslims "despaired of getting justice" and
would pray to "God that he gives justice in his own way."
The article went on to say that in response to questions the
subject stated that Muslims obey the law, do not carry firearms
and are never the aggressors but if attacked have their God-
given right to defend themselves.

The May 24, 1962 edition of the *Los Angeles Herald Dispatch* contained an article which reflected that a protest rally
against police brutality was held in Los Angeles on May 20,
1962, at the Park Manor Auditorium which was sponsored by
the "County Civic League," the latter being described in the

article as an independent organization dedicated to the protection and preservation of the black community.

The article reflected that the subject spoke at this meeting and is quoted as saying "... Not a Muslim but a black man was shot down." The article indicted that the subject reiterated the importance of not letting religious, political, social or economic differences divide the blacks. He further stated, according to the article, "For you're brutalized because you're black and when they lay a club on the side of your head, they do not ask your religion. You're black, that's enough."

At this above mentioned rally held on May 20, 1962, [BUREAU DELETION] during the subject's speech, he said that black people all over the world are uniting. Socialists, Communists and Liberalists [*sic*] all are coming together to get rid of the common enemy with white skin.

[BUREAU DELETION] that early in June, 1962, [BUREAU DELETION] at the Holman Methodist Church, Los Angeles, California, during which a bulletin was passed out that had on its back "A Manifesto for Clergymen of the Los Angeles Area." [BUREAU DELETION] the bulletin indicated that this manifesto was being issued as a result of the killing of a Muslim by the LAPD. This manifesto indicated that the Negro Ministers did not condone police brutality but that they were in no way related to or in sympathy with the Muslim movement.

The June 6, 1962 edition of the *Los Angeles Herald Examiner* contained an article which reflected that news media of Southern California were asked by Los Angeles Mayor SAMUEL W. YORTY to publicize statements made by the subject at an NOI meeting in Los Angeles, California. The article indicated that Mayor YORTY, during a press conference in his office, played a tape recording of the NOI meeting which included a speech by the subject during which the latter said in regard to the crash of a jet airliner in Paris, France, in which all the passengers were killed:

I would like to announce a very beautiful thing that has happened. As you know, we have been praying to Allah. We have been praying that he would in some way let us know that he has the power to execute justice upon the heads of those who are responsible for the lynching of Ronald Stokes on April 27.

And I got a wire from God today (laughter) wait, all right, well somebody came and told me that he really had answered our prayers over in France. He dropped an airplane out of the sky with over 120 white people on it because the Muslims believe in an eye for an eye and a tooth for a tooth (cheering and applause).

Many people have been saying, "Well, what are you going to do?" And since we know that the man is tracking us down day by day to try and find out what we are going to do so he'll have some excuse to put us behind his bars, we call on our god. He gets rid of 120 of them in one whop. But thanks to God, or Jehovah or Allah, we will continue to pray and we hope that every day another plane falls out of the sky (cheering and applause). I want to just let you understand this.

Whenever you read in the paper or hear on the television about accidents in which these good, blessed, blue-eyed people have lost their lives, you can say amen for that's God's work. God knows you are cowards; God knows you are afraid; God knows that the white man has got you shaking in your boots. So God doesn't leave it up to you to defend yourself.

God is defending you himself. They don't know what makes those airplanes come down; they start looking for mechanical failure. No, that's godly; that's "divinely failure."

Following the playing of the above recording the article indicated that Mayor YORTY stated that he did not believe that MALCOLM X or the black Muslims had the support of the Los Angeles Negro community and urged that wide publicity be given to this statement of MALCOLM X so the public could understand the threats of this philosophy.

Animosity Between Subject and the
Family of ELIJAH MUHAMMAD

On several dates during February, March and April, 1963, [BUREAU DELETION] there was developing a feeling of resentment and animosity against the subject by members of ELI-

JAH MUHAMMAD's family. This resentment apparently stems from MALCOLM's taking charge and running the NOI Convention in Chicago, Illinois, on February 26, 1963, when illness precluded ELIJAH MUHAMMAD's attendance. The family was especially resentful of subject's attempts to advise and tell the family what to do and of statements he was allegedly making against ELIJAH and his family.

This resentment was further aggravated, [BUREAU DELETION] by subject's remaining in Chicago for several weeks after the convention where he made numerous appearances and speeches in the Chicago area. On the request of members of the family, ELIJAH MUHAMMAD, who was still in Phoenix, Arizona, ordered subject to return to New York City, which he did on March 10, 1963, canceling his future scheduled appearances around Chicago. The excuse utilized for leaving the Chicago area was that subject had to return home and assist his wife who had fallen and broken her leg, which in fact she had done.

A possible incident reflecting the reason for some of this resentment is indicated below:

At the NOI Convention in Chicago, Illinois, on February 26, 1963, subject's speech was interrupted several times by an apparent request to allow ELIJAH's son WALLACE MUHAMMAD, to speak. Subject refused to heed this request and stated that due to the late start it would not be possible for WALLACE to speak. However, subject did introduce those members of ELIJAH's family who were present.

2/4/63

AIRTEL
TO: DIRECTOR, FBI (25–330971)
FROM: SAC, WFO (100–22829)
NATION OF ISLAM
IS-NOI
(OO:CG)

During a simultaneous release of a filmed interview on radio and television stations WMAL, Washington, D.C., on 2/3/63, at 7:00 P.M., MALCOLM X, New York City, described as the official spokesman for the black Muslims and Minister of Muhammad's Mosque, No. 7, New York City's Harlem District, made some comments as follows:

The honorable ELIJAH MUHAMMAD teaches that the black man is closer to God and is actually superior physiologically, psychologically, socially and numerically.

The religion of Islam eliminates drunkenness, dope addiction, vice, immorality, smoking, drinking, stealing, lying, cheating, gambling, and disrespect for womanhood.

Regarding violence, Muslims are taught to obey the law, respect the law and to do unto others as "We would like them to do unto us," but that after having religiously obeyed the law, the Muslims are within their rights to defend themselves when attacked.

Muslims are never involved in riots and are never involved in violence unless attacked.

ELIJAH MUHAMMAD has never advocated the overthrow of the government. If the black man cannot go back to his own people and his own land, ELIJAH MUHAMMAD is asking that a part of the United States be separated and given to the Muslims so they can live separately. ELIJAH MUHAMMAD is the only man the white people can deal with in the solving of problems of the so-called Negro, as ELIJAH MUHAMMAD knows his problems.

Communism does not support the Muslim ideology.

The FBI spends twenty-four hours daily in attempting to infiltrate the Muslims and after Muslim meetings are held, the FBI goes from door to door asking about the meetings. The FBI goes far beyond its duty in the "religious suppression" of the Muslims.

The NAACP has existed for fifty-four years, during which period it has always had a white man as president. MALCOLM believes that the organization is not developing leadership among the black people or it is practicing discrimination.

There is a group of Muslims in every Negro community.

Financial support from the white people is not desired, but would be accepted because it would represent what the white "forefathers" robbed from the black "forefathers" during the 310 years that the Negro spent in bondage while working without pay for the white people.

The above interview was conducted by MATTHEW WARREN and MALCOLM LA PLACE, reporters for WMAL News.

A more complete account of the interview will be furnished to the Bureau, CG and NY when it has been assembled.

Mr. W. C. Sullivan   February 4, 1963

[BUREAU DELETION]
NATION OF ISLAM
INTERNAL SECURITY-NOI
MALCOLM X LITTLE
INTERNAL SECURITY-NOI

My memorandum 2/1/63 advised a scheduled program called "Black Muslim" would be presented at 7 P.M., Sunday, 2/3/63 on Channel 7, WMAL Television, Washington, D. C. "Black Muslims" is the term used by the news media in referring to the Nation of Islam (NOI). WMAL, the *Evening Star* (a Washington, D. C., daily newspaper) station, advised that one of the reasons they were presenting the program was because they felt it presented MALCOLM X and the "Black Muslims" in a "bad light."

During the program MALCOLM X did refer to the FBI on one occasion. He said:

The FBI spends twenty-four hours a day infiltrating or trying to infiltrate Muslims and after we hold our religious services they go from door to door and ask questions of persons who come to the meetings to try and harass them and frighten them. The FBI really goes way beyond the call of its duty in the religious suppression of the Muslims in this country. We have many occasions where they have tried to threaten and frighten Negroes from becoming Muslims, but it doesn't work. Today they have a new Negro on the scene and the more harassment and threats the FBI or the police or anyone gives toward Islam or toward the Negro, it only makes us grow that much faster.

OBSERVATIONS:

In carrying out our responsibilities in the security field [BUREAU DELETION]. However, the statements concerning harassment and threats are absolutely false and are additional examples of wild untrue statements made to influence the Negro.

The program did not put MALCOLM X or the "Black Muslims" in a "bad light." The "answers" given by MALCOLM X were not questioned. He was allowed to expound the NOI program in such a way that he created interest in the NOI. This is another example of the effect of publicity concerning the NOI. While it was intended to have an adverse effect, it created interest in the organization which was out of proportion to its importance.

RECOMMENDATION:

It is recommended that we continue to follow the approved policy of taking no steps which would give them additional publicity.

3/13/63
DIRECTOR, FBI (100–439895)
SAC, CHARLOTTE (100–4273)
NATION OF ISLAM
IS–NOI

[BUREAU DELETION] made available to SA [BUREAU DELETION] a recording of the speech made by MALCOLM X LITTLE at the Hi-Fi Country Club in Charlotte, N. C., on 1/30/63.

[BUREAU DELETION]

Hearing the actual speech of MALCOLM X enables the listener to discover the type of argument and logic employed by a hate peddler. The resulting effect is clearly heard in the background of this particular tape.

[BUREAU DELETION] The listener can hear audience reaction in the background as MALCOLM X stimulates his listeners to the release of their prejudices, grievances and wishes. Some of the content of the tape underlines the inhibitions and repressed attitudes of a segment of Negroes in general and of Charlotte Negroes in particular. These bitternesses are easily identified on the tape through crowd outbursts as MALCOLM X underlines some of the causes of Negro unrest.

This taped speech [BUREAU DELETION] shows clearly how MALCOLM X unites the individuals into an emotional entity, how he achieves rapport, reaches common understanding and responsiveness as he fuses individuals into a unit.

It is interesting to listen to the method of using statements of fact to set a favorable state of mind as he interweaves easy catch phrases of hate into the content of his speech. He continually throws irritants into an atmosphere of growing disapproval of the white race.

MALCOLM X uses his skill as a speaker to direct emotions and hatreds of his audience toward white people whom he sets up as a scapegoat for Negroes, described by him as a people severed from their racial heritage.

The apolitical stance of Elijah Muhammad and the NOI leadership in response to the Ronald Stokes incident was not discrete. Rather it typified the official NOI position on all social issues outside the Black Muslim community, no matter how significantly they affected America's black population as a whole. The NOI may have preached Armageddon, but, an essentially separatist religious organization, it totally divorced itself—and Malcolm X—from the civil rights movement.

Malcolm had once said that Islam gave him wings. When the ties between him and the NOI were irreversibly severed, Malcolm underwent another metamorphosis. The suspended Muslim minister emerged from his ninety days of silence as a dynamic black nationalist ready to engage himself in the struggle of African Americans for human rights.

In the following selection James Cone examines the effects of Malcolm's break with Elijah Muhammad on his political consciousness and personal mission in the last year of his life.

from *Malcolm and Martin and America*
A Dream or a Nightmare
by James Cone
" 'Chickens Coming Home to Roost'
(1964–1965)"

*We are not fighting for integration, nor are we fighting for
separation. We are fighting for recognition as human beings.*

Malcolm X
New York City
8 April 1964

A bloodbath is on its way in America.

Malcolm X
Afro-American
18 July 1964

*I'm for truth, no matter who tells it. I'm for justice, no matter
who it is for or against. I'm a human being first and foremost,
and as such I'm for whoever and whatever benefits humanity
as a whole.*

Malcolm X
Autobiography
1965

*Sometimes, I have dared to dream . . . that one day, history may even
say that my voice—which disturbed the white man's smugness, and
his arrogance, and his complacency—that my voice helped to save
America from a grave, possibly even fatal catastrophe.*

Malcolm X
Autobiography
1965

More than any black leader during the 1950s and 1960s, Malcolm X persistently and passionately warned America about the imminent eruption of the nightmare which African-Americans experienced daily in the ghettos of its cities. He contended that America could not survive as a *segregated nation,* sharply divided between whites and blacks, with the latter being treated as if they were less than human beings. Malcolm informed whites that African-Americans would not remain passive, nonviolent, and law-abiding as the U.S. government crammed them into filthy, rat-infested ghettos which were unfit for human habitation. "Retaliation in self-defense to the maximum degree of our ability," he contended, was a natural reaction and a normal response of human beings whose dignity was not publicly recognized and respected in the nation of their birth.

Malcolm's conception of the nightmare about which he spoke was strongly influenced by the biblical idea of the judgment of God. As a black Muslim minister, he did not believe that America could continue its exploitation of the poor and the weak, here and abroad, and not experience the full force of the wrath of God as described in the Scriptures and as discernible throughout human history. He believed deeply in the biblical God of justice, the One who "put down the mighty from their seats and exalted them of low degree" (Luke 1:52 KJV). Malcolm was a black prophet who told America, in the language and style of his biblical predecessors, that *repentance now* was the only way to escape God's coming judgment: "If America will repent and do this [justice], God will overlook some of [its] wicked deeds (as in the days of Nineveh) ... but if America refuses ... then, like the biblical houses of Egypt and Babylon (slave empires of the bible), God will erase the American government and the entire [white] race ... from this planet." Repent or die—these are the nation's only alternatives. "White America," Malcolm warned, "wake up and take heed, before it is too late!"

As a follower of Elijah Muhammad, Malcolm did not believe that America would "wake up" in time to avoid "that Great Doomsday." As shown in the preceding chapter, he proclaimed America's coming destruction with the passion and certainty of an eschatological prophet: *"White America is doomed!"* he said, sometimes with apparent delight and at other times with great anger. Malcolm warned the "so-called Negroes" about the "day of slaughter . . . for this sinful white world." He told African-Americans that it was foolish of them to seek integration into a white world that would soon be destroyed in a "lake of fire."

In lieu of integration, Malcolm urged blacks to separate themselves completely from whites and join with their own kind so that they together, under the leadership of Elijah Muhammad, could either return to their African homeland or build a black nation in the Western hemisphere. "God has . . . prepared a refuge," Malcolm explained, "a haven of salvation, for those who will accept his last Messenger and heed his last warning."

As long as Malcolm functioned as the mouthpiece of Elijah Muhammad, he was not allowed to participate in the political activities of the civil rights movement. But after his break with the Nation of Islam, which he announced to the public on 8 March 1964, a new Malcolm began to emerge—independent and free of the narrow straitjacket of the religious philosophy of Elijah Muhammad. His views about America and the black struggle changed. Moreover, he moved toward Martin King (and King toward him) and closer to the mainstream of the civil rights movement.

In this chapter, I will examine Malcolm's reluctant break with Elijah Muhammad and his decisive movement toward Martin King during the last and most important year of his life, concentrating chiefly on his warning about the imminent explosion of "America's racial powder keg."

BREAK WITH ELIJAH MUHAMMAD

Malcolm's fanatic commitment to the liberation of the black poor alienated him not only from most whites and many persons in the black middle class, but also, as it turned out, from his own religious community and from Elijah Muhammad as well. In a soul-wrenching experience he was separated from his spiritual father and teacher, the Messenger of Allah, to whom he had given his complete allegiance.

From the moment of his sudden conversion in 1948, Malcolm had defined his whole life in total devotion to building the Nation of Islam into a force to be reckoned with. He promoted Muhammad as the "second Moses," sent by the "Great God Allah" to separate the so-called Negroes from the coming destruction of white America. Often working eighteen to twenty hours daily, he traveled throughout the country, recruiting new members and organizing temples, interpreting Muhammad's teachings, and contributing in other ways to the advancement of the Black Muslim philosophy of separation. He surpassed all his co-religionists, even Muhammad, in time and energy devoted to the organization.

Elijah Muhammad rewarded Malcolm for his outstanding service to the Nation by providing him with a car and house, support for his family, and freedom to travel wherever he wished and to say whatever he thought the occasion demanded. In late 1963 Muhammad bestowed upon Malcolm the title of "National Minister," a unique distinction among his fellow ministers, and one that had never been given. When Muhammad announced Malcolm's new status before a Philadelphia rally, he embraced him and said: "This is my most faithful, hardworking minister. He will follow me until he dies."

The relationship between Malcolm and Muhammad was close and their affections for each other were so deep that the mood of one influenced the other. "Mr. Muhammad and I were so close," Malcolm recalled, "that I knew how he felt by how I felt. If he was nervous, I was nervous. If I was relaxed, then I knew he was relaxed." It appeared that the Malcolm-Muhammad bond was unbreakable. Many observers assumed that Malcolm was the heir apparent to the Black Muslim movement. He was frequently referred to as the "number two man" in the Nation.

What went wrong? What precipitated the break? The *official* reason, issued by Elijah Muhammad and spokesmen of the Nation, for Malcolm's ninety-day silencing and later his permanent separation, was that he had seriously disobeyed Elijah Muhammad. The episode cited was connected with Kennedy's assassination on 22 November 1963. Muhammad gave his ministers explicit instructions not to comment on the tragedy. On 1 December 1963, Muhammad gave Malcolm permission to replace him as the featured speaker for a Black Muslim rally in New York City. He also reminded Malcolm of his directive regarding the Kennedy assassination.

Malcolm spoke on the subject "God's Judgment of White America." Unlike his "Grass Roots" speech about two weeks earlier, it was a typical Black Muslim speech, similar to many he had given before, and no different from what Muhammad had taught him. It was strong on religion and weak on political engagement. The main theme was "divine justice," that is, "as you sow, so shall you reap," or more specifically, "how the hypocritical American white man was reaping what he had sowed." Although Malcolm referred to the "late President" several times (repeating his standard comments about Kennedy's control of the March on Washington), he did not comment on the assassination in his address.

However, "during the question-and-answer period" after the address, Malcolm made his now-famous characterization of the Kennedy assassination as an instance of the "chickens coming home to roost." "Somebody asked [him] what [he] thought of the assassination of President Kennedy." "Being an old farm boy myself," he said with the wide, merciless smile that had become his trademark, "chickens coming home to roost never did make me sad; they've always made me glad." Malcolm, of course, was referring to "America's climate of hate," "the seeds that America had sown—in enslavement, in many things that followed since then—all these seeds were coming up today; it was harvest time."

Predictably the media were not interested in Malcolm's ideas on either white oppression or God's justice, but only in his apparent disrespect for the assassinated president. The *New York Times* headlines read: "Malcolm X Scores U.S. and Kennedy: Likens Slaying to 'Chickens Coming Home To Roost.' " It also referred to the "loud applause and laughter" of the audience.

Soon afterward, making his "regular monthly visit to Muhammad," Malcolm discovered to his great dismay that the closeness between them had vanished. "Did you see the papers this morning?" Muhammad asked. When Malcolm answered, "Yes, sir, I did," he could feel the tenseness growing between him and "the man ... who had treated [him] as if [he] were his own flesh and blood." "That was a very bad statement," Muhammad told him. "The country loved this man. . . . A statement like that can make it hard on Muslims in general." Distancing himself even further from his chief spokesman, Muhammad said, "I'll have to silence you for the next ninety days—so that the Muslims everywhere can be disassociated from the blunder."

Malcolm could hardly believe what he had heard. Muhammad knew that silencing Malcolm was like taking a fish out of water. No disciplinary measure could have been worse. It was a cruel punishment, not commensurate with the nature of Malcolm's error in judgment. It was, however, consistent with Muhammad's arbitrary exercise of authority in the Nation.

After his initial shock, Malcolm regained his composure and then reflected momentarily about the "many times" he had said to his "own assistants that anyone in a position to discipline others must be able to take discipline himself." Following his own advice, he accepted his punishment—willingly and completely. "Sir," he said to Muhammad with a contrite and humble attitude, "I agree with you, and I submit, one hundred percent."

However, upon his return to New York from Chicago, Malcolm discovered that more was involved in his suspension than his ill-timed statement about the Kennedy assassination. A conspiracy had been set in motion by the "Chicago officials," as Malcolm referred to them, to oust him from the Black Muslim movement. According to Malcolm and Elijah's son Wallace, who also split with Elijah Muhammad, the Chicago officials wanted Malcolm out because of their jealousy of his public popularity and their envy of his power within the Nation, which was derived from his closeness to Muhammad. "Those officials were jealous of Malcolm's power and popularity," Wallace said, "and they wanted him out of the way. They planted suspicions in my father's mind, telling him that Malcolm wanted to take over the organization.''

The Black Muslim leadership was also troubled by Malcolm's black nationalist philosophy, which often involved the Nation of Islam in national and international politics, thereby creating more confrontations with the "white power structure," especially the police and the FBI. "Malcolm abandoned the *religion* to become a *political sociologist,''* said Black Muslim minister Henry X. He and other ministers criticized Malcolm for injecting "the political concept of 'black nationalism' into the Black Muslim movement," which was "essentially religious in nature when Malcolm became a member.''

Malcolm's adversaries in the Nation were correct in their accusation that he was moving the organization away from its exclusively religious focus toward an engagement of issues in the mainstream of the socio-political life of America and the world. Malcolm believed that the Nation's philosophy of separation and self-defense was a better method for achieving black unity and freedom than the integrationist, nonviolent philosophy of the civil rights organizations. That was why he claimed that Elijah Muhammad, and not Martin King, was the "most powerful black man in America." Unlike the "Chicago officials," who viewed the Nation mainly as a competitor with Christian churches, Malcolm envisioned it primarily as a competitor with the civil rights organizations. He viewed the Nation as a religio-political organization, the one that was best suited for achieving "freedom, justice, and equality" for blacks in America.

Elijah Muhammad, along with most of his ministers, did not share Malcolm's political philosophy. Elijah consistently refused to allow Malcolm to involve the Nation in the politics of the civil rights movement. The Nation's nonengagement policy caused many blacks to say: "Those Muslims *talk* tough but they never *do* nothing, unless somebody bothers Muslims." The Muslims' acts of physical retaliation were meted out primarily in the black community (especially toward persons who left the Nation), and only *verbal* retaliation was directed toward whites. For example, when the Los Angeles police invaded a Muslim temple, killing a minister and wounding several other people,

Muhammad did not allow Malcolm to implement the Black Muslim philosophy of retaliation. Instead he instructed his followers to leave the vengeance to God. As a result several young members whom Malcolm had recruited left the Nation, greatly disappointed with its passive response to blatant police brutality. Even Malcolm found Muhammad's claim that God would punish the white man for his evil deeds difficult to accept and to explain to others. While vigorously denying any differences between himself and Muhammad, Malcolm nonetheless had to admit that he and other younger Muslims were becoming impatient with the exclusively religious teachings of the Messenger. "But I tell you this," he said in an interview with Louis Lomax during his period of suspension, "the Messenger has seen God. He was with Allah and was given divine patience with the devil. He is willing to wait for Allah to deal with this devil. Well, sir, the rest of us Black Muslims have not seen God, we don't have this gift of divine patience with the devil. The younger Black Muslims want to see some action."

It was not that religion was secondary to Malcolm's political concerns. On the contrary, like Martin King, religion was primarily in defining Malcolm's life and thought. His religious commitment, however, was inseparable from his concern for the political liberation of blacks. "I believe in a religion that believes in freedom," he told Harlem blacks. "Any time I have to accept a religion that won't let me fight a battle for my people, I say to hell with that religion."

Malcolm viewed the Nation as the "divine solution" to the black people's sociopolitical oppression in America, countering Christianity's antiblack and pro-white ideology that fed the oppression of blacks. The Nation of Islam dealt with the moral decay in the black community, providing African-Americans with the spiritual power to abstain from drugs, alcohol, gambling, and crime. Beyond that, Malcolm thought the Nation was a great *political* force in America. It was this theo-political principle that led him to reject Christianity and to accept the teachings of Elijah Muhammad and later to split with the Messenger and to embrace orthodox Islam. "If I harbored any per-

sonal   disappointment   whatsoever,''   he   said   in   his
Autobiography,

> it was that privately I was convinced that our Nation of
> Islam could be an even greater force in the American black
> man's overall struggle—if we engaged in more *action.* By
> that, I mean I thought privately that we should have
> amended, or relaxed, our general non-engagement policy.
> I felt that wherever black people committed themselves, in
> the Little Rocks and the Birminghams and other places,
> militantly disciplined Muslims should also be there—for
> all the world to see, and respect, and discuss.

Elijah Muhammad and other Muslim officials, however, did
not view the Nation of Islam as a political organization. They
pointed to ''God's solution'' as the *only* answer to the problem
of injustice that whites inflict upon blacks in America and
throughout the world. Muhammad prophesied that 1970 was the
year of the great day of reckoning, the time when Allah would
bring the rule of the white race to an end and blacks, the Original People, would inherit the earth.

As the rapidly growing membership eagerly waited for ''the
War of Armageddon,'' the ''Showdown'' between God and the
devil, the Black Muslim leadership (especially Muhammad's
family) took for themselves an inordinate share of the material
benefits of the economic growth of the Nation. Not wishing to
lose their new perquisites through confrontation with the white
power structure, they were determined to deal firmly with Malcolm's attempt to insert the Nation into the politics of black
liberation.

In addition to jealousy and envy in the Nation and to Malcolm's black nationalist politics, Elijah Muhammad's moral hypocrisy contributed significantly to Malcolm's definitive rupture
with the Black Muslims. The moral code of the Nation was
strict and the punishment for breaking it was severe. For ''fornication or adultery,'' it was not unusual for Elijah Muhammad
''to mete out sentences of one to five years of 'isolation,' if
not complete expulsion from the Nation.'' Malcolm internalized

deeply the moral principles of the Nation, teaching them "so strongly," he said, "that many Muslims accused me of being 'anti-woman.' The very keel of my teaching, and my most personal belief was that Elijah Muhammad in every aspect of his existence was a symbol of moral, mental, and spiritual reform among the American black people." Malcolm referred to his "own transformation" as the "best example" of "Mr. Muhammad's power to reform" the lives of black people. From the time he entered prison in 1946 to his marriage to Betty in 1958, Malcolm "never touched a woman." He also rigidly observed other moral principles, refusing to smoke or drink alcohol even in the company of close friends outside the Nation. At no time did he trivialize the morality which Elijah Muhammad taught.

However, "as far back as 1955," Malcolm, to his great distress, "heard hints" about the "immoral behavior of Mr. Muhammad." "Why, the very idea made me shake in fear," Malcolm recalled. It was so "insane-sounding" that he could not even consider believing it. He simply ignored it *"Adultery! Why any Muslim guilty of adultery was summarily ousted in disgrace,"* as were Malcolm's brother Reginald, several of Muhammad's secretaries, and many others.

"But by late 1962," it became impossible for Malcolm to ignore the gossip about Muhammad's moral failure. Muslims began to leave the Chicago Mosque, and "the ugly rumor was spreading swiftly—even among non-Muslim Negroes." When Wallace Muhammad, Elijah's son, personally confirmed the truth of the accusation against his father, Malcolm became greatly troubled about the moral integrity of the Black Muslim movement. How could he explain to the Nation's membership and to the non-Muslim public the great moral contradiction between what Muhammad said publicly and what he did privately?

Malcolm felt that the survival of the Nation was at stake. "I desperately wanted to find some way—some kind of bridge— over which I was certain the Nation of Islam could be saved from self-destruction," he recalled. In his search of the Quran and the Bible, with the assistance of Wallace Muhammad, he believed that he had found the answer. "Loyal Muslims could be taught that a man's accomplishments in his life outweigh his personal, human weakness.'' David's and Moses' adultery, Lot's incest, and Noah's drunkenness were less important than the positive contributions they made to their people. Could not the same be true of the Messenger Muhammad? This solution, however, gave Malcolm only temporary relief from his spiritual torment.

Nothing was more important to Malcolm than living according to the message one preached. He regarded America as morally worse than South Africa because the latter practiced what it preached—apartheid. America, in contrast, preached freedom and democracy but practiced racial discrimination against its people of color. He made a similar distinction between southern, white conservatives and northern, white liberals, referring to them respectively as ''wolves'' and ''foxes.'' What passes for democracy in America, according to Malcolm, is nothing but ''disguised hypocrisy,'' which he also frequently called ''tricknology,'' ''a science of tricks and lies.'' For twelve years, Malcolm, before black and white audiences, on television and radio, vented his rage against the calculated deception of white America. *Now* to discover beyond any doubt that Elijah Muhammad, the ''Dear Holy Apostle,'' was a trickster and that he himself was a dupe shook the foundation of Malcolm's faith. ''I can't describe the torments I went through,'' he wrote in his *Autobiography.*

Malcolm's spiritual crisis was so deep that he also ''broke the rule,'' ''looked up,'' and ''talked with three of the former secretaries to Mr. Muhammad'' ''in 'the isolated state.' '' They not only confirmed what he already knew; they also told him what he did not know, namely that Muhammad was deceitful in his relationship with him.

From their own mouths, I heard their stories of who had fathered their children. And from their own mouths I heard that Elijah Muhammad had told them I was the best, the greatest minister he ever had, but that someday I would leave him, turn against him—so I was ''dangerous.'' I learned from these former secretaries . . . that while he was praising me to my face, he was tearing me apart behind my back.

Early in 1963, feeling that he had to discuss the matter face to face, Malcolm wrote Muhammad a letter "about the poison being spread about him." In April Muhammad invited Malcolm to Phoenix to talk about the matter. "Plainly, frankly, pulling no punches," Malcolm confronted Muhammad with what was being said about him. "And without waiting for any response from him," Malcolm told Muhammad that "with his son Wallace's help" he "had found in the Quran and the Bible that which might be taught to Muslims—if it became necessary—as the fulfillment of prophecy."

Muhammad responded with an expression of appreciation for Malcolm's insight. "Son, I'm not surprised,' he said. "You always have had such a good understanding of prophecy, and spiritual things. You recognize that's what all of this is—prophecy." Muhammad then proceeded to give his own theological explanation of his moral laxity. "I'm David," he told Malcolm. "When you read about how David took another man's wife, I'm that David. You read about Noah, who got drunk—that's me. You read about Lot, who went and laid up with his own daughters. I have to fulfill all of those things."

After Malcolm discovered the truth about Muhammad's immorality and found biblical references to explain it as the fulfillment of biblical prophecy, he still found the Messenger's moral failings difficult to accept. He spoke less about the *religion* of the Nation and more about the politics of black liberation. Of course, Malcolm's shift from religion to politics in his preaching did not go unnoticed. It seemed that Elijah Muhammad, under the influence of the Chicago officials, could no longer trust Malcolm. Muhammad, therefore, merely waited for Malcolm "To make a move that would enable him to suspend [his well-known spokesman] and get the support of the public in doing so." The opportunity came with his incautious remark about the Kennedy assassination.

It seems in any case that the break between Malcolm and Muhammad could not have been avoided. Malcolm was too political and honest, and Muhammad was too religious and hypocritical for them to sustain their relationship. Muhammad knew it. But Malcolm was too naive to see it soon enough to avoid its disastrous consequences.

During Malcolm's suspension a chain of events occurred that could be interpreted only as a determined effort by the Nation's leadership to put him out of the Black Muslim movement. He was prevented not only from speaking publicly among non-Muslims but also at Muslim temples, including Number Seven, which he headed.

Malcolm also discovered, to his great surprise and dismay, that his enemies not only wanted to put him out of the Nation but out of existence as well. While the Nation's leadership denied making any attempts against Malcolm's life, there is much evidence to support their complicity and very little to contradict it. According to Malcolm, one plot against his life was revealed to him by the person who was supposed to carry it out. "This first direct death-order was how, finally, I began to arrive at my psychological divorce with the Nation of Islam." "The death talk," Malcolm said, "was not my fear."

> Every second of my twelve years with Mr. Muhammad, I had been ready to lay down my life for him. The thing to me worse than death was the *betrayal*. I could conceive death. I couldn't conceive betrayal—not of the loyalty which I had given to the Nation of Islam, and to Mr. Muhammad. During the previous twelve years, if Mr. Muhammad had committed any civil crime punishable by death, I would have said and tried to prove that I did it— to save him—and I would have gone to the electric chair, as Mr. Muhammad's servant."

The experience of betrayal by his religious community was psychologically devastating. "I was in a state of emotional shock," he said. He compared it to "someone who for twelve years had had an inseparable, beautiful marriage—and then suddenly one morning at breakfast the marriage partner had thrust across the table some divorce papers." It affected him physically. "My head felt like it was bleeding inside. I felt like my brain was damaged." He even consulted his physician, who recommended rest.

Fortunately, his newly found friend, Cassius Clay (now Muhammad Ali), who later sided with Muhammad against Malcolm, offered him and his family a vacation in Florida, where he was training for the heavyweight fight against the then-champion Charles "Sonny" Liston. This vacation gave Malcolm time to assess his place in the Nation of Islam and also to start his psychological move toward independence. He did not want to break with Muhammad. "I still struggled to persuade myself that Mr. Muhammad had been fulfilling prophecy." What broke his faith with Muhammad was his moral hypocrisy.

> Try as I might, I couldn't hide, I couldn't evade, that Mr. Muhammad, instead of facing what he had done before his followers, as a human weakness or as fulfillment of prophecy—which I sincerely believe that Muslims would have understood, or at least they would have accepted— Mr. Muhammad had, instead, been willing to hide, to cover up what he had done. That was my major blow. That was how I first began to realize that I had believed in Mr. Muhammad more than he believed in himself.

Malcolm's break with Muhammad set him off on his own as leader with no organization and very few public followers. Even though he had many sympathizers, most were afraid to be associated with him because of his public image as a teacher of hate and fomenter of violence against whites. Since Malcolm had neither initiated nor anticipated his break with the Nation, he had not developed a religious philosophy which clearly distinguished his views from Muhammad's. Even his political philosophy, though partly different from Muhammad's, was closely linked to and dependent upon the Nation of Islam. Malcolm tried desperately to remain a minister within the Black Muslim movement, and failing that, he wanted to separate from it without bitterness or rancor.

But that was not to be. At the end of Malcolm's ninety-day

suspension, he wrote a letter to Muhammad asking for clarification of his status in the Nation. Muhammad's reply indicated that his suspension would remain in effect "for an indefinite period." Malcolm concluded that the "national officials" in Chicago had successfully poisoned the Messenger with misinformation against him. He, therefore, decided to make a public break by creating his own movement, which he called the Muslim Mosque Incorporated. He initially conceived the organization as a complement to and not in competition with the Nation of Islam. In a telegram to Muhammad, he told him that "you are still my leader and teacher, even though those around you won't let me be one of your active followers or helpers." Malcolm wanted Muhammad to know that he was pressured out of the Nation and did not leave of his own free will. "I have reached the conclusion," he said on the occasion of his public declaration of independence, "that I can best spread Mr. Muhammad's message by staying out of the Nation of Islam and continuing to work on my own among America's 22 million non-Muslim Negroes." Malcolm's separation from the person who rescued him from the depths and placed him in the religious community which defined his ministry was a painful and difficult decision. He left Muhammad's Nation only because he had no other alternative.

Upon his departure from the Nation, Malcolm did not project himself as a divine man like Elijah Muhammad or as an educated leader like Martin King. "My sincerity is my credentials," he said at the 12 March 1964 press conference at New York's Park Sheraton Hotel.

MOVEMENT TOWARD MARTIN

As he slipped out of Muhammad's "straightjacket" religious philosophy, Malcolm was seen increasingly as an independent political leader of the black masses in the urban ghetto. His thinking moved further toward the politics of black nationalism as the necessary alternative to the integrationist, nonviolent philosophy of Martin King. What is remarkable, however, is that in this final stormy year of his life Malcolm revealed not only differences with Martin but also many similarities. Neither their differences nor their similarities remained static but were constantly in a process of change and development, strongly influenced by their awareness of each other, as they searched for the meaning of black freedom in America and the best method for achieving it.

Before the break, Malcolm's public reactions to the leadership and philosophy of Martin King passed through two stages: "mostly silence" during the 1950s and "open attack" during the early 1960s. In both stages he was complying with Elijah Muhammad's instructions. After Malcolm got the green light to criticize King's movement, his remarks were harsh, particularly in 1963. King was a "chump" for using children in the Birmingham demonstrations, a "traitor" for advocating nonviolence, and a "clown" for participating in the March on Washington, which was controlled by whites.

Having been educated in the streets of Roxbury and Harlem, Malcolm was not accustomed to restraining his language in his attempt to state the truth about black-white relations in America. His language was particularly harsh against King and other civil rights leaders, whom he perceived as adjusting the black liberation struggle to ethical guidelines laid down by whites. His lack of verbal restraint was both an asset and a liability. It was an asset in that it enabled him to speak the truth from the perspective of blacks in the urban ghetto in sharp, uncomplicated language. But it was a liability in that it alienated him from Martin and other civil rights leaders as well as from the vast majority of blacks, especially Christians in the South. In addition Malcolm's straightforward language made it easy for the white media to project him as a demagogue.

As Malcolm moved out of the Nation of Islam and began to plot his own course, he consciously moved toward the politics of Martin King and the civil rights movement. "Now that I have more independence-of-action I intend to use a more flexible approach toward working with others to get a solution to this problem," he said. Malcolm decided to enter the civil rights movement as a supporter of blacks everywhere who were fighting against segregation. While he continued to reject integration and to advocate separation, Malcolm concluded that the return to Africa or the creation of a separate state in the Western hemisphere was "still a long range program." In the meantime, the short range goal must be achievement of "better food, clothing, housing, education, and jobs *right now.*"

In order to participate in the civil rights movement, of which Martin King was the most visible symbol, Malcolm realized that he had to change his Black Muslim image. He issued a call for unity among all black leaders and organizations. "I am not out to fight other Negro leaders or organizations," he said. "We must find a common approach, a common solution, to a common problem. As of this minute, I've forgotten everything bad that the other leaders have said about me, and I pray they can also forget the many bad things I've said about them."

"THE BALLOT OR THE BULLET"

Malcolm's classic statement of his emerging political vision is his well-known speech entitled "The Ballot or the Bullet." He gave it many times to mostly black audiences, in such places as New York, Cleveland, and Detroit. It was one of his best talks, rivaling his great "message to the Grass Roots," especially in terms of the enthusiastic response of his audience.

Malcolm began "The Ballot or the Bullet" speech by clarifying his religious status: "I'm still a Muslim," he said. "I still credit Mr. Muhammad for what I know and what I am." But in the interest of black unity Malcolm stopped proselytizing or even discussing religion because of its propensity for creating divisions. While he was still deeply committed to Islam as the only true religion of blacks, his negative experiences in Muhammad's Black Muslim movement had showed him the limitations of religious fanaticism. As a consequence, Malcolm turned toward Martin King as a model for the political direction in which he was now moving. "Just as ... Dr. Martin Luther King is a Christian minister ... who heads another organization fighting for the civil rights of black people in this country," Malcolm said, "I myself am a ... Muslim minister" following a black nationalist line of action. "I don't believe in fighting today on any one front but on all fronts," he continued. "In fact, I am a black nationalist freedom fighter."

Using language similar to his "Grass Roots" speech, Malcolm emphasized a concept of unity that was based on the common plight of black people and not on his Islamic religion. "It's time for us to submerge our differences and realize that ... we have the same problem, ... a problem that will make you catch hell whether you're a Baptist, or a Methodist, or a Muslim, or a nationalist." As Malcolm saw it, "whether you're educated or illiterate, whether you live on the boulevard or in the alley," the consequences of being black in America were pretty much the same. "We're all in the same boat," he said. "They don't hang you because you're a Baptist, they hang you because you're black. They don't attack me because I'm a Muslim, they attack me because I'm black. They attack all of us for the same reason. All of us catch hell. . . . We're in the same bag. . . . We suffer political oppression, economic exploitation, and social degradation ... from the same enemy"—"the white man."

"The Ballot or the Bullet" speech was Malcolm's initial attempt to develop a political vision that was continuous with his black nationalist, Muslim past, while also showing the new directions in his thinking that would enable him to enter and expand the civil rights movement. The "bullet" in the phrase represented the *continuity* in Malcolm's perspective. It accented his militancy. It referred to his firm belief that no people can be recognized and respected as human beings if they are not prepared to defend their humanity against those who violate their God-given rights.

On the occasion of his declaration of independence, Malcolm created much controversy when he said: "In areas where our people are the constant victims of brutality, and the government seems unwilling or unable to protect them, we should form *rifle clubs* that can be used to defend our lives and our property in times of emergency." He contended that it is "criminal" to teach nonviolence to blacks when they are routinely the victims of white violence. With these comments, Malcolm wanted the whole world to know that his break with Elijah Muhammad and move toward Martin King and the civil rights movement did not mean that he was going to urge blacks to be nonviolent with people who were violent toward them. He wanted to enter the civil rights movement in order to *expand* it, that is, to give it a "new" and "broader interpretation," thereby making it more militant by including the principle of self-defense or, as he often called it, the "by any means necessary" philosophy.

Malcolm was especially careful to stay within the bounds of the law. He wanted only to affirm the ethical principle of self-survival for African-Americans, a right which whites took for granted, both legally and morally. Malcolm never once advocated aggressive violence against whites. "We should be peaceful, law-abiding," he said during his declaration of independence and on many other occasions. "But the time has come for the American Negro to fight back in self-defense whenever and wherever he is being unjustly attacked." Malcolm knew that whites, especially the government, would not like what he was saying. That was why he concluded his statement with the comment: "If the government thinks I am wrong for saying this, then let the government start doing its job."

Like Malcolm's comment about the "chickens coming home to roost," his reference to "rifle clubs" created quite a stir among civil rights groups, law enforcement officials, and in the media throughout the country. Many interpreted the remark as meaning that Malcolm was advocating violence. "Broader Malcolm: His Theme Now Is Violence" was the headline in *U.S. News & World Report*. The report in the *Chicago Defender* read: "Negroes Need Guns, Declares Malcolm X." The editorial in the New York *Amsterdam News* was entitled "Reckless Orbit." "We don't hesitate to say that the solution to the problems of minorities does not lie in hysterical sword rattling and wild statements about the need and use of shotguns in race relations," the editorial said. "The founding fathers long ago made clear the right of the minority to speak out, demonstrate and protest against injustice. And we stand squarely behind and support such protests when the cause is just and the aim is plain. But," it continued, "in the light of the progress that has been made and is being made through nonviolence, it's downright silly to start preaching violence now." "To Arms with Malcolm X" was the heading for the *New York Times* editorial. The editorial said: "His is a call to break the law; to take the law into one group's own hands that would hold firearms; to erect a private militia. His is a call to arms against duly constituted police forces." Calling him an "embittered racist" and "irresponsible demagogue," the *Times* went on to assure its readers that "Malcolm X will not deceive Negroes in New York or elsewhere."

The FBI alerted its agencies and the local police in many cities to be on the lookout for blacks buying firearms and forming rifle clubs. The New York *Amsterdam News* reported on the organization of a "Negro Rifle Club" in Cleveland by a city employee, Louis Robinson. The FBI in Chicago reported that an unknown Negro placed an order for eleven to fifteen .22 caliber magnum automatic rifles with fixed telescopes, stating that he was organizing a rifle club. According to Ray Davis, a columnist for the *Michigan Chronicle,* Malcolm "denied the leadership of the Medgar Evers Memorial Rifle Club, being formed in cities, but declared the constitutional right of such clubs to exist if they are the only means by which Negroes can secure protection."

The predictable negative reactions to Malcolm's statement about blacks protecting themselves with "rifles and shotguns" confirmed, for him, once again that whites did not regard blacks as human beings. "Not a single white person in America would sit idly by and let someone do to him what we black[s] have been letting others do to us," Malcolm said during his third appearance at the Harvard Law School Forum. "The white person would not remain passive, peaceful, and nonviolent." In an interview with the *Washington Star* Malcolm said that like any white person who would defend his or her humanity at all costs, he "reserve[d] the right to do whatever, wherever, whenever, and however is necessary to get results." He made a similar point in response to a question at the Militant Labor Forum, which had a predominantly white audience: "I'm the man you think you are. . . . If we're both human beings we'll both do the same thing. And if you want to know what I'll do, figure out what you'll do. I'll do the same thing—only more of it.''

White people's refusal to acknowledge the right of blacks to defend themselves against persons who violated their humanity was perhaps the main reason that Malcolm could never accept Martin King's idea of nonviolence and its capacity to prick the moral conscience of whites. He urged blacks to stop trying to appeal to the good will of whites because it was useless. ''Don't change the white man's mind,'' Malcolm told blacks. ''You can't change his mind, and that whole thing about appealing to the moral conscience of America—America's conscience is bankrupt. She lost all conscience a long time ago. Uncle Sam has no conscience. They don't know what morals are.'' The only language that whites understand is the language that they themselves use—violence. ''They don't try to eliminate evil because it's evil, or because it's illegal, or because it's immoral; they eliminate it only when it threatens their existence.''

While Malcolm did not think that it was possible to change white people's minds, he was hopeful that he could revolutionize the political consciousness of black people. As was true with his ''Grass Roots'' speech, Malcolm's ''Ballot or Bullet'' talk was designed to inspire blacks to take charge of their own political destiny by reshaping their lives, rejecting their assigned role as passive sufferers, and accepting their God-given role as active freedom fighters. ''It was not necessary to change the white man's mind,'' Malcolm assured blacks. ''We've got to change our own minds about each other. We have to see each other with new eyes,'' that is, ''as brothers and sisters. We have to come together with warmth so we can develop unity and harmony that's necessary to get this problem solved ourselves.''

To persuade blacks to adopt the self-help philosophy of black nationalism, Malcolm believed that he had to show them that they would never get their freedom as long as they put their trust in the government and white liberals. ''The government has failed us—you can't deny that,'' he frequently said. He knew that many blacks would not accept his sweeping condemnation of the government, especially since the Kennedy and Johnson administrations supported the Civil Rights Bill. Still,

he told them how misguided they were to think of the government as their ally rather than their main opponent: "Anytime
you're living in the twentieth century and you're walking
around here singing 'We Shall Overcome,' the government has
failed you. ... White liberals who have been posing as our
friends have failed us. Once we see that all these other sources
to which we have turned have failed, we stop turning to them
and turn to ourselves."

As Martin King and other integrationists accented their
American identity, Malcolm refused to identify with the country
of his birth. "We're not Americans, we're Africans who happen
to be in America," Malcolm told a Harlem audience. "We were
kidnapped and brought here against our will from Africa. We
didn't land on Plymouth Rock—that rock landed on us." Without fail, Malcolm aroused the resentful feelings of integrationists when he spoke like that. No persons tried to be *Americans*
more than integrationists. They have been called "super Americans" and "exaggerated Americans." When they heard Malcolm denying his American identity, they were greatly
embarrassed because he contradicted what they had been telling
whites that blacks wanted. How could the black advocates of
integration explain Malcolm's philosophy of separation to their
white friends in government and the civil rights movement?

Malcolm, however, could not resist exposing what he regarded as the sheer stupidity of black, middle-class leaders talking about America as it if is "*our* country." "I am one,"
he said, "who doesn't believe in deluding myself." Malcolm
compared being a citizen with being a diner. "I am not going
to sit at your table and watch you eat with nothing on my plate,
and call myself a diner," he said. "Sitting at the table doesn't
make you a diner, unless you eat some of what's on that plate."
Likewise, "being born in America doesn't make you an American. Why, if birth made you an American, you wouldn't need
any legislation, you wouldn't need any amendments to the Constitution, you wouldn't be faced with civil-rights filibustering in
Washington, D.C., right now."

Malcolm reminded blacks that European immigrants do not
need legislation to make them Americans. "Those Hunkies that

just got off the boat, they're already Americans,'' he said. ''Everything that came out of Europe, every blue-eyed thing is already an American. And as long as you and I have been here, we aren't Americans yet.''

NEW DIRECTIONS

While the "bullet" symbolized the continuity in Malcolm's thinking, the "ballot" signaled an important change. It represented his movement away from the narrow skin-nationalism of the Black Muslims to an affirmation of blackness which enabled him to cooperate with Martin King and others in the mainstream of the civil rights movement. "We will work with anybody, anywhere, at any time, who is genuinely interested in tackling the problem headon," he said. "We'll work with you on the voter-registration drive, ... rent strikes, ... and school boycotts."

When Malcolm was Elijah Muhammad's minister, his religious beliefs defined the heart of his public discourse about America, while his political ideas were kept private. He had been separated from the American political process and from the civil rights movement which sought to integrate African-Americans into it. His advocacy of complete separation was based on an act of faith and not on an option in the American political process. After his break the situation was reversed. He relegated religion to the "private" sphere and placed politics in the center of his public discourse.

This radical change provided an opportunity for a more fruitful dialogue between him and Martin. Malcolm not only cast aside his "true believer" attitude, which had encouraged Martin to avoid him; he also tempered his critique of Martin and other civil rights leaders. Furthermore he put forward an idea of black nationalism that was exclusively devoted to the political, social, and economic development of the black community. Malcolm compared his advocacy of black nationalism with Billy Graham's preaching of Christianity, which he called "white nationalism." Graham "circumvents the jealousy and envy that he would ordinarily incur among the heads of the church" by limiting his activity to "preaching Christ" and urging the converts "to go to any church wherever you find him." "Well," said Malcolm, "we are going to do the same thing, only our gospel is black nationalism." His point was that once one was converted to black nationalism, he or she was free to join any organization or church where it was preached. "Don't join a church where white nationalism is preached," Malcolm told an audience of blacks in Detroit. "You can go to a Negro church and be exposed to white nationalism. When you go in a Negro church and you see a white Jesus and a white Mary and white angels, that Negro church is preaching white nationalism."

As a Black Muslim, Malcolm normally would have sharpened his critique of the black church, for he saw little liberating potential in it and took many opportunities to say so. The "new Malcolm," however, curtailed his critique of the black church in the interest of black unity, defined by the politics of black nationalism. Using conciliatory language that surprised even some of his critics, he said: "When you go to a church and you see the pastor of that church with a philosophy and a program that's designed to bring black people together and elevate black people, join that church!" Malcolm also applied that same principle to civil rights organizations: "If you see where the NAACP is preaching and practicing that which is designed to make black nationalism materialize, join the NAACP." He also mentioned CORE in the same connection. "Join any kind of organization—civic, religious, fraternal, political or otherwise—that's based on lifting ... the black man up and making him master of his own community."

It is true that as a Black Muslim Malcolm had issued calls for unity, holding many "Unity Rallies" in Harlem and inviting Martin and other black leaders to present their solutions to the black condition in America. He also spoke on unity at Black Muslim and non-Muslim community meetings throughout the country. The unity theme was the core of all types of black nationalist philosophies. However, it was one thing to issue calls for unity and quite another to create the wholesome conditions necessary for its achievement. For example, as a Black Muslim, Malcolm's idea of unity was based on the African-American community's acceptance of the Nation of Islam as the true religion of black people and Elijah Muhammad as their leader who was sent by Allah to save them from the imminent destruction of white America. It was not surprising that little unity could be achieved on that basis. Elijah Muhammad had neither the vision nor the integrity to be an appropriate symbol for unity in the African-American community. This insight grew in Malcolm during the 1960s as he began to see the limitations of Muhammad's sectarianism.

Martin King and the civil rights movement were much more successful in establishing solidarity among blacks than were Malcolm and the Black Muslims. Malcolm knew that and was sometimes jealous of Martin's influence in the black community. Despite his own rhetoric Malcolm knew that Martin's influence was not always supported by the federal government and the white media. Martin's prestige in the black community was primarily the result of his ability to transcend many petty differences among civil rights leaders and effectively speak to the everyday needs of black people. Therefore, when Malcolm became an independent leader, his inspiration was derived more from Martin than Muhammad, as he sought to build an organization that could include a broad range of blacks with different political and religious orientations. He tried hard to develop a unity message that would enable him to be involved in civil rights activities which previously had been closed to him. In this aim he was only partly successful.

As one might have expected, there were mixed responses to Malcolm's split from the Black Muslims and his subsequent attempt to enter the civil rights movement. In a *New York Times* article appropriately entitled "Negroes Ponder Malcolm's Move: Differ over Significance of His Political Effort," Fred Powledge reported several reactions among civil rights leaders to Malcolm's attempt to join them. James Farmer of CORE focused on Malcolm's "rifle club" statement and suggested that he was "proposing a race war that Negroes could not win." However, most observers, including Farmer, agreed with Bayard Rustin: "There are many elements in the Negro community . . . who out of frustration with the current situation, have been

deeply attracted to Malcolm's analysis . . . of the evils that are
being practiced on the Negro people." But only a very few
accepted Malcolm's idea of "non-nonviolence." Richard A.
Hildebrand, then pastor of Bethel AME Church and president
of the New York branch of the NAACP, expressed the senti-
ments of many: "I welcome anybody who is going to help the
civil rights struggle, but I cannot condone violence. Malcolm
X is a brilliant person. I have the feeling that we can work
together as long as we can contain that philosophy of violence."

Malcolm's initial participation in civil rights activities occurred in the New York area. He supported the school boycott
that was led by Milton A. Galamison, a militant civil rights
activist who was pastor of Siloam Presbyterian Church in
Brooklyn. Malcolm's support was unsolicited. In view of his
"violent" image, largely created by the media, Galamison accepted it with much caution. "The boycott is being operated
under a philosophy of nonviolence," Galamison said. "I have
not talked to Malcolm X. If he adheres to nonviolence, he will
be welcome at the boycott. We don't want to reject any legitimate support, but I want it to be legitimate." Malcolm did not
march in the picket line. As a "believer in '*non-violence*,' "
he explained, "if I got in line, other believers of non-violence
would join it, and when we met up with white non-nonviolence
believers, there would be violence."

Malcolm also addressed a "rent strike rally" sponsored by
the Community Council on Housing under the leadership of
Jesse Gray, a militant activist. Gray spoke at several of Malcolm's meetings as well. Both appeared frequently in the pages
of the *New York Times* and the New York *Amsterdam News* as
harsh critics of Police Commissioner Michael J. Murphy.

Galamison and Gray were among several locally based "militant civil rights leaders" who found the national, established
leadership too "conservative," that is, too "anxious 'to please
white people.' " They were largely located in the North, and
still committed to nonviolence. But they were urging more militant confrontations with the white power structure, such as the
New York school boycott, initiated by Galamison without the
support of the NAACP and CORE. Besides Galamison and Gray,

other militants included Stanley E. Branch, head of the Committee for Freedom Now in Chester, Pennsylvania; Lawrence Landry, an organizer of school boycotts in Chicago; and Gloria Richardson, chairperson of the Cambridge [Md.] Nonviolent Action Committee.

The militants invited Malcolm to speak at a meeting in Chester, Pennsylvania. About sixty persons were present. He made his standard comments about the right of blacks to defend themselves when the government failed to protect them in the exercise of their human rights. Although the group was "militant," they gave a cautious response to Malcolm's talk about the "firearms and 'rifle club' organizing bit." The headline of the *Afro-American* read: "Malcolm's Gun Idea Gets Cool Response: Even Militant 'Militants' Fail to Warm Up to Plan." According to Stanley Branch, the group supported Malcolm's desire and aim for racial unity as a "good thing." But "Malcolm's firearms ideology was the 'furthest thing from our minds.' "

However, some persons in the group, such as Gloria Richardson, welcomed both Malcolm's call for self-defense and his cooperation with civil rights groups. "Malcolm is being very practical," she said.

> The resisting white community takes advantage of our commitment to nonviolence and uses this against us. Throughout the nation colored citizens are at the boiling point. Self-defense may actually be a deterrent to further violence. Hitherto, the government has moved into conflict situations only when matters approach the level of insurrection. Self-defense may force Washington to intervene sooner.

The "militant civil rights activists" formed a new organization called ACT! (not an acronym) to show its contrast with the "passive" approach of the national Negro leadership. "The sole qualification for membership in ACT! is that one must act or utilize direct action to resolve civil rights disputes," said Lawrence Landry, who was elected president of the group.

Using language similar to that of Malcolm X, Landry told the group that "1963 had established the principle that Negroes want to be free, and in 1964, we established the principle that Negroes will do whatever is necessary to be free." ACT! turned to Malcolm for inspiration and named him, along with Adam Clayton Powell, Jr., and Dick Gregory, as a consultant to the group.

Another important development was the invitations Malcolm received to speak at the meetings of several clergy groups, including the Brooklyn Methodist Ministers Association (a mixed group of blacks and whites) and a gathering of about twenty black ministers who called their group the Interdenominational Ministers Meeting of Greater New York and Vicinity. To the Methodists Malcolm spoke on the "gospel of black nationalism," repeating his Billy Graham analogy, and reiterating his affirmation of self-defense. When a white minister asked him "whether he thought there were any good white people," Malcolm replied, "I do not say that there are no sincere white people, but rather that I haven't met any."

At the Interdenominational Ministers gathering, the session was polite, with Malcolm and the ministers "twitting each other." He warned them of the coming nightmare in their own communities. "1964 is explosive," he said, "and I'm afraid that most of the leaders have gotten so out of touch with the people that they don't know the powder keg they're sitting on." Asked if his critical attitude toward Christianity had changed within the last year, Malcolm replied: "I don't care what I said last year. That was last year. This is 1964."

It is important to note that some ministers supported Malcolm and appeared on the platform with him. Albert B. Cleage, Jr., a clergyman of the United Church of Christ and pastor of the Shrine of the Black Madonna in Detroit, was a close friend of Malcolm and appeared with him many times. Malcolm introduced Nelson C. Dukes, pastor of the Fountain Spring Baptist Church in New York, as a "strong Black Nationalist." The *Amsterdam News* reported that C. Asapansa-Johnson (originally an AME minister from Sierra Leone who organized and became pastor of the Bethel Community Church in Staten Island) agreed

"85 percent with Malcolm X." As president of the Interdenominational Ministers Meeting of Greater New York and Vicinity, he contended that "Negroes should fight in defense of their lives, homes and rights because 'until we're willing to die, we'll never receive freedom.'" Like Malcolm, he claimed that no people can gain freedom as long as they are paralyzed by fear. "The majority of Negroes are afraid to die," he proclaimed to an assembly of black ministers. "They're taking it too easy. They must be told they must die—shed blood—for freedom."

Other ministers strongly objected to Malcolm's advocacy of "rifle clubs" and rejected his offer to join the civil rights movement. Among them was Robert M. Kinlock. Kinlock—a highly controversial Harlem community activist who later was appointed and then relieved of his duties as the chairman of the Commission for the Elimination of Racism, which was sponsored by the Council of Churches for the City of New York— "called Malcolm's position ridiculous." According to Kinlock, the so-called new Malcolm is not new. "He's still preaching the same philosophy under a new name." A similar position was taken by Irvin C. Lockman, pastor of Mount Calvary Methodist Church, and W. Eugene Houston, pastor of Rendall Memorial Presbyterian Church, both churches located in Harlem. Houston succeeded Asapansa-Johnson as the president of the ministerial group. Both Houston and Lockman opposed Aspansa-Johnson at the Interdenominational Ministers gathering. "It would be suicidal for minority Negroes to fight majority whites through armed conflict to attain first-class citizenship." Lockman advocated that blacks should follow the "moral leadership of Dr. Martin Luther King, Jr." He even claimed with confidence that "the victory (of the rights struggle) has been won—all we need do now is to mop up."

Of the mainline civil rights organizations, the young activists of SNCC were influenced the most by Malcolm's philosophy of black nationalism. Many of them grew increasingly impatient with Martin King's "conservative," nonviolent, and charismatic leadership role. James Forman, the executive director of SNCC, said that Malcolm's new position "opens up possibilities for people who certainly thought that Muslims had something to

say but who reject the whole concept of a separate state and
the religion. That cat does have a lot of followers outside the
[Muslim] temple." John Lewis, SNCC's national chairman,
called Malcolm a "great person," but unlike the majority of
the other SNCC leaders, he was ideologically closer to King.
"SNCC will not support a movement to take up arms," he said,
"because we believe in nonviolence as a philosophy of life."

Elsewhere in the civil rights movement Adam Clayton Powell, Jr., who referred to himself as a friend of Malcolm X and
invited him to speak several times at Abyssinian Baptist Church,
where he served as pastor, said that Malcolm's "suggestion . . .
that colored people arm themselves with guns and rifles has run
afoul of the civil rights movement." He "labeled the scheme
'totally and completely wrong,' " because "the whole power
of the black revolution is based upon nonviolence." Roy Wilkins and Whitney Young shared a similar view.

No one was more concerned about Malcolm's call to arms
than Martin King. In his speech to the spring luncheon of the
United Federation of Teachers, held at New York's Americana
Hotel, Martin acknowledged that "race relations had reached a
crisis but that he was certain that 'the white majority was willing to meet the Negro half-way.' " When he was asked about
Malcolm's "formation of the Black Nationalist Party and his
call for Negroes to arm themselves," Martin said "I think it is
very unfortunate that Malcolm X continues to predict violence"
because "it would be very tragic . . . for the Negro to use
violence in any form. Many of our opponents would be de-
lighted." Furthermore, he continued, "if we would take up
arms, it would give them an excuse to kill up a lot of us."

Despite Malcolm's "violent" language, Martin sensed that
he should not be taken too literally and thus might be opened
to tactical nonviolence since he was no longer accountable to
the narrow sectarian philosophy of Elijah Muhammad. That was
why Martin told the media that he would probably talk with
Malcolm about his "call to arms" and seek to convince him
of the futility of violence. Cautious in his initiative, Martin,
three months later, took a few more steps toward Malcolm,
which we will discuss shortly.

In contrast to Martin's cautious approach, Malcolm was bold in his efforts to meet with Martin. He visited Martin's SCLC office in Atlanta several times, but the latter was never there. Malcolm attended civil rights events that featured Martin as a speaker and frequently talked with SCLC staffers. Malcolm also initiated their only encounter in Washington, D.C., during the Senate debate of the Civil Rights Bill. While Malcolm was trying to meet with Martin in order to form a black united front against racism, Martin was shrewdly avoiding him because of his "violent" image.

Since neither King and the civil rights movement nor Muhammad and the Nation responded positively to Malcolm's overtures of unity and peace, he decided to make the Hajj, the required pilgrimage to Mecca, followed by visits to several independent countries in Africa, in order to search for spiritual and political directions. From 19 April to 21 May, he traveled, read, and conversed with many orthodox Muslims and revolutionary Africans about Islam and the worldwide black liberation struggle.

Malcolm's trip to Egypt, Lebanon, Saudi Arabia, Nigeria, Ghana, Morocco, and Algeria made an enormous impact upon his understanding of Islam and his perspective on the politics of black nationalism. In Mecca he discovered that Elijah Muhammad's Islamic teachings—especially the idea that white people were devils by nature—contradicted orthodox Islam. Malcolm saw white Muslims in Mecca treating persons of other races, including himself, as brothers and sisters, showing no prejudice whatsoever. The experience of racial harmony, among many shades of humanity, from all over the world, shocked him. He was told by many Muslims that Islam, the religion of God, is also the religion of "brotherhood." It requires its adherents to treat all persons as human beings, without regard to race or color. Islam, Malcolm was informed, cannot tolerate any form of racial discrimination.

Malcolm spoke of his experience in Mecca as a "spiritual rebirth" which revolutionized his attitude toward white people. "What I have seen and experienced," he wrote in his *Autobiography*, "has forced me to *rearrange* much of my thought patterns previously held, and to *toss aside* some of my previous conclusions.'' Malcolm rejected completely the racial ideology which he had advocated as a Black Muslim. He wrote many letters to friends back in the United States, describing the ''unexpected drastic changes'' in his perspective. ''Never before have I witnessed such . . . overwhelming spirit of true brotherhood as is practiced by people . . . here in this ancient holy land.'' He wrote: ''They were of all colors, from blue-eyed blonds to black-skinned Africans. But we were all participating in the same ritual, displaying a spirit of unity and brotherhood that my experience in America had led me to believe could never exist between the white and the non-white.''

Since Malcolm X went to the Middle East in 1959 as Elijah Muhammad's emissary, he must have seen blacks and whites associating with each other in a manner similar to what he saw in 1964. Also, several representatives of Islam had informed him of its principle of ''brotherhood'' and how it contradicted Muhammad's teachings about whites. Why then did Malcolm act as if he was hearing and seeing these things for the first time? As a Black Muslim, Malcolm was not permitted to think for himself but only for Muhammad. ''I had blind faith in him,'' Malcolm said as he reflected back. ''My faith in Elijah Muhammad was more blind and more uncompromising than any faith that any man has ever had for another man. And so I didn't try and see him as he actually was.'' Thus while Malcolm saw and heard new things about Islam in 1959, he could only view them in the light of his absolute commitment to the Messenger of Allah. After his break, however, Malcolm became a free thinker, in search of new directions. With an openness to hear and see new things, he heard and saw them in Mecca, and they changed his life.

From Mecca, Malcolm journeyed to Nigeria and Ghana. As orthodox Islam challenged his theology of race, his African experience caused him to rethink his politics of black nationalism. Malcolm met many revolutionaries who ''to all appearances'' were white. His strong talk on black nationalism, stressing black control of the economy, politics, etc., made communication difficult with white revolutionaries in Africa. Malcolm spoke often of his encounter with the Algerian ambassador to Ghana, Taher Kaid, who was, according to his description, an "extremely militant" "revolutionary." "When I told him that my political, social, and economic philosophy was black nationalism," Malcolm recalled, "he asked me very frankly, well, where did that leave him?" An African with "all appearances" of "a white man" showed Malcolm how his black nationalist philosophy was "alienating people who were true revolutionaries." "So," Malcolm said, "I had to do a lot of thinking and reappraising of my definition of black nationalism."

Of course, Malcolm knew that many people (friends and foes alike) would be greatly surprised by the radical change in his views regarding whites. Anticipating their surprised reaction, Malcolm wrote: "You may be shocked by these words coming from me. . . . [But] I have always been a man who tries to face facts, and to accept the reality of life as new experience and new knowledge unfolds it." He discussed his new perspective in several letters to friends and acquaintances and in his published essays, interviews, and *Autobiography*. He also spoke of it many times in speeches before black and white audiences when he returned to the United States. "My whole life had been a chronology of—*changes*," he wrote in his *Autobiography*. "I have always kept an open mind, which is necessary to the flexibility that must go hand in hand with every intelligent search for truth."

Malcolm's trip to Mecca and Africa not only transformed his thinking about race; it also deepened his international outlook, reinforcing his conviction that the black freedom movement in America could not be separated from African liberation struggles on the continent. Malcolm had previously recognized the cultural links between African-Americans and Africans. He had urged the former to "submerge their little petty differences" and create a unity based on a "common enemy," using the Bandung conference as a model. However, after his conversations with African peoples, including several heads of state, Malcolm became convinced as never before that the African-American struggle for freedom in the United States and African liberation struggles on the continent were *one and the same struggle*, with the success of each dependent on the success of all. He believed that no black could be free anywhere in the world until blacks everywhere achieved freedom.

While Malcolm's understanding of "black" referred primarily to persons of African descent, it nonetheless had always included all peoples of color throughout the world. His travels abroad reinforced this international perspective and even enlarged it so that he began to speak increasingly of the "human being" without regard to race or nationality. When he returned to the United States, he spoke less of black nationalism and civil rights and more and more of the human rights of all peoples. "I am not a racist," Malcolm said repeatedly. "I am against every form of racism and segregation, every form of discrimination. *I believe in human beings*, and that all human beings should be respected as such, regardless of their color."

The contrast between Malcolm's perspective before and after his trip abroad attracted the attention of Martin King. In an uncharacteristic move, Martin, with the assistance of his legal counsel Clarence B. Jones, who was also a friend of Malcolm, tried to arrange a meeting between them "as soon as possible on the idea of getting the human rights declaration" of the United Nations to expose America's inhuman treatment of its black inhabitants. Malcolm informed his caller (a woman speaking for Jones) that he was eager to meet with "Rev. King," because he was in the process of launching his recently conceived Organization of Afro-American Unity (patterned after the Organization of African Unity), whose "basic aim . . . is to lift the whole freedom struggle from civil rights to the level of human rights, and also to work with any other organization and any other leader toward that end." Malcolm gave the caller his complete schedule, and they tentatively set the meeting time between himself and Martin for the afternoon of the next day. The meeting did not take place."

About a month later Clarence Jones, in the aftermath of the Harlem and Rochester riots and in light of Martin's and Malcolm's initiatives toward and openness to each other, "forecast eventual cooperation between [them]." The occasion of Jones's prediction was a meeting of "a group of Negro writers and artists and intellectuals." They met in order "to access the meaning of the Harlem and Rochester riots and their probable effect on the future of civil rights organizations." In a statement to the news media, Jones said: "I think it is an irony and a paradox in terms of the national Negro community that two Negroes of such opposing views as Dr. King and Malcolm X should have such great mass appeal. . . . The Negroes respect Dr. King and Malcolm, because they sense in these men absolute integrity and know they will never sell them out." He predicted that "Malcolm is going to play a formidable role, because the racial struggle has now shifted to the urban North."

Jones was "warmly supported" by the well-known playwright and actor Ossie Davis. "The Negroes," he said, "have depended on the goodwill of the whites to help advance their cause of civil rights. Dr. King's doctrine of nonviolence implied that the white people must do the main job. Cooperation between Dr. King and Malcolm is a possibility."

Novelist John Oliver Killens also predicted cooperation between Martin and Malcolm. "If Dr. King is convinced that he has sacrificed 10 years of brilliant leadership," he said, "he will be forced to revise his concepts. There is only one direction in which he can move, and that is in the direction of Malcolm. . . . Politics make strange bedfellows."

Despite the optimistic forecasts by Jones, Davis, Killens, and others, it was not likely that Martin's white benefactors would have allowed public cooperation between him and Malcolm to take place. Several of his advisers expressed their displeasure to Jones for implying that King and Malcolm would work together. For white liberals Malcolm was still too unpredictable and thus not subject to their control. When Martin and Malcolm merely shook hands in Washington, several white liberals questioned Martin about it, fearing that the white public might view it as a symbolic act of unity.

Malcolm departed for another trip abroad on July 9 in order to pursue his United Nations project. He was not present to ignite, observe, or stop the "Harlem explosion" he had predicted; nor was he present to pursue ways in which he might cooperate with Martin King and the civil rights movement. He flew to Cairo in order to attend the second meeting of the Organization of African Unity. His chief concern was to "appeal to the African Heads of State" on behalf of "the interests of 22 million African-Americans whose *human rights* are being violated daily by the racism of American imperialism." Despite the opposition of the U.S. State Department, especially the CIA and the U.S. Information Agency, Malcolm was given the status of an observer and allowed to submit an eight-page "memorandum" to the delegates.

Malcolm planned to stay abroad only about two weeks, but he got so caught up in his mission of bridging the gap between African-Americans and Africans on the continent that he did not return to the United States until 24 November. Shortly after his return, he gave a major speech as his "Homecoming Rally of the OAAU" (29 November 1964) and then departed again (3 December 1964) for Britain, mainly to participate in an Oxford Union debate and other events. Coincidentally, Martin was also present in London during that time, en route to receive the Nobel Peace Prize. Speaking to four thousand Britons at St. Paul's Cathedral, Martin, with an obvious reference to Malcolm, repeated his standard comment that "the doctrine of black supremacy is as great a danger as the doctrine of white supremacy." The implication regarding Malcolm was false, as King should have known. But the words were pleasing to the white world that had bestowed upon Martin one of its highest honors—Nobel Laureate. Malcolm was of course aware of Martin's presence in London. Desirous of building a black united front, he was restrained in his comments about Martin. The *Manchester Guardian Weekly* characterized Malcolm's comments as "barbedly generous to Mr. King." Speaking to three hundred Islamic students, he said: "I'll say nothing against him. At one time the whites in the United States called him a racialist, an extremist, and a Communist. Then the Black Muslims came along and the whites thanked the Lord for Martin Luther King." In a radio talk, however, he labeled Martin's nonviolence "bankrupt" and referred to South African Nelson Mandela's turnabout as evidence.

Malcolm also was present on 17 December 1964 when Harlem honored King upon his return from receiving the Nobel Prize. Despite his new aims and outlook, Malcolm could not resist commenting negatively. "Imagine that?" he said. "Getting a peace prize . . . and the war's not over!" "If I have to follow a general who is fighting for my freedom and the enemy begins to pin peace medals on him before I've gotten my freedom, I'm afraid I'll have to find another general, because it's impossible for a general to be at peace when his people don't get no peace."

During a lecture engagement at Tuskegee Institute of 3 February 1965, SNCC activists invited Malcolm, against the wishes of SCLC staffers, to speak at a voting rights rally the next day in Selma. There was much tension in the air. Martin was in jail, and SCLC people pondered whether Malcolm would inflame the situation with his militant talk. James Bevel and Andrew Young took Malcolm aside and asked him to focus solely on the single issue of voting. As they walked toward Brown Chapel AME Church where he was to speak, Malcolm said, "Remember this: nobody puts words in my mouth."

During his speech, Malcolm expressed wholehearted support for the civil rights struggle to achieve the right to vote. "I believe that we have an absolute right to use whatever means are necessary to gain the vote," he said. "I don't advocate violence," he told his audience, "but if a man steps on my toes, I'll step on his." "If [Sheriff James] Clark brutalizes Negroes, he should be brutalized." Malcolm also gave his well-known analysis of the house Negro/field Negro during slavery.

As was true in every lecture he gave after his travels abroad, Malcolm was critical of the U.S. involvement in the affairs of Third World nations, especially the Congo; he berated the American government for "slaughtering innocent black men . . . under the guise of a rescue operation" in the Congo. Both blacks and whites raised questions about the relevance of his international perspective for the right of blacks to go to the polls in Dallas County. But for Malcolm the two issues were the same.

Malcolm viewed himself as a warrior against worldwide white supremacy. He wanted whites in Selma to know that they had an alternative. They could either listen to Martin King or they would have to deal with him and other "non-nonviolent" blacks. "Whites better be glad Martin Luther King is rallying the people because other forces are waiting to take over if he fails." By threatening whites with his presence, Malcolm believed that he was helping Martin. Greatly disappointed that his flight schedule to Europe did not permit him to visit Martin in jail, Malcolm told Coretta King: "I want Dr. King to know that I didn't come to Selma to make his job difficult. I really did come thinking I could make it easier. If the white people realize what the alternative is, perhaps they will be more willing to hear Dr. King."

From Selma Malcolm made another trip to Britain "to address the first congress of the Council of African Organizations in London." Then he went to Paris for a scheduled speech for the Congress of African Students, but he was denied entrance into France. "General de Gaulle had too much gall in keeping me out of France," he quipped. Malcolm returned to Britain for a speech at the London School of Economics where he spoke about the "shrewd propaganda" of the press—propaganda that makes the criminal look like the victim and the victim look like the criminal. Again his chief examples were U.S. involvement in the Congo and black-white relations in America. Malcolm also went to Birmingham for a private meeting with Islamic students at Birmingham University. During his stay, the British Broadcasting Corporation was assailed for "conducting" Malcolm "around Smethwick," the town on the outskirts of Birmingham that has become a symbol of Britain's racial problems. "If the colored people here continue to be oppressed," Malcolm said, "it will start off a bloody battle."

Malcolm arrived back in New York on Saturday, 13 February. A few hours later, "Sunday morning about 3:00 A.M. somebody threw some bombs inside [his] house." Fortunately no one was hurt. (Malcolm was convinced that it was the work of the Black Muslims.) After he got his family a place to stay, he left again for Detroit and gave a speech which has been called "The Last Message." "Clad in a loose-fitting gray suit without a tie," exhausted and heavily dosed with medicine (due to his exposure to the cold when he hurriedly vacated his bombed house), Malcolm, speaking to "a small gathering at Ford Auditorium," rambled as he talked about the "African revolution" and proclaimed that "1965 will be the longest and hottest and bloodiest year of them all. It has to be, not because . . . I want it to be . . ., but because the conditions that created these explosions in 1963 . . . [and] in 1964 are still here." The next day he lashed out at Elijah Muhammad and the Muslims in a talk at the Audubon Ballroom in New York City, one of the few times he spoke against his mentor.

During the last week of his life, he went to Rochester, New York, for lectures at Colgate-Rochester Divinity School and Corn Hill Methodist Church. He reminded both audiences that "our problem was no longer a Negro problem or an American problem but a human problem." He also rejected nonviolence: "We don't believe that we can win in a battle where the ground rules are laid down by those who exploit us. We don't believe that we can carry on our struggle trying to win the affection of those who for so long have oppressed and exploited us. . . . Our fight is just." He stated that the criminals were those people who exploit black people. Therefore, "we believe that we're within our rights to fight those criminals by any means necessary."

Back in New York City, Malcolm gave his standard lecture on "The Black Revolution and Its Effect upon the Negroes in the Western Hemisphere" at Barnard-Columbia (Thursday, 18 February 1965) and sat for an important interview the next day with Gordon Parks of *Life* magazine. Knowing that death was closing in on him, Malcolm refused to back down from his commitment to justice for all human beings. "It looks like this brotherhood I wanted so badly has got me in a jam," he told Parks.

As one seeks to understand Malcolm, it is important to keep in mind that his perspective was undergoing a radical process of change and development during the last year of his life. He gradually discarded his Black Muslim beliefs about race and religion and moved toward a universal perspective on humanity that was centered on his commitment to the black liberation struggle in America. He was struck down by assassins' bullets before he arrived at the point of view toward which he was moving. ''I am out in outer limbo,'' he said in June 1964. While acknowledging the limitations of his previous black nationalist views, Malcolm, as late as 18 January 1965, expressed his inability to state precisely his perspective: ''I still would be hard pressed to give a specific definition of the overall philosophy which I think is necessary for the liberation of black people in this country.''

Eleven months was too short a time to arrive at that definition, particularly as he was trying to save his life from the lethal intentions of the Black Muslims. What was amazing in the circumstances was his ability to do so much so quickly. A similar observation must be made about Martin King. Although Malcolm was severely critical of Martin's nonviolent approach to social change, he realized that both were fighting for the same goal and were equally subject to violent death. ''It is anybody's guess which of the 'extremes' in approach to . . . black men's problem might *personally* meet fatal catastrophe first—'nonviolent' Dr. King, or so-called 'violent' me,'' Malcolm wrote in his *Autobiography* shortly before his assassination. It was after Malcolm's death that Martin began to make his radical turn away from his vision of the American dream and to gaze at the horror of Malcolm's nightmare.

In December 1964, just six weeks before the assassination, Claude Lewis interviewed Malcolm X. At that time Lewis was a reporter at the New York Post, *and Malcolm, as Lewis writes in his introduction, "was worried. He knew he hadn't long to live. The word had been given. But he had much to get done in whatever time was left.... He wanted to get something 'on the record.'..."*

Malcolm had telephoned Lewis at the Post *offices late one night and requested the interview. They had met at the 22 West Coffee Shop on 135th Street in New York City, which, as Lewis writes, "was crowded with people he knew and who respected him. He wanted to be among friends throughout his final days.... [We] sat in a booth along with Malcolm's personal bodyguard. The outspoken leader reflected [on] many concerns, including his image, his organization, his public stance and his impending death."*

Lewis's interview with Malcolm appeared eighteen years later, on June 2, 1983, in a Special Report of The National Leader. *In his introduction Lewis, then the editor and publisher of the* Leader *(he is now a syndicated columnist for* The Philadelphia Inquirer), *wrote that this interview "places Malcolm in perspective and reveals how much he changed toward the end of his life, though that change was rarely reflected in the daily press."*

"Final Views"
An Interview with Malcolm X
by Claude Lewis

CLAUDE LEWIS: I notice you're growing a beard. What does that mean? Is it a symbol of anything?

MALCOLM X: It has no particular meaning, other than it probably reflects a change that I've undergone and am still undergoing.

CLAUDE LEWIS: Then will you shave it off one day?

MALCOLM X: Certainly. I might leave it on forever, or I might shave it off in the morning. I'm not dogmatic about anything. I don't intend to get into any more straitjackets.

CLAUDE LEWIS: What do you mean, any *more* straitjackets?

MALCOLM X: I don't intend to let anybody make my mind become so set on anything that I can't change it according to the circumstances and conditions that I happen to find myself in.

CLAUDE LEWIS: I see. You've been traveling a good deal recently. Can you tell me a little bit about the experiences relative to your movement? Where you've been and . . .

MALCOLM X: Well I was in Cairo, in Mecca, Arabia; in Kuwait, in Beirut, Lebanon; Khartoum, Sudan; Addis Ababa in Ethiopia, Nairobi in Kenya, Zanzibar, Dar es Salaam in what is now Tanzania and Lagos, Nigeria; Accra in Ghana, Monrovia in Liberia and Conakry in Guinea, and Algiers in Algeria. And during my tour of those various cities, or countries, I spent an hour and a half with President Nasser in Egypt; I spent three

195

hours with President Nyerere president of Tanganuika or Tanzania; I spent several days with Jomo Kenyatta and in fact I flew
with Jomo Kenyatta and Prime Minister Milton Obote of
Uganda from Tanganyika, from Dar es Salaam to Kenya. I saw
Azikwe and I had an audience with Azikwe; also with President
Nkrumah and I lived three days in Sekou Toure's house in
Conakry. And I cite this to show that everywhere I went I found
people at all levels of government and out of government with
open minds, open hearts, and open doors.

CLAUDE LEWIS: I see. How long was the trip?

MALCOLM X: I was away almost five months.

CLAUDE LEWIS: And do you think you've learned very
much?

MALCOLM X: Oh yes, I've learned a great deal. Because in
each country that I visited, I spoke with people at all levels. I
had an open mind. I spoke with heads of state, I spoke with
their ministers, I spoke with cabinet members, I spoke with
kings; I was the guest of State again when I re-visited Saudi
Arabia, I spoke with members of King Faisal's family—I don't
know how many foreign ministers I spoke with in the Middle
East and in Africa and all of them discussed our problems
quite freely.

CLAUDE LEWIS: The Negro problem in America?

MALCOLM X: Oh yes, yes!

CLAUDE LEWIS: Did they seem to know much about it?

MALCOLM X: Oh yes. Not only did they seem to know much
about it, but they were very sympathetic with it. In fact, it's
not an accident that in the United Nations during the debate on
the Congo problem in the Security Council, that almost every
one of the African foreign ministers tied in what was happening
in the Congo with what's happening in Mississippi.

CLAUDE LEWIS: Do you think this changes the minds of any
of the Mississippians here in this country?

MALCOLM X: Well, the Mississippian—it's not a case of
changing the mind of the Mississippian as much as it's a case
of changing the mind of the Americans. The problem is not a
Mississippi problem, it's an American problem.

CLAUDE LEWIS: Do you think that it's getting any better, the situation here?

MALCOLM X: No! It'll never get any better until our people in this country learn how to speak the same language that the racists speak. If a man speaks French, you can't talk to him in German. In order to communicate, you have to use the same language he's familiar with. And the language of the racist in the South is the language of violence. It's the language of brutality, and power and retaliation.

CLAUDE LEWIS: You think this is what the Negro should subscribe to?

MALCOLM X: The Negro should—if he's going to communicate—subscribe to whatever language the people use that he's trying to communicate with. And when you're dealing with racists, they only know one language. And if you're not capable of adopting that language or speaking that language, you don't need to try and communicate with those racists.

CLAUDE LEWIS: Dr. Martin Luther King, the other night, was honored in Harlem after receiving the Nobel Peace Prize. And he said, if I can quote him, "If blood must flow on the streets, brothers, let it be ours."

MALCOLM X: I was sitting in the audience. I heard him say that.

CLAUDE LEWIS: What do you think of that statement?

MALCOLM X: I think that if there's going to be a flowing of blood, that it should be reciprocal. The flow of blood should be two ways. Black people shouldn't be willing to bleed, unless white people are willing to bleed. And black people shouldn't be willing to be nonviolent, unless white people are going to be nonviolent.

CLAUDE LEWIS: Well, do you think the majority of Americans are nonviolent?

MALCOLM X: No. If the majority of Americans were nonviolent, America couldn't continue to exist as a country. Is America nonviolent in the Congo, or is she nonviolent in South Vietnam? You can't point to a place where America's nonviolent. The only people that they want to be nonviolent are American Negroes. We're supposed to be nonviolent. When the world becomes nonviolent, I'll become nonviolent. When the white man becomes nonviolent, I'll become nonviolent.

CLAUDE LEWIS: I've heard talk recently about Negroes getting money together and hiring a mafia to take care of some of the murderers ...

MALCOLM X: You don't need to hire a mafia but units should be trained among our people who know how to speak the language of the Klan and the Citizens Council. And at any time any Ku Klux Klan inflicts any kind of brutality against any Negro, we should be in a position to strike back. We should not go out and initiate violence against white indiscriminately, but we should *absolutely* be in a position to retaliate against the Ku Klux Klan and the White Citizens Council. Especially, since the government seems to be incapable or unwilling to curtail the activities of the Klan.

CLAUDE LEWIS: Can you tell me a little bit about your new program, if you have a new program?

MALCOLM X: We're not unveiling our new program until January. But I will say this, that the Organization of Afro-American Unity, which I'm the chairman of, intends to work with any group that's trying to bring about maximum registration of Negroes in this country. We will not encourage Negroes to become registered Democrats or Republicans. We feel that the Negro should be an independent, so that he can throw his weight either way. He should be nonaligned. His political philosophy should be the same as that of the African, absolute neutrality or nonalignment. When the African makes a move, his move is designed to benefit Africa. And when the Negro makes a move, our move should be designed to benefit us; not the Democratic party or the Republican party or some of these machines.

So, our program is to make our people become involved in the mainstream of the political structure of this country but not politically naïve. We think that we should be educated in the science of politics so that we understand the very workings of it, what it should produce, and who is responsible when that which we are looking for doesn't materialize.

CLAUDE LEWIS: Do you tell people what they want to hear, essentially?

MALCOLM X: I tell them what I've got on my mind to tell them, whether they like it or not. And I think that most people would have to agree. I don't think anybody could ever accuse me of telling people just what they want to hear. Because most of them don't want to hear what I'm ... (chuckle), especially white people.

CLAUDE LEWIS: Do you think the Negro can succeed in America through the vote?

MALCOLM X: Well, independence comes only by two ways; by ballots or by bullets. What you read historically—historically you'll find that everyone who gets freedom, they get it through ballots or bullets. Now naturally everyone prefers ballots, and even I prefer ballots but I don't discount bullets. I'm not interested in either ballots or bullets, I'm interested in freedom.

I'm not interested in the means, I'm interested in the objective. So I believe that black people should get free by ballots or bullets. If we can't use ballots to get free, we should use bullets. Yes, yes, I believe that black people should be just as quick to use bullets as ballots.

The white man has not given us anything. It's not something that is his to give. He is not doing us a favor when he permits us a few liberties. So I don't think we should approach it like that; I don't think we should approach our battle like we're battling a friend. We're battling an *enemy*. Anybody who stands in the way of the black man being free is an enemy of the black man, and should be dealt with as an enemy.

CLAUDE LEWIS: Would you say there are some blacks in that group?

MALCOLM X: Oh, yes. A lot of black people in that group. But they are not independent, they're puppets. You don't worry about the puppet, you worry about the puppeteer.

CLAUDE LEWIS: You've been threatened; do you take those threats lightly?

MALCOLM X: I don't take anything lightly. I don't take *life* lightly. But I never worry about dying. I don't see how a Negro can start worrying about dying at this late date. But I think that Negro organizations that talk about killing other Negroes should first go and talk to somebody about practicing some of their killing skill on the Ku Klux Klan and the White Citizens Council.

CLAUDE LEWIS: What do you think of Dr. King?

MALCOLM X: He's a man. He's a human being that is trying to keep Negroes from exploding, so white folk won't have too much to worry about.

CLAUDE LEWIS: Would you say that he's getting in the way of Negro progress?

MALCOLM X: Of Negro what?

CLAUDE LEWIS: Progress?

MALCOLM X: Well the Negro will never progress nonviolently.

CLAUDE LEWIS: What were your thoughts when King was receiving the (Peace) award last week?

MALCOLM X: Well, to me it represented the fact that the struggle of the Negro in this country was being endorsed at the international level and that it was looked upon as a problem that affects the peace of the world. And it was looked upon as a human problem or a problem for humanity, rather than just a Mississippi problem or an American problem.

To me, King getting that Nobel Peace Prize—it wasn't King getting it—it represented the awareness on the part of the world that the race problem in America could upset the peace of the world. And this is true.

If King can get—see I don't think that King got the prize because *he* had solved our people's problem, cause *we* still got the problem. He got the Peace Prize, and *we* got the problem. And so I don't think he should have gotten the medal for that. On the other hand, if Negroes can get it nonviolently, good.

CLAUDE LEWIS: Are you in favor of that?

MALCOLM X: I'm not in favor of anything that doesn't get the solution. But if Negroes can get freedom nonviolently, good. But that's a dream. Even King calls it a dream. But I don't go for no dream. And the only way that you can think Negroes can get it nonviolently, is dream. But when you get out here and start facing the reality of it, Negroes are the victims of violence every day. So I'd rather get violent, right along with the white man.

CLAUDE LEWIS: Have you ever received an award of any kind for your work?

MALCOLM X: No ... Yes, I've received an award. Whenever I walk the street and I see people ready to get with it. That's my reward (chuckle). Whenever people come out, they know in advance what I'm going to talk about. And if they show any sign of interest in it or agreement with it, that's my reward. And when they show that they're fed up with this slow pace, you know, that's my reward.

CLAUDE LEWIS: When King received his medal, did you sort of wish that it was yours?

MALCOLM X: I don't want the white man giving me medals. If I'm following a general, and he's leading me into battle, and the enemy begins to give him awards, I get suspicious of him. Especially if he gets the peace award before the war is over.

CLAUDE LEWIS: You don't propose that Negroes leave the U.S.?

MALCOLM X: I propose that we have the right to do whatever is necessary to bring about an answer to our problem. And whatever is necessary, if it's necessary to leave to get a solution then we should leave. If we can get a solution staying here, then we should stay. The main thing we want is a *solution*.

CLAUDE LEWIS: Well, do you think things have changed very much since you grew up?

MALCOLM X: They've changed in this sense. If you're a butler for a poor white man, you're a butler and you live but so well and you eat but so well. But if your master becomes rich, you begin to eat better and you begin to live better, but you're still a butler. And the only change that has been made in this society—we occupied a menial position twenty years ago. Our position hasn't changed. Our condition has changed somewhat, but our position hasn't changed. And the change that has been brought about, has been only to the extent that this country has changed. The white man got richer, we're living a little better. He got more power, we got a little more power, but we're still at the same level in his system. You understand what I'm saying?

CLAUDE LEWIS: Oh yes. Oh yes.

MALCOLM X: Our position has never changed. If you sit at the back of the plane and it's going a hundred miles an hour, and you're on the back of the plane, well it can start going a thousand miles an hour; you're going faster, but you're still at the back of the plane. And that's the same way with the Negro in this society, we started out at the rear and we're still in the rear. Society is going faster, but we're still in the rear. And we think we've made progress because *they've* made progress.

CLAUDE LEWIS: Why do you stay in America? Wouldn't it be easier for you to . . .

MALCOLM X: I was offered some good positions in several countries that I went to. Good positions, that would solve my problems personally. But I feel pretty much responsible for much of the action and energy that has been stirred up among our people for rights and for freedom. And I think I'd be wrong to stir it up and then run away from it myself.

CLAUDE LEWIS: Do you expect further riots next year?

MALCOLM X: Yes. I expect that the miracle of 1964 was the degree of restraint that Negroes displayed in Harlem. The miracle of 1964 was the ability of the Negroes to restrain themselves and contain themselves. Because there is no place where Negroes are more equipped and capable of retaliation than right here in Harlem.

CLAUDE LEWIS: Can you give me a capsule opinion of some of the following people? Adam Clayton Powell.

MALCOLM X: Powell is actually the most independent black politician in America. He's in a better position to do more for black people than any other politician.

CLAUDE LEWIS: Is he doing it?

MALCOLM X: And the reason that he's in that position is because he's in an area where people support him. They support him, whereas many other Negro politicians don't get that type of support. People in Harlem are just independent-minded. They just vote for a black man, whether the machine likes it or not. So Powell is in a tremendous position. And with his position also goes responsibility. I think that he should see his responsibilities with the same clarity that he sees his powerful position.

CLAUDE LEWIS: What about Roy Wilkins?

MALCOLM X: Well, I heard Roy say at the rally the other night that he was three-fourths or one-fourth Scandinavian. And he seemed to be lost in that Scandinavian dream somewhat, that night.

CLAUDE LEWIS: Martin Luther King, well—we've talked about him.

MALCOLM X: Well, everytime I hear Martin he's got a dream. And I think the Negro leaders have to come out of the clouds, and wake up, and stop dreaming and start facing reality.

CLAUDE LEWIS: Do you ever think of Whitney Young?

MALCOLM X: Whitney seems to be more down to earth, but he doesn't spend enough time around Negroes. He seems to be down to earth; he's a young man for one thing. But not enough Negroes know him. When I say he needs to be around Negroes, not enough Negroes know Whitney Young. Whitney Young could walk around Harlem all day long and probably no more than five people would know who he was. And he's supposed to be one of our leaders. So he should make himself more known to those who are following him.

CLAUDE LEWIS: Where are you headed from here? Where do you think your future lies?

MALCOLM X: I think one of the most sincere of those big six is James Farmer. You missed asking me about him. I think James Farmer seems to ... He seems sincere. And I get the impression when I watch Farmer that he could be another Mandela. Mandela, you know, was a man who advocated nonviolence in South Africa, until he saw that it wasn't getting anywhere and then Mandela stepped up and had to resort to tactical violence. Which showed that Mandela was for the freedom of his people. He was more interested in the end than he was the means. Whereas many of the Negro leaders are more straight-jacketed by the means rather than by the end.

CLAUDE LEWIS: Where are you headed? What do you suppose your future is from here?

MALCOLM X: I have no idea.

CLAUDE LEWIS: You have no idea?

MALCOLM X: I have no idea. I'm for freedom. I can capsulize how I feel. I'm for the freedom of the twenty-two million Afro-

Americans *by any means necessary. By any means necessary!*
I'm for freedom. I'm for a society in which our people are
recognized and respected as human beings and I believe that
we have the right to resort to *any means necessary* to bring
that about. So when you ask me where I'm headed, how can I
say? I'm headed in any direction that will bring us some immediate results. Nothing wrong with that!

CLAUDE LEWIS: I think it's going to take a tremendous public relations job to change your image. And you may not be
interested in changing your image, but everybody else is. I agree
with a lot that you say, but I don't see how people can sign
up with you.

MALCOLM X: They don't need to sign up. The most effective
part of the trees are the roots. And they're signed up with the
tree but you don't ever see them. They're always beneath the
ground. And the reason that you never see me worry about my
image is because that image puts me in a better position than
anybody else. Because I'm able to walk through the street or
anywhere else and really find out where people are at. In a
silent sort of way, I know where they are, in a silent sort of
way. I think that the sympathies are deeply rooted, many of
them. Plus also it puts me in a position wherever I go, people
know where I stand in advance. And doors that would normally
be closed for American Negroes, I don't find them closed for
me anywhere. It doesn't make any difference. Anywhere.

CLAUDE LEWIS: So you're saying because of your outspo-
kenness, your honesty . . .

MALCOLM X: People know where I stand. They know where
I stand. And you see I'm not standing in an unjust position.
This is the thing. Whatever I say I'm *justified*. If I say the
Negroes should get out of here right tomorrow and go to war,
I'm justified. Really! It may sound *extreme*, but you can't say
it's not *justified*. If I say right now that we should go down
and shoot fifteen Ku Klux Klansmen in the morning, you may
say well that's insane, but you can't say that I'm not justified.
This is what I mean. I think that the stand that I'm taking is
justified. Many others might not take it.

CLAUDE LEWIS: What I'm trying to do is find out if there is a new Malcolm X?

MALCOLM X: Well, there is a new one in the sense that, perhaps in approach. My travels have broadened my scope, but it hasn't changed me from speaking my mind. I can get along with white people who can get along with me. But you don't see me trying to get along with *any* white man who doesn't want to get along with me. I don't believe in that. Now you got to get another religion.

CLAUDE LEWIS: When you get old and retire . . .

MALCOLM X: I'll never get old.

CLAUDE LEWIS: What does that mean?

MALCOLM X: Well, I'll tell you what it means. You'll find very few people who feel like I feel that live long enough to get old. I'll tell you what I mean and why I say that. When I say by any means necessary, I mean it with all my heart, and my mind and my soul. But a black man should give his life to be free, but he should also be willing to take the life of those who want to take his. It's reciprocal. And when you really think like that, you don't live long. And if freedom doesn't come to your lifetime, it'll come to your children. Another thing about being an old man, that never has come across my mind. I can't even see myself old.

CLAUDE LEWIS: Well, how would you like to be remembered by your black brothers and sisters around the world—twenty years from now?

MALCOLM X: Sincere. In whatever I did or do, even if I make mistakes, they were made in sincerity. If I'm wrong, I'm wrong in sincerity. I think that the best a person can be—he can be *wrong*, but if he's sincere you can put up with him. But you can't put up with a person who's *right*, if he's insincere. I'd rather deal with a person's sincerity, and respect a person for their sincerity than anything else. Especially when you're living in a world that's so hypocritical.

This is an era of hypocrisy. The times that we live in can rightfully be labeled, the Era of Hypocrisy. When the white folks pretend that they want Negroes to be free, and Negroes pretend to white folks that they really believe that white folks want them to be free (laughter). An Era of Hypocrisy, brother. You fool me and I fool you. This is the game that the white man and the Negro play with each other. You pretend that you're my brother and I pretend that I really believe you're my brother (laughter).

CLAUDE LEWIS: Do you think there are going to be more killings and more bombings in Mississippi and Alabama?

MALCOLM X: In the North as well as the South. There might be even more in the North because I'll tell you one of the dangers of Martin Luther King. King himself is probably a good man, means well and all that. But the danger is that white people use King. They use King to satisfy their own fears. They blow him up. They give him power beyond his actual influence. Because they want to believe within themselves that Negroes are nonviolent and patient, and long suffering and forgiving. White people want to believe that so bad, 'cause they're so guilty. But the danger is, when they blow up King and fool themselves into thinking that Negroes are really nonviolent, and patient, and long suffering, they've got a powder keg in their house. And instead of them trying to do something to defuse the powder keg, they're putting a blanket over it, trying to make believe that this is no powder keg; that this is a couch that we can lay on and enjoy.

So that's it. Whatever I do, whatever I did, whatever I've said, was all done in sincerity. That's the way I want to be remembered because that's the way it is. . . .

Alex Haley was writing a Reader's Digest *piece on the Nation of Islam when he first became acquainted with Malcolm X. He was then commissioned to do a* Playboy *interview with "the militant major-domo of the Black Muslims," as the magazine tagged Malcolm in its May 1963 issue. The following year Haley and Malcolm began their collaboration on* The Autobiography *of Malcolm X, which has never been out of print since its publication in 1965. As Malcolm himself had predicted, he did not live to see the book in print.*

In October 1992, just a few months before Haley's death, David Gallen spoke at length with him about his association with Malcolm X. Over a period of two years, in more than fifty interviews, Haley had had the opportunity to observe Malcolm outside the public arena, away from the rally podium and the microphone, and to appreciate the more private man. He generously shared his recollections of that time.

"Alex Haley Remembers Malcolm X"
An Interview with David Gallen

DAVID GALLEN: Did you first meet Malcolm when you were doing your piece for *Reader's Digest*?

ALEX HALEY: Yes, that was the initial meeting. I was very suprised when I was given the assignment of writing about the very controversial Nation of Islam—or more colloquially, Black Muslims,—by the arch-conservative *Reader's Digest*. But the *Digest* editors wrote me a letter in which they said we would like you to do a piece in which you say what is said against this organization and, in fairness, what they say of themselves. I took that letter to Malcolm X at the Nation of Islam restaurant in Harlem on, I think it was, 116th Street and 7th Avenue.

DAVID GALLEN: What were your initial impressions of him?

ALEX HALEY: My first impressions of Malcolm were that he was cagey and wary and suspicious of me. He did not do anything to soften that impression. I think his first statement to me was, "I suppose you know that we know you are a spy for the white man who has come here under the disguise of wanting to write an article about us." I showed him the letter from the *Reader's Digest* and he said, "Well, you should certainly know that nothing the white man writes and signs is worth the paper it is written on." Then he asked if I didn't know anything about the treaties the Indians had signed long years before.

DAVID GALLEN: Was Malcolm what you had expected him to be?

ALEX HALEY: To some degree; I say that because I hadn't really known what to expect. I had heard of their leader, Elijah Muhammad, who was kind of mysterious, and of his minister, Brother Malcolm, who was most articulate, even eloquent, as an orator who spoke the cause of the Nation of Islam most ably.

DAVID GALLEN: Did he say or do anything that stands out particularly vividly when you were interviewing him for the *Digest?*

ALEX HALEY: One thing that would qualify there is that he told me right up front that he would not talk to me, that he would not take that responsibility, since I was obviously a spy and that I would have to get the approval of his leader, the Honorable Elijah Muhammad, which meant that I would have to go to Chicago to meet with him. I asked him if he would arrange this, and he said he would. So I called the *Digest* and told them I would have to make the trip; they approved the travel. Then I called back Malcolm X. It was arranged, and I went to Chicago and spent, I think, two days there. I visited two or three times with Mr. Muhammad, who never directly questioned me; he would just obliquely talk about this, that, or the other. Finally he indicated that I should go back to New York, which I did. By this time, he had, of course, called Malcolm and indicated that he felt it would be okay for him to talk with me. And Malcolm did begin to talk with me—cagily, reluctantly. He seemed sometimes awed when I would ask him questions. Every other sentence would contain "I was taught this by the Honorable Elijah Muhammad," or something like that.

DAVID GALLEN: Did you have much contact with Malcolm between the time you were doing the *Reader's Digest* piece and your 1963 *Playboy* interview with him?

ALEX HALEY: Not very much. I would guess we probably came into actual contact maybe three or four times, usually by chance, when we would happen to be at some event at the same time, probably because we both knew Louis Lomax, who was a very aggressive kind of journalist, a black fellow. Malcolm enjoyed Louis Lomax; he used to get a twinkle in his eye when he would say about Lomax, "Every time I see him, he's hurrying somewhere; he's either into something or on to something." Lomax was, always looking to see if he couldn't find an angle to make a story that would get media attention. Louis Lomax was involved in early television; he was a colleague of Mike Wallace. Lomax was in contact with Malcolm more in fact than I was. But Lomax was usually the reason I happened to be at some occasion, and Malcolm also came there, and of course Malcolm and I would speak, though we often didn't know what to speak of.

DAVID GALLEN: Did he seem any different to you during the *Playboy* interview with him?

ALEX HALEY: I would say he seemed somewhat more familiar, that was about all, simply because we had had these fleeting kinds of contacts. Also, I should say that after the *Reader's Digest* piece came out, I received a letter from Mr. Muhammad—a copy had gone to Malcolm as well—and the letter commended me because in fact the article had been as the letter had said it would be, and Mr. Muhammad repeated, "So you did say what others say against us, but you also did say what we said of ourselves." That approval from Mr. Muhammad served to improve relations somewhat with Malcolm.

DAVID GALLEN: Had his racial, political, and religious beliefs changed in any way?

ALEX HALEY: Not visibly; up to this point, no. He was still the spokesman for the Nation of Islam by the time I was doing the *Playboy* interview, and the *Playboy* interview reflects that.

DAVID GALLEN: Had he changed in his attitude towards you? Did he treat you differently? Did you begin to feel that he trusted you?

ALEX HALEY: Well, he changed his attitude towards me—somewhat. It was simply the fact that he, I think, trusted me a little more. I would never say that he trusted a lot, certainly not at this point, but he did think I was not trying to undo him or double-cross him, and probably one reason he thought that was because I wasn't.

DAVID GALLEN: In what year and month did you and Malcolm begin to collaborate on the book? Who was the publisher that suggested you do an autobiography with Malcolm? What was the *modus operandi* for your collaboration? When did Malcolm last proofread the manuscript for the autobiography?

ALEX HALEY: I can't answer that specifically. It would probably have been, I would say, 1962. I'm guessing, because I know we spoke for two years, and I worked one of the two years interviewing him. Malcolm would come down to my place in Greenwich Village. I was in 92 Grove Street, off Sheridan Square. He would come down there about twice a week, at night. He would get there say about nine o'clock, after his busy day. He would instantly pick up my phone and call his wife; he would sort of review the day with her and say little pleasantries to her and ask about the children. And then he would stay with me until about eleven-thirty, something of that nature, when again he would call his wife and tell her that he was on the way to traveling home in the blue Oldsmobile. But that would have probably been, I'm guessing, in 1962, because I know I spent two years with him, one year interviewing, one year writing. The book was published in 1965, and given the fact that it takes nine months to publish, they must have had the manuscript in 1964. So I'm guessing again, but I think I'm correct: 1962.

The publisher that suggested I do the autobiography with Malcolm was Doubleday. The editor was the venerable, Ken McCormick—he is an editor emeritus now—who's beloved across the whole of publishing. It was he who read the *Playboy* interview and who somehow got in touch with Malcolm X and took to him the question if he would be willing to tell his life, his own personal story, at book length. Malcolm demurred for some time, then finally agreed that he would, but with lots of stipulations. One was that the money, his money, whatever he got, would go to the Nation of Islam, I think. And then Malcolm asked that I write the book. The reason was, he said, that he had studied what I had written, and of course we had shared two experiences, one with *Reader's Digest* and the other with *Playboy*, so he kind of knew me by now. He said, "I checked through your work and I think, one, you can write and secondly

I don't believe you are the kind of writer who would try to get in my story and try to out-Malcolm me." In any event, he asked me, and I was pleased, honored, flattered to take the job.

I had never done a book. I was intimidated by the idea of doing a book. I was very familiar with writing articles, though, because I'd been doing them for years. How I was able to deal with it finally was after a great number of interviews with Malcolm, when I was separating the material into chronological order, it occurred to me that each section was like a magazine article. And so I sort of saw the book in terms of successive magazine articles that would flow together. That was how I came to conceive of the chapters for the book.

As for the *modus operandi* for our collaboration, I think I told you he would come down to the house about twice each week and we would work together. One thing that is kind of interesting is that I have a friend, George Sims. We grew up together in Henning, Tennessee, our hometown. George has all his life been a heavy reader. As a kid, he used to read the labels on tin cans. George and I got back in contact again after World War Two. We met one day, quite by accident, in the New York Public Library, after not having seen each other for a couple of decades. Little by little, when I began to get more and better writing assignments, I got George to become a researcher for me. George is a great . . . not a scholar, but a buff on Shakespeare. Well, nobody knew it, certainly I didn't know it and George didn't know it, but so was Malcolm. One night he just kind of dropped something like "Didn't Shakespeare say it?"—or whatever it was—and George, well, he rose to that like a trout to a fly and said something like Shakespeare also said whatever. And George and Malcolm were suddenly almost like bonded in their love for Shakespeare. And it got to be after that that almost every night that Malcolm would come down to my place—sometimes he'd had a day that just left him angry as he could be, and he was uptight and he was mad—he and George would get into something about Shakespeare or some of the other people way back in literature and that would temper Malcolm. His anger would kind of go away and he would become more, I guess, more malleable, from an interviewer's point of view. And after he had talked long enough, I would say, "Look, fellas, you know we got to talk about Mr. Malcolm here," and then I would start questioning him. But that little session they would have at the outset of Malcolm's arrival each evening was most helpful; it just kind of cleared the air and eased what might otherwise have been a lot of tension.

We had an agreement, and it was certainly kept, that nothing would be in the book he did not want in the book, and that anything he wanted to be in the book would be in the book. I would go through three to four drafts, and when I thought it was okay, I would give it to him. He would read it and go over it and the next time he would come back he would bring it with him. Then we would go over it together, and if there was something he wanted to change we would do so. This wasn't always just done flatly; sometimes I'd challenge him about a particular event, how he remembered it, but nothing serious. And what he wanted ultimately was dealt with, and then, and only then, would he put his MX at the bottom of the page, and it was those manuscripts that went to the publisher, those with his MX at the bottom of each page.

DAVID GALLEN: Were there any events while you were working together that caused him to trust you more fully? What were they? When did he start to be more open with you? How did your feelings change towards him?

ALEX HALEY: I can think of one thing that maybe made him a little bit more warm toward me. Naturally, I had a little list of dates for this and that and the other, and my basic notes. And one day I happened to come upon the fact that the next day was his eldest daughter Attallah's birthday, and I just knew Malcolm, as busy as he was and as guilty as he was about not spending much time with his family and what not—he just felt awful about that, and he practically revered his wife, Sister Betty, and she just went on taking care of things at home while he was away—I just knew he'd forget. So that afternoon before the day I knew was the birthday for Attallah, I just went uptown and I bought a large brown doll with all kinds of little froufrou around her frock, with ruffles and frills and so forth, and I put it into a closet. And Malcolm came that night and we had our regular interview, and when he was getting ready to leave, I just sort of quietly said—I just went to the closet and I said—"You know, Brother Malcolm, I just happened to be looking at my notes and I noticed that tomorrow is the birthday for Attallah, and I know as busy as you are you just simply haven't had time to stop and pick her up something. I knew you'd want to; so I got this for you," and then I handed him the doll. That was as close as I ever saw Malcolm to tears, when he took the doll. He didn't say much of anything, but I knew he was deeply moved. And then he went on out.

Sometimes later Sister Betty was on the phone. She and I used to talk sometimes on the phone at night when Malcolm was traveling. He permitted that; we didn't do that till he said it was all right for us to do so. We would talk on the phone, we would exchange recipes—things like that. I used to be a cook, and Sister Betty is a good cook. And she told me one night how much Attallah liked the doll, and in subsequent years Attallah herself has told me how much she enjoyed it. As a matter of fact, she still has it, she told me. Attallah is my godchild.

DAVID GALLEN: What were Malcolm's feelings regarding himself and his own significance?

ALEX HALEY: I think that Malcolm was embarrassed, genuinely embarrassed, by a lot of his prominence in media. I know he was discomfited by it because—I didn't know this until later—his prominence in the media was what some others in the movement were using to undermine him with Mr. Elijah Muhammad. You know, things were said, so I later heard and learned; they were saying things to Mr. Muhammad like Malcolm, it seemed, wanted to take over the organization, that his picture was in the paper more than the leader's was. And this was very, very true. It was also true that it was Malcolm's job; he was the one who spoke for the organization, who represented the organization. He took on the interviews and all these kinds of things that hardly anyone else within the organization would have been able to take on, and do, I would imagine—certainly not in the way he did—but it was, as I said, discomfiting to him. He was frustrated by the fact that he was expected to be the vibrant, vocal spokesman and that it was causing him to be cut away at, defiled even, chewed away, by those who were envious or jealous of his prominence. So he had a lot of bitterness about this thing of being out there in the public eye as much as he was.

DAVID GALLEN: Were you surprised when he told you, "I don't want anything in this book to make it sound that I think I'm somebody important"?

ALEX HALEY: No, not at all. That's exactly what he said numerous times in different ways, and that's what he manifested in his actions. He would have liked, I think, to have been much less prominent than he was, if he could have gotten the message across some other kind of way.

DAVID GALLEN: Was Malcolm a very different person away from the microphone? How?

ALEX HALEY: Not a whole lot, not a whole lot. Somewhat; we all are somewhat different away from the microphone. But Malcolm was always ready to take the microphone on issues about black people. He lived, at least in my experience, very close to the microphone in such instances and was ready always to leap to the defense of the black people.

DAVID GALLEN: How would you describe Malcolm's personality?

ALEX HALEY: He was sincere, he was sensitive, he was loyal. I would say he was all three of those things. I genuinely feel that he never pursued any of the numerous opportunities he might have in order to gain for himself what he would have regarded as carnal enclosure, or something like that. God knows that there were enough young ladies and old ones, and older ones as well. They took every opportunity to get his attention and Malcolm made a great point of avoiding anything he thought might be suspicious—he had no part of that.

DAVID GALLEN: What events do you remember that might illustrate his sincerity and loyalty?

ALEX HALEY: Well, I guess none would be better than how he would stay up so late night after night, how he would go out and try to help recruit somebody who was teetering, some Christian black, a Baptist or Catholic or Methodist, who was teetering on the edge of leaving their church to come to the Nation of Islam. Malcolm would go visit these people late at night—I know I said late; I'm not talking eleven or twelve, but you know, eight-thirty, nine o'clock—and he would tell me often about how he had done that. This would, of course, be on the nights he was not with me. It's just one example that he really cared about the individuals he was talking to, trying to guide them to the light of Islam, and he would speak of them in such a warm way.

DAVID GALLEN: Were you surprised that he was so touched when a young black couple named their child Malcolm after him?

ALEX HALEY: No, no. That was the Malcolm that would be touched. Very much so.

DAVID GALLEN: Did Malcolm change significantly during the period you were working together?

ALEX HALEY: Absolutely. Malcolm almost went full-circle in his thirty-nine years. I didn't know him all those years before, but from what he told me I could piece together an idea of what his earlier life had been like. And yes, he did change. Very much so. Probably the greatest change was brought to my attention when he went to Mecca. He sent to me a card on which he had written in fine handwriting: "Dear Alex Haley: I have eaten from the same plate with fellow Muslims whose eyes were bluer than blue, whose hair was blond, blonder than blond, whose skin was whiter than white, and we were all the same." I don't think anything I ever saw or heard connected with him gave me the feeling or impact that that did of how much he had changed, because that would not have been the Malcolm I had known earlier. There is no way he ever would have written or thought or felt that earlier. So he was changing very much.

DAVID GALLEN: Did he ever regret any statements he had made as a member of the NOI?

ALEX HALEY: I would say yes; there's one that comes to mind: There was this young white lady who came to him at the Muslim's restaurant and asked him something like what could she do for him and his cause, and all he said was "Nothing.'' She turned away, weakened, and left. But Malcolm worried about it; he played it back and wished it had been played differently.

DAVID GALLEN: Was Malcolm very upset when he was suspended by the NOI, or did he view this turn of events as a possibility to move forward and to accomplish more for his people without the restrictions of the NOI?

ALEX HALEY: Yes, extremely upset. I didn't know he was in trouble with the NOI until the split became public knowledge. He had never breathed a word of it to me, and I was pretty close to him—which gave me good sense of Malcolm's self-discipline. He wouldn't tell even those close to him things that were going on and were wrecking him, anguishing him. I don't know that he saw this as an opportunity to move forward. It became an opportunity for him to create his own organization. That was the OAAU, the Organization of Afro-American Unity. It was never able to grow, certainly not as he had hoped it would grow, but he had had to create some organization of his own, because his power base was gone. This power base had been the Nation of Islam.

DAVID GALLEN: What character traits in other people were most important to Malcolm?

ALEX HALEY: The first thing that comes to mind is punctuality. I don't know anybody who was so time-conscious as Malcolm. If you had an appointment with him at ten o'clock or two o'clock or six o'clock or whenever, please be there at that time. He had kind of out-of-the-ordinary, almost hyper responses to people who were late. If you were late, you were exhibiting a whole lot of negative things in his view: that you were not to be trusted; that you did not really care seriously; that you were not serious at all. That would be the first thing. Other things would be standard, like people who told the truth and who didn't try to double-cross you, but the most conspicuous thing was his acute sense of time, I would say.

DAVID GALLEN: Whom among his friends and associates did he most respect, and why?

ALEX HALEY: I would say there wasn't really anyone as close to him as Mr. Muhammad, whom he revered, absolutely adulated. There were two other people that he highly respected during this period of time. One of them was a young fellow who had been a folk singer or a popular singer [Gene Louis Walcott] and had become a member of the Nation of Islam and was very popular and highly liked. Malcolm called him "my little brother," and this young man said he was Malcolm's little brother. They both were most fond of each other, and this was Louis Farrakhan, as he is known today, and I think that is what he was termed then, although he was probably called Louis X or had a number of Xs, I don't know how many, but that is one person he was really close to. And Malcolm was very proud of being the big brother, so to speak, of little brother Farrakhan. And similarly, there was another young fellow who got to know Malcolm and vice versa, and they just had a marvelous attachment to each other and that was the young Cassius Clay. I remember Malcolm being there when Cassius Clay fought Sonny Liston way back. Cassius wasn't going to have it any other way. Malcolm called me before the fight and said it was sure to be one of the greatest upsets in modern times, or something like that. And afterwards he called me back, and you could hear all this whooping and hollering going on in the background of the dressing room. Malcolm could not have been higher in his life than when he and Cassius Clay were so close as they were. And then they fell out, when Malcolm was ejected from the Nation of Islam. Cassius Clay stayed with the Messenger, Mr. Muhammad. I know that one of the most down experiences in Malcolm's life was subsequent to when he went on a trip to Mecca; he was coming back, I think, too happy, and he was in some airport in one of the African countries. He was walking through the airport; he turned left, and then saw that there was Muhammad Ali—Cassius had changed his name— and they came towards each other and their eyes met, and Malcolm saw Muhammad Ali look away from him and walk past him without speaking, and that just ripped Malcolm up and down. I don't think he ever got over the hurt of that.

DAVID GALLEN: What was it like to walk through the streets of Harlem with Malcolm? How did people respond to him, and he to them?

ALEX HALEY: Exciting, to say the very least. Exciting, for several reasons. He was dangerous to be around, because so many people would bother him. Also the thing that happens when you are with a star—I used to experience this when interviewing major personalities for *Playboy*; their presence generates energy and excitement in the people around them—would happen with Malcolm. People would come and bow before him, people would shake his hand, people would smile broadly; there was every kind of approval, adulation, admiration.

One day, I recall, we were in his car riding the streets of Harlem. Malcolm liked to move around from street to street in the car; he'd say, "I'm just making my little daily rounds," that was his expression. And this day, all of a sudden, he slammed on the brakes. The car screeched, jerked to a stop; I was sure somebody had hit us. By the time I got my wits together Malcolm was out on the driver's side and he was standing like an avenging devil; there were three young men who had been shooting craps, and he was just staring them down. He said, "Other people are in their pajamas studying you and your people, trying to learn more about them. That [the Countee Cullen Library] which houses the Schomburg Collection is the greatest repository of information about the black man in existence, and what you are doing? The best you can do is to be out here down on your knees shooting craps against the door." They were young street men—nineteen, twenty, twenty-one, that age range—and just about anyone else who dared interrupt them so rudely like that would have had some severe physical problems, I would suspect. But not Malcolm; because of his charisma, because of the power of his image. Those young men went slinking away because it was Malcolm who talked to them like that. And I have often thought of that; I have often thought about how young black people talk, you know, this or that about Malcolm. But you don't hear much about the deep, feverent thing he had about young black people who had educated themselves.

I remember one time we were all on a train, a pullman, going, I think from Washington back to New York, or maybe it was the other way around. I remember how, when we walked in, people just froze and Malcolm said to me out of the corner of his mouth, "Take a deep breath. They don't know what to say. They are scared in the presence of a proud black man,"—things like that. I remember also there were black porters, and finally, one of them, a man in his fifties, a very dignified man, very deliberately walked up to Malcolm, stuck out his hand, shook hands with Mr. Malcolm, and said, "I'm glad to have you in my car, and I want to say if you need anything, please buzz me," or something like that. Malcolm stood up and said, "Well, I appreciate your saying this, and if I do I certainly will, but at the moment I am most comfortable." But everybody else in there was like a wind-up toy, the tension was so great. After a while, as we rolled along, a young white man got up and walked over and stuck out his hand at Malcolm. He said something like, "I don't agree with everything you say, but I do want to say I appreciate the courage you've shown for your people." And Malcolm said something like, "No people have ever achieved any gain unless they have fought for their rights." Then he brought up the American Revolution, that if the colonists had not fought for their rights, this country wouldn't be here. It was never dull traveling with Malcolm.

DAVID GALLEN: Do you think Malcolm ever truly hated all white people?

ALEX HALEY: No, I don't think so. I know he cared for individual white people. He would talk nostalgically of people he had known in Mason, Michigan, where he was a student, and you couldn't detect anger in his memory of students and teachers alike, but you could detect care. And there were people like M.S. Handler of *The New York Times*. Malcolm really, really cared about this man, and respected him and admired him. He enjoyed Mike Wallace, too; he enjoyed the verbal sparring that they would have from time to time. Malcolm appreciated Mike Wallace's brain, his cleverness. And there were others. Malcolm really rather looked forward to his next jousting with them. He had a professional respect for them, a professional debator's respect for them.

DAVID GALLEN: Did Malcolm ever speak to you about the death threats made on him?

ALEX HALEY: Yes, he did. He would speak of them rather matter-of-factly. He would just say, "Brother, I don't think I'm going to live to read this book in print." There were times he described, like the time he had been in Los Angeles, in a car with some brothers, and they came to some kind of tunnel. That's when they saw another car behind them, in which they knew were people who were enemies—they were all members of the Nation of Islam but they were all anti-him—and as this other car drew closer Malcolm took his cane—he had a cane, a walking cane—and he slipped that cane out of the back window and worked it from behind so that it looked like a rifle barrel. And the other car fell back rapidly, and they got away without difficulty.

DAVID GALLEN: Did he look more tired as you neared the end of the book?

ALEX HALEY: Of course he did, because he was under just insane pressure.

DAVID GALLEN: Did he seem distracted or preoccupied? Did he feel he was nearing the end of his life?

ALEX HALEY: Yes, same reason, same thing. He didn't ever say to me that he was nearing the end of his life, but I would imagine that, yes, he probably felt that he was.

DAVID GALLEN: When was the last time you saw Malcolm? The last time you spoke with him? What did he say?

ALEX HALEY: I don't remember when I last saw Malcolm, not specifically, but I do remember the last time I spoke with him. It was the Saturday before his death. His home had been bombed. He called, and it was the first time in all our acquaintance that I did not understand, I did not recognize, his voice when he called. You know how you know the voices of people you know, but he sounded like someone that was under a deep, heavy cold, and now I'm pretty sure that it was stress to some degree. He tried to make something jocular of it. He said something like, "You know, nobody would lend me a penny. Nobody would make me a loan in a bank. Nobody would write any insurance on me." And he said that his house had been bombed—I knew that—and he said that he had nowhere for his wife and children to go. And he adored, I couldn't overstate how much he adored, his wife and children, and how guilty he felt that he wasn't doing the things he should, that he wasn't able materially to give them the things he would have liked to. When he called me this day, he said that his home had been bombed and he had to get some place for his family to live. And then in this heavy, heavy, strained voice he asked if I would go to the publisher, if I would go back to Ken McCormick and ask him if it was possible that Doubleday might advance, I think it was twenty thousand dollars, so he could get a home, and that was when he said, "You know, nobody, no bank, would make me a loan." And nobody would write insurance on him. I told him I would do the best I could, and he just said, you know, "I'd appreciate it if you would do that." And that was the last time I spoke with Malcolm, because the next day he was shot to death in the Audubon Ballroom.

DAVID GALLEN: What do you think is Malcolm's legacy to young people today?

ALEX HALEY: I would say that Malcolm today offers to young blacks a clean, stellar, solid, articulate, courageous black image—or role model, if you will. He is clean, as the expressions goes. His image is unsullied. So now he comes more to the fore than ever. He is embraced by those who were in many cases not yet born when he was around. He is hailed for the things he said. You see his face on sweatshirts, you see his words on T-shirts—words like "By any means necessary." That was one of his master lines; it's up to you to interpret it as you have your own feeling about what he meant, but all he said was "By any means necessary." He was a master of that sort of statement. Interesting thing: Malcolm X was synonymous with violence in the public view, that was his image, whereas Dr. King was imaged as the man of peace, Ghandi's follower, when in fact, it was Dr. King, the man of peace, who met the water hoses and the dogs and the sheriffs, and who spent time in all the jails, while Malcolm, the man associated with violence, never got a scratch. He was adroit in his way of fighting the black battle. He made tremendous impressions, but never at the cost of personal or physical confrontations. He used lines like "By any means necessary" and got people excited so that they would follow him and join the Nation of Islam.

DAVID GALLEN: What do your readers most ask about Malcolm?

ALEX HALEY: That's easy. They come to me and say, "Tell me, what he was really like?" I've heard that hundreds of times, and my answer is the truth: Everything I know about Malcolm is in that book, *The Autobiography*, particularly in the afterword. After he was killed, for the next five days writing was my dirge as I tried to put down everything I knew or had heard having to do with him, so that the book would hold between its two covers the life of one man. The book began when Malcolm was not yet born; I think it started something like, "When my mother was pregnant with me . . ." And in the afterword I recounted how he was assassinated and described his funeral services. I'm proud of the ending now. Endings are important for a writer; you have to find what works, what sentences to use. But I am so glad that I wrote what I did—something, I think, like what he would have wanted me to write of him—and now I leave him to the scholars and I leave him in the hands of the young people, the students, some of whom will become scholars, and I just feel good that I was able to write his life as he would have it written, from his own words, because otherwise the true story of his life would have been lost in apocrypha.

"There were some crazy things going on then. You wouldn't believe!" Benjamin Karim told an interviewer. He was referring to the random freakish incidents that were occurring during the last edgy weeks before Malcolm's assassination.

To forward the human rights program of the Organization of Afro-American Unity Malcolm had flown to Cairo in July 1964 to attend the African Summit Conference, where he had appealed to the delegates of the thirty-four member nations to bring the cause of twenty-two million African Americans before the United Nations. After the conference he had extended his stay to garner commitments of support from the African nations. By October he had visited eleven Asian countries. He had talked with their heads of state and addressed their parliaments, but he had not readily won their support. Africa, after all, had strong economic and political ties to the United States. Malcolm had been gone 138 days when he flew back to the United States on November 24. The weather had already turned cold and wintry. That winter, as Benjamin Karim recalls in the following excerpt from his memoir, would be cruelly cut short for Malcolm X.

from *Remembering Malcolm*
by Benjamin Karim
"Winter"

He knew that he was not going to die an old man. He knew, too, that time for him that winter was fast running out.

I remember a day not long before the end. I was walking with Malcolm from the Hotel Theresa to his car. It had been snowing. Malcolm was wearing a heavy, dark overcoat. He had pulled the flaps of his beaverskin hat down over his ears and a woolen scarf protected his throat and neck. Still, he shivered a little when he told me that he had been refused a life insurance policy because the company considered him too high a risk. Outright they had refused him; they had not even bothered with the formality of a physical.

Malcolm didn't try to hide his concern. He had no bank account. He had no money. The *Autobiography* had not yet been published, and he owned nothing else that he could sell. If he died uninsured, he would be leaving his wife and their four daughters penniless. "They refused to insure my life," he said. He paused, and I could hear the clink-clink of the metal clasps on Malcolm's galoshes as we trudged along the sidewalk. Malcolm had tucked his trousers into the tops of his galoshes. "That tells you how much my life is worth," he added.

The slush sloshed beneath our feet. "No, Brother Minister," I replied, "your life is invaluable to us." Malcolm smiled. In his eyes I saw the concern that included all of us, all his people.

His people were his mission. We were the reason Malcolm came back from Africa. He came back with hundreds of photographs from the many African nations he had visited, but in terms of beauty, no country had impressed him or his photographer's eye more than Ethiopia. "You know," he said one night when he was showing me the pictures he had taken in Africa, "if it wasn't for you all here in this country, I would have stayed there, in Ethiopia." His friends there had feared for Malcolm's life in America. They had tried to persuade him not to return to the United States. They had offered him a home there and the Ethiopian government had promised him sanctuary. Malcolm loved Ethiopia, but, he said, his mission did not lie there. It lay here, among us. "You are the only reason I didn't make Ethiopia my home," he said.

The autumn sunlight on the hills of Ethiopia had faded for Malcolm into a snowy, gray Harlem day. Bundled up in his beaverskin hat, a scarf and heavy overcoat, with his trousers tucked into his galoshes, Malcolm hesitated a moment at the door to his car. That day, like many days that winter, solemn thoughts weighed heavily on Malcolm's mind. He was haunted by uncertainty. It sat beside him every time he turned the key in the ignition to his car. It followed him when he brought his Oldsmobile to a stop at a traffic light, when another car—out of nowhere, it would seem—might pull up beside him and in a quick blaze of gunfire he might be dead. He knew his end was coming, but he didn't know how, or when.

Malcolm got in his car and turned the key.

Throughout the winter death threats to Malcolm arrived in the mail or over the phone. Assassination plots were frequently rumored. On the freeway in Los Angeles, in New York's Lincoln Tunnel, assassination attempts were initiated and failed. The Chicago leadership was calling for an end to the "scandalizing" of Mr. Muhammad by the hypocrite Malcolm X, and the Boston mosque, for one, was actively responding with plots against Malcolm's life.

The news from Boston was rarely good. Early in February Malcolm was planning to meet in Boston with Muslim sisters and brothers who had defected from Farrakhan's Mosque Number Twelve there. In New York, meanwhile, we received word that Muslim zealots from Farrakhan's mosque had plans of their own for Malcolm. Rumor had it that Malcolm would not be returning from Boston alive. Malcolm still wanted to attend the meeting, but we objected. Brother John and Luqman then volunteered me to go in Malcolm's place. For me, it was an honor.

I flew to Boston. Brother Busby met me at the airport and we arrived at the meeting without any incidents. It was held at the house of Malcolm's half-sister Ella Collins. I spoke with the brothers and sisters whose dissatisfaction with the national officials and sympathy with Malcolm had driven them from the Boston mosque. I thanked Malcolm's sister for her hospitality and then headed back to the airport with Busby and Malcolm's cousin in an old tank of a Cadillac.

It was late. Malcolm's cousin was driving. It was his car, it was his single-barrel shotgun lying at our feet in the back. I had noticed the new 1965 Lincoln earlier. It had pulled up along the deserted roadside and let us pass. Now it was beginning to overtake us. It passed us just as we were reaching the Callahan Tunnel. When we entered the tunnel, the Lincoln was blocking our path. Malcolm's cousin braked hard. Busby grabbed the shotgun. Four Muslim brothers from Number Twelve had left the Lincoln and were heading toward us when we screeched to our stop. Immediately Malcolm's cousin started backing up his all-steel Cadillac. The four Muslims lunged after it and were trying to grab hold of the door handles when Malcolm's cousin suddenly shifted gears. He gunned the Cadillac forward. He rammed the shiny new Lincoln broadside, then backed up again. He had thrown the four Muslims off their balance, but they were still scurrying after us. I was grappling with Busby for the shotgun—he wasn't using it—when, abruptly, the Cadillac jerked forward and slammed again into the Lincoln. The next time the Cadillac attacked we practically tore off the Lincoln's simonized fender. By then Busby had the shotgun aimed out the window and the four Muslims were hightailing back to their battered car. Malcolm's cousin reversed, advanced, rammed,

and inched his Cadillac past the Lincoln. We sped the rest of
the way to the airport.

At the Eastern Airlines terminal Busby and I leapt out of the
car without even noticing that Busby still had a loaded shotgun
clutched under his arm and trigger finger. It was eased away
from him when we were apprehended by the police inside the
terminal. Someone had called the police and informed them
of an incident in progress at the Callahan Tunnel; it's in an
FBI report.

Someone had called the telephone company. The number I had
dialed, said the recording, had been temporarily disconnected.
Certainly it had not been disconnected by Malcolm. He had just
left an MMI meeting and I had told him that I would call to
see that he'd gotten safely home. The recording aroused all our
suspicions. We feared for Malcolm's safety.

There were maybe twenty of us—Earl Grant, Brother James,
Brother Ivory, Calvin, Luqman, me, others—and we decided to
head that minute for Queens. In our bulky winter clothes we
crammed ourselves and our weapons into four cars. We had all
started carrying weapons that winter, for our own defense and
Malcolm's, so when we hit the toll booths at the Triborough
Bridge, four carloads of us, with assorted guns pointing in every
direction and rifle barrels jutting out the windows, we must
have looked like something sent by Pancho Villa. We drove up
to Malcolm's house on 97th Street in East Elmhurst. We
knocked on Malcolm's door. He answered it. He was all right.
I told him what he himself had already discovered, that his
telephone number had been cut off. He had also already contacted the telephone company. Their information showed that
Malcolm himself had ordered the interruption of service, supposedly because he was going to be out of town for an indeter-
minate length of time. Malcolm corrected their information, and
his telephone service was being restored.

Incidents like this did not help any of us to rest easier. Nor
did Malcolm's weapon. All he had to protect himself and his
family was a bolt-action rifle, the same caliber and make as the
one Lee Harvey Oswald had used in Dallas. So that Malcolm

would not have to pull the bolt back to eject the empty shell and then push the bolt forward to insert a new round, I insisted that he take my automatic rifle instead. I tried to convince him that an M-1 carbine with a thirty-round banana clip—it was much like the one I had used in Korea—would serve him better in an emergency. Malcolm agreed with some reluctance, but he agreed. We traded weapons.

That settled, I joined the brothers in their routine check of the neighborhood. That was when we detected the car parked about seventy-five feet down the block. Two men were sitting inside it. Our weapons raised, the twenty of us took positions on either side of the lamplit street. We motioned for the car to pull forward. Slowly it moved toward us. Slowly it advanced between our two columns. Then we roadblocked it. We discovered the two men were police officers who had been assigned to monitor the area and to provide Malcolm and his family protection. Malcolm knew nothing about it. We let the two officers pass. They waved as their unmarked car gathered speed and disappeared into the city's streets. A few minutes later we were heading back to Harlem. We left some brothers behind to stand guard outside Malcolm's house through the night. A quiet night, as it turned out, on Malcolm's block in Queens.

The block was quiet, too, the early morning hours of Sunday, February 14, and Malcolm's household lay in unsuspecting sleep. Then the firebombs hit. Around 2:45 A.M. the interior of Malcolm's house burst into flames that endangered the lives not only of Malcolm and Sister Betty but also of four children ranging in age from six months to six years. Malcolm angrily accused the NOI of the firebombing. The NOI, which held the title to 23–11 97th Street, in turn accused Malcolm himself of setting the blaze in order to gain publicity and to avoid eviction from the house by court order on February 15. Later, after thinking more calmly about the incident, Malcolm began to doubt the NOI's responsibility for the death threats and the recent actions against him. He couldn't believe that the NOI would in fact risk killing his wife and children in their attempt to kill him, or that they would risk killing innocent children, period. I may have shared his doubts then, but not now. I have been informed that there are recordings on tape of a former NOI official from the New York mosque actually bragging about issuing the orders for the firebombing to Number Seven's FOI. Malcolm, I think, wanted to believe that the evil of the NOI against him knew a limit. But it didn't. They would not have hesitated to burn down his house even at the cost of his family's lives. Muslim zealots could be so blinded by their allegiance to the NOI, I think, that they would not only commit arson but also, in their fanaticism, blindly violate Islamic laws that in fact protect the lives of women, children, and the elderly. To set fire to a house inhabited by innocent children is not Islamic; it's Satanic.

Muslim zealots in the FOI are capable of any act that they believe is justified by the Nation. The Muslims who tossed the firebombs through the windows of Malcolm's house, like those who had attempted on several occasions to assassinate Malcolm and like those who would eventually succeed, all believed one hundred percent that Mr. Muhammad had been taught by God and spoke for Allah. They believed that America would be destroyed by Allah in Mr. Muhammad's lifetime. They believed that after Armageddon the faithful would be led by Allah's One True Messenger out of this place into the Promised Land and that the planet would then belong to Islam: The Nation would rule the Earth. They believed that Fard was God. They believed that Mr. Muhammad would not die. They believed without doubt or question that Malcolm was a hypocrite, a speaker of lies and rumors about their infallible, morally flawless leader, and they had been taught to kill the hypocrite wherever they might find him. That they themselves might be killed in fulfilling their mission would not in any way dissuade them, for they had been given a sacred cause. They had been called upon by the very top officials in the NOI whose leadership they devoutly honored and whose orders they eagerly obeyed. Neither the FBI nor any other federal agency or criminal organization had to contrive Malcolm's assassination. The NOI did it for them. Ultimately the NOI had Malcolm killed not for spreading lies but for speaking the truth, as he did when he told Mike Wallace about Mr. Muhammad and the secretaries on national television. Only in death could the NOI finally silence Malcolm X.

The silence fell on February 21, a Sunday, at an OAAU rally in Harlem's Audubon Ballroom. Malcolm's promise earlier in the month that he would present the OAAU charter at the rally on the twenty-first was attracting a good-sized crowd that afternoon. It was a mixed crowd, too, much of it non-Muslim. Malcolm had directed the MMI brothers at the rally not to carry weapons that particular Sunday because, he said, he didn't want to alarm the non-Muslims in the OAAU membership and he didn't want any of the more trigger-happy Muslims among us starting any incidents on this important occasion. At least one of the brothers, Reuben X Francis, disobeyed; he concealed a .45 pistol on himself when he came into the meeting. Malcolm had also instructed us not to check the person of anyone attending the rally for weapons or alcohol. "Anyone who comes, let them in," he had told us. Anyone who came that aroused the suspicions of the MMI brothers, however, would have been checked, despite our instructions, so as to ensure Malcolm's well-being.

The rally was late getting started. Both the Reverend Dr. Galamison, a civil rights activist, and Ralph Cooper, a popular disk jockey and well-known talent scout with ties at the Apollo Theater, had been booked by the OAAU secretary to open up the rally. It was nearing two o'clock, and neither of them had shown up as yet at the Audubon. Nor had the singing group that Cooper had planned to try out before a Harlem audience that day. Unpunctuality upset Malcolm. Unmet commitments upset Malcolm, and not only had Cooper and Galamison failed to appear but also Malcolm's drafting committee had failed to complete the OAAU charter. So Malcolm was already upset when Brother James came backstage to tell Malcolm that Ralph Cooper had called to say that he couldn't make it. Still, I would never have predicted Malcolm's reaction. He exploded. Why hadn't Brother James told him immediately, he wanted to know, and when Brother James said he had tried to reach Malcolm at home and had left the message with Sister Betty, Malcolm flew into a blind rage. After screaming at Brother James that he should know better than to tell Sister Betty anything, Malcolm burst out at all of us. "Get out!" he bellowed. "Everybody! Get out!!"

Only one time before had I seen Malcolm truly angry, the day he discovered that John Ali had misappropriated the New York mosque's funds, but even then he had not so totally lost his rationality and composure. Nor had I, until that gray February afternoon, seen Malcolm more distraught than he had been upon learning of Mr. Muhammad's infidelities, when he had felt as if his brain cells were bleeding. A sense of terrible foreboding had overcome me backstage at the Audubon. Neither singly nor together could Galamison's failure to appear or Cooper's cancellation or the unfinished charter fully explain Malcolm's behavior. God, we are told, does not burden a soul with more than it can bear, but I had thought as I'd stood there before his fury that Malcolm's soul could not bear much more. A metaphysical weight, it seemed, was sitting heavily on his back and shoulders. I felt the weight myself, on my own shoulders, but I knew it did not lighten the burden for him. I didn't know, either, what could.

Some minutes after Malcolm's outburst, the OAAU secretary came looking for me. She told me that Malcolm wanted me to open up the rally.

"How are you going to open up?" Malcolm asked me for the first time in the eight years that I had been assisting him.

"How do you want me to open up?" I responded, surprised that he had not said, as he usually did, simply to follow my own mind. Then I suggested that I prepare the audience for his announcement regarding the failure of his committee to complete its draft of the OAAU charter. I said that I would speak about voyages and the disappointments we experience when unexpected circumstances prevent a ship from reaching its destination on time. As I spoke to him, though, I thought that I was looking at a man who could voyage no farther, a man who had come to a dead stop and could neither turn back nor move forward. He could only stand there beneath the weight of his overburdened soul.

"Okay," said Malcolm. "Make it plain."

I looked into Malcolm's face. Again I felt the heaviness in his soul bearing down upon me. It lay upon me with such weight that I thought I couldn't even move my feet. I felt dazed, I wanted to perspire. Unsteady, I made my way to the podium onstage at the Audubon.

I talked about a ship voyaging the Atlantic. I talked about ocean storms that it sometimes rode and that other times it had to circle. I talked of trade winds and doldrums, of the many unforseen delays that might keep even a well-captained ship from arriving in port at its scheduled time. I talked about Columbus who asked for the Great Khan of China when he landed another entire continent and ocean away from the destination he had charted. When I finished, the weight seemed only heavier on my shoulders, and under my suit I could feel the perspiration rising on my back. I turned away from the podium.

I was going to take the stage chair that Malcolm had been sitting in, but he stopped me. He put his hand on my arm and spoke into my ear. He instructed me to go to the green room just offstage and to have Brother James and the OAAU secretary inform him the minute that Reverend Galamison arrived. Somewhat perplexed—it seemed apparent to me that Galamison would not appear—I left the stage. As I stepped into the green room I felt beads of perspiration beginning to dampen my forehead. I shut the door behind me before telling James and the secretary what Malcolm had said. Then I sat down. I heard a sound like firecrackers, I heard panic, I heard blasts of gunfire—all in a matter of seconds. The perspiration broke out of every pore in my body. I knew that he was gone.

I knew that he was gone before the door from the stage to the green room burst open and someone came running through. I just sat there, stunned, staring through the open doorway at the body on the stage. I couldn't move. Malcolm was lying on the floor of the stage, his face up, and I thought for a moment that he was trying to breathe, but his eyes were fixed—it seemed almost that they were fixed on me—fixed and unblinking; and I couldn't move. Then, all at once, it left me, the weight on my shoulders, and I felt a great relief come over me, Malcolm's

relief from all his suffering. Death ends a thing on time. Whatever may be the instruments to bring it about, when it comes,
it comes on time.

How long I sat there I don't know. When I got up from the
chair in the green room and walked back out onto the stage,
everyone had left the Audubon. My eyes scanned a deserted
ballroom, an empty stage, the podium, the microphone, an overturned chair. On the floor of the stage I noticed a ring. I picked
it up. The onyx stone was inscribed with *Allah* in Arabic. It
was Malcolm's ring. A bullet had shot it off his finger. I put
it in my pocket; later I gave it to Sister Betty. I stood at the
podium. The microphone was dead and my mind was as vacant
as the place. I didn't even wonder what time it was.

We had started late. It was after two o'clock when I began
the opening. I spoke for twenty or maybe twenty-five minutes,
so it must have been close to three o'clock when Malcolm
offered the audience his salaams. Just as he was about to begin
his address, a man near the center of the audience started a
commotion. Pushing back his chair, he leapt up and said loudly
to the person next to him, "Nigger, get your hand out of my
pocket!" On top of the accusation, from the same area, came
a few rapid shots that sounded like firecrackers. "Hold it!"
Malcolm shouted from the podium; you can hear it on the tape
of the rally. "Hold it!" he shouted into the blasts of gunfire
not fifteen feet away from him. A bullet cut through Malcolm's
microphone. He reeled back, he fell. It had happened in a matter
of seconds.

The audience had panicked. Chairs were flung helter-skelter
across the ballroom as three hundred people, most of them
screaming, scrambled for the door. Another hundred ran blind.
Some fell to the floor. Sister Betty swept her children under a
table; her head down, she covered them with herself and her
coat. A Muslim audience would not have panicked. It would
have responded to the situation with military discipline, not like
a herd of cattle in a thunderstorm. Had the audience not stam-
peded, the Muslim brothers who were present could probably
have taken all five assassins. Instead, Luqman ended up with a

bullet in his coat after trying to stop one of the assassins by hurling a chair at him, and another brother got hit in the stomach. Reuben X Francis, however, had his .45. He wounded the one assassin who was taken that day at the Audubon—Talmadge Hayer, a member of the Newark mosque and a resident of Paterson, New Jersey.

Not until four or five days later did the police pick up Thomas 15X Johnson and Norman 3X Butler, both of whom were charged with murder in the case of Malcolm X. Neither Johnson nor Butler had gone with Malcolm when he left the Nation, so either of them could probably have been enlisted by the NOI to assassinate Malcolm under the Muslim code of honor. Neither of them, however, had attended the rally at the Audubon that Sunday. If they had, I would have spotted them from the platform when I was opening up. Luqman or any of the other brothers at the door would have recognized them if they had entered the ballroom. As any current NOI member was considered suspect by us, both Johnson and Butler would have been checked for weapons at the door and, in all likelihood, been barred from the meeting. (In March 1965 I testified both to the assistant district attorney and before a grand jury that as I had left the stage, I had not in fact witnessed the assassination and therefore had not seen the assassins themselves. I was nevertheless certain, I testified further, that neither Butler nor Johnson could have been involved in the assassination as neither was present that day at the Audubon. I stated, too, that in my view, the assassins were NOI Muslims but were not members of the New York mosque. Had they been, I pointed out, Luqman, James, I, or any of the other MMI brothers at the meeting would have recognized them. I was not called by the defense to testify at the trial itself.)

I don't know how Betty Shabazz or anybody else was able to positively identify the suspects Butler and Johnson and thus place them at the scene. Especially Butler. That Sunday morning, the very day of the rally, Butler had been in the hospital to have work done on his knee. Despite the fact that he couldn't have made the assassins' swift escape through the crowded, chaotic ballroom with his injury, Butler was indicted. Butler was incriminated mostly by his old tweed coat. That old tweed coat of his was the only coat I had ever seen Butler wear. Unfortunately for him one of the assassins had decided to wear tweed that day.

From the outset both suspects denied the charges against them. When they came to trial the following year Talmadge Hayer testified under oath to the innocence of his two codefendants. All three were nonetheless convicted on March 11, 1966, of murder in the first degree. The case was closed. It stayed closed, too, when Hayer later named his four accomplices, all of them members of the Newark mosque and all of them duped, like Hayer himself, by their Muslim zealotry. Hayer had testified that he got ten thousand dollars for assassinating Malcolm X. I don't believe, however, that Hayer or any of them did it for money. They did it for the Nation. They were devoted, they had been given a sacred mission. Around three o'clock on Sunday afternoon, February 21, 1965, they accomplished it.

At 3:30 that dark Sunday afternoon Malcolm X was pronounced dead on his arrival at the Vanderbilt Clinic of Columbia-Presbyterian Hospital. His death made news for days in the press, on the radio, on television. You couldn't escape it. For days I could not pronounce the death that had emptied my soul. I couldn't eat, I couldn't sleep. I'd stay awake most of the night, then at five or six in the morning, just before sunrise, I'd find my way home and fall into bed. For an hour or so I'd drift in and out of shallow sleep while time, it seemed, unraveled inside my head. For weeks time seemed only to move backward, as everything seemed now to belong to history. I lived for weeks inside the cloud of my own grief.

In Harlem, at the Unity Funeral Home, I viewed the body of our Brother Minister. Wrapped in a seamless white garment, it lay in a modest casket. On the morning of February 27, still half in a daze, I attended the funeral services at the Bishop Alvin S. Child's Faith Temple Church of God in Christ. Ossie Davis presided. In his eulogy he praised "our own black shining Prince," a phrase that for me did not capture the man I knew: the minister, from the Latin word for servant; our counselor, healer, judge, and peacemaker; the teacher at the blackboard with a world in his mind and a piece of chalk in his hand. After the service I went with the procession to Ferncliff Cemetery. A body in a modest casket was lowered into the ground.

A love died inside me that day. No longer could I bear love for all brothers in Islam, not for those who had conspired to kill Malcolm, or for Hayer and his four unknown accomplices who had been the instruments of Malcolm's death, or for the NOI officials in Chicago who had manipulated all of them by turning the minds of the Nation against its most admired minister. Those of us who had stood closest to Malcolm talked among ourselves of retaliation. We laid plots and we drew up strategies. Nothing ever came of them, not out of fear or inadequacy but out of respect for Malcolm himself. Malcolm would have preferred justice.

The courts denied Malcolm his justice. They convicted three codefendants, but, I believe, only one assassin. Four other men with Malcolm's blood on their Muslim souls went free. The police, the FBI, the district attorney, the court, they all wanted a quick conviction and got it. They tied their case up fast. They preferred expediency.

Immediately after the assassination of Malcolm X at the Audubon Ballroom on Sunday afternoon, February 21, 1965, FBI agents in the field began teletyping reports on the shooting to their regional Bureau offices. Details varied, but in essence the reports agreed. A version of the violent events took shape. An FBI report dated March 12, 1965, collated much of the information that appeared in the initial teletyped accounts and provided further detail about suspects and the evidence gathered in the days following Malcolm's death.

from *Malcolm X: The FBI File*
from section 16

UNITED STATES DEPARTMENT OF JUSTICE
FEDERAL BUREAU OF INVESTIGATION

New York, New York
March 12, 1965
Malcolm K. Little
Internal Security—MMI

On February 21, 1965, at 3:10 P.M. [BUREAU DELETION] advised that Malcolm X had just been shot in the Audubon Ballroom, New York City, while addressing an OAAU public rally. [BUREAU DELETION] that Reuben X Francis, one of Malcolm's officers, fired back at those shooting at Malcolm X. [BUREAU DELETION] a Negro male (later identified as Talmadge Hayer) was captured outside the Audubon Ballroom immediately after the shooting.

[BUREAU DELETION] advised on February 21, 1965, that at approximately 3:10 P.M., this date, he received a call at the station that a homicide was committed at the Audubon Ballroom, 564 West 166th Street, New York City.

He stated that Patrolman [BUREAU DELETION] New York City Police Department, advised the same date that Malcolm

X, Negro, male, age 39, of Suite 128, Hotel Theresa, 7th Avenue and 125th Street, New York City, while on the stage of the Audubon Ballroom, was shot and killed by unknown persons. Patrolman [BUREAU DELETION] stated that Malcolm X was pronounced dead on arrival by [BUREAU DELETION] at Vanderbilt Clinic, Presbyterian Hospital at 168th Street and Broadway, New York City, on February 21, 1965. [BUREAU DELETION] stated that the Police Department determined that the shooting of Malcolm X occurred at about 3:10 P.M., February 21, 1965.

On February 21, 1965, [BUREAU DELETION] and [BUREAU DELETION] both of the [BUREAU DELETION] advised that Malcolm X was shot that afternoon during a rally of the OAAU at the Audubon Ballroom. They stated that [BUREAU DELETION] was on patrol on Broadway when he heard shots coming from the Audubon Ballroom. He immediately proceeded in that direction where he saw people coming out of the said ballroom shouting that Malcolm X had been shot. Others were shouting "Don't let him get away." [BUREAU DELETION] at that time arrested person identified as Thomas Hagan as he was running out of the ballroom. When arrested, Hagan (true name Hayer) had in his pocket a .45 caliber automatic clip containing four rounds. Hayer had been shot in the left leg.

[BUREAU DELETION] further stated on February 21, 1965, that the Police Department obtained two witnesses immediately after the shooting, namely [BUREAU DELETION] both freelance reporters and photographers of [BUREAU DELETION].

[BUREAU DELETION] stated that [BUREAU DELETION] and [BUREAU DELETION] gave statements in which they say they saw Hayer with a gun in his hand while Malcolm X was on the stage speaking. They said Malcolm X suddenly called out "Hold it" and after this, [BUREAU DELETION] dropped to the floor and did not actually see Malcolm X shot, but stated before they dropped to the floor, they saw Hayer with a gun in his hand pointing it towards Malcolm X. The next thing they saw was Hayer trying to run out of the ballroom with a gun in his hand. According to [BUREAU DELETION] as Hayer ran out, one of Malcolm's group shot three times at Hayer with an automatic pistol. Hayer did not have the pistol on him when he was arrested outside the ballroom.

[BUREAU DELETION] also stated that [BUREAU DELE-TION] who was sitting in the front row in the Audubon Ball-room was shot in the foot during the shooting spree in which Malcolm X was shot. He also stated that [BUREAU DELE-TION] was also hit during the shooting spree in the ballroom and both [BUREAU DELETION] and [BUREAU DELETION] were treated at Columbia Presbyterian Hospital, New York City.

[BUREAU DELETION] later advised that the police found a 12 gauge sawed-off double-barrel shotgun manufactured by J. C. Higgins, model 1017, also bearing the number 5100. The police advised, upon examination, that the shotgun had been fired and left at the scene.

At approximately 7:45 P.M., on February 21, 1965, [BU-REAU DELETION] advised that Hayer was being detained in the prison ward at Bellevue Hospital, under guard. He stated that Hayer had one bullet in him which entered his left thigh and shattered the thigh bone. He stated the hospital plans to put Hayer's left leg in traction and that the bullet would stay in the leg for about two weeks until such time as the bone would be healed enough to permit an operation.

On February 21, 1965, [BUREAU DELETION] New York, contacted the office of the Federal Bureau of Investigation (FBI) at New York City and stated that he had one of the pistols used to kill Malcolm X. [BUREAU DELETION] was at that time in [BUREAU DELETION] and asked that Bureau Agents meet him at the [BUREAU DELETION] address as soon as possible. [BUREAU DELETION] when contacted the same date by Agents of the FBI, [BUREAU DELETION] was in the back of the Audubon Ballroom, the same date, to hear Malcolm X speak. He stated that he is a member of the OAAU. He said Malcolm X was just introduced and began to speak when some people began to scream somewhere about eight rows from the front of the auditorium. He said people in that area began to move away and Malcolm X put up his hands as though to quiet the people down and was heard to say "Keep your seats." Just then, [BUREAU DELETION] shots rang out, but [BUREAU

DELETION] could not see who was doing the shooting. After the shots were fired [BUREAU DELETION] the persons shooting headed for the exit. Some of the people in the audience tried to stop them by throwing chairs at them or in their way. At this time, two of Malcolm X's men were shooting at the assailants as they were trying to leave the ballroom. [BUREAU DELETION] said the two men involved in the shooting passed him, but as the other two men involved were running towards the exit, one turned to fire back at Malcolm X's men. As this man then turned to run through the exit, [BUREAU DELETION] threw a "body block" into him knocking him down the stairs, at which time, this person dropped a .45 caliber pistol. [BUREAU DELETION] picked up the gun and attempted to shoot the man he knocked down as he was running down the stairs, but the gun jammed and he ran out of the building. [BUREAU DELETION] said he checked the gun and noticed that three rounds were still in the clip. [BUREAU DELETION] then turned over to Special Agents of the FBI a .45 caliber automatic pistol, serial number 335055, containing a clip with three rounds of ammunition.

At 10:15 P.M., February 21, 1965, [BUREAU DELETION] came to the office of the FBI, at which time, they were furnished a .45 caliber automatic pistol, which was obtained by Agents of the FBI from [BUREAU DELETION].

[BUREAU DELETION] stated that Hayer, who was arrested immediately after shooting Malcolm X, has been charged with homicide and that Reuben X Francis, a member of Malcolm X's group, was charged with felonious assault and possession of a deadly weapon.

[BUREAU DELETION] also stated that the Police Department has a witness who identified Francis as the person firing back at assailants of Malcolm X. He said Francis was believed to have fired a shot which struck Hayer in the leg. He said Francis is suspected of being the person who fired a .32 caliber pistol, which has never been recovered by the Police Department. [BUREAU DELETION] stated that it is estimated that up to four persons may be involved in the killing of Malcolm X.

[BUREAU DELETION] further advised that an autopsy performed on Malcolm X reflected that he had ten bullet wounds in his chest, thigh and ankle plus four bullet creases in the chest and thigh. The autopsy located one nine millimeter slug and one .45 caliber slug, and several shotgun pellets in the body of Malcolm X.

[BUREAU DELETION] said that when the Police Department examined the Audubon Ballroom after the shooting they found a sawed-off double-barrel shotgun wrapped in a green suit coat. In the suit coat pocket was found a key for a Yale lock, a package of Camel cigarettes and an empty eyeglass case bearing the optometrist name ''M. M. Fine, Main Street, Flushing.'' The shotgun contained two discharged Remington express shells, single O buckshot shells, and there were indications that the gun was recently fired.

[BUREAU DELETION] also stated that in the ballroom were found three .45 caliber shells and slugs, six nine millimeter shells and two slugs, and three .32 caliber slugs and 10 pieces of lead, presumably fired from the shotgun.

The FBI Identification Division, on February 22, 1965, identified prints of the person arrested in the shooting of Malcolm X as Talmadge Hayer, who up until then, was known to the Police Department only as Thomas Hagen. Identification records reflect that Hayer, FBI #142496F, is a male, Negro, born March 16, 1942, at Hackensack, New Jersey, last known residing at 347 Marshall Street, Paterson, New Jersey. [BUREAU DELETION]

[BUREAU DELETION] that Malcolm X arrived at the Audubon Ballroom, February 21, 1965, in white 1965 Cadillac. Malcolm X was surrounded by his bodyguards and was then escorted into the front corridor of the Audubon Ballroom and then to the stage. When Malcolm X began to speak, a disturbance occurred between two men. Up in the front near the stage, Malcolm X's bodyguards started to move towards the two men causing a disturbance, when Malcolm X said ''Hold it.'' Without hesitation, two men occupying the front seats, left side, middle aisle, looking towards the stage, got into a crouched position and fired several shots in the direction of Malcolm X. The fire ''spitting'' from the guns ''crashed'' into the chest of Malcolm X and he fell backwards as if knocked down by a

sudden powerful force. Still in the crouched position, the gunmen hastily moved toward the exit in the back of the hall,
stepping over persons who were laying on the floor. It is believed that approximately twenty shots in all were fired during
the shooting.

[BUREAU DELETION] reviewed a photograph of Talmadge
Hayer and identified him as one of the persons who shot and
killed Malcolm X on February 21, 1965, at the Audubon Ballroom.

[BUREAU DELETION] advised on that date Hayer's finger-
prints were found on the clip of the .45 caliber pistol that was
picked up by [BUREAU DELETION] at the Audubon Ballroom
the day Malcolm X was killed and turned over to the FBI.

On February 26, 1965 [BUREAU DELETION] Norman 3X
Butler, 661 Rosedale Avenue, Bronx, New York, was arrested at
3:00 A.M., same date, by the New York City Police Department,
as one of the assassins in the killing of Malcolm X on February 21,
1965. [BUREAU DELETION] said that three witnesses including
[BUREAU DELETION] placed Butler in the Audubon Ballroom
at the time that Malcolm X was shot and he was identified as one
of the persons who actually shot at Malcolm X.

[BUREAU DELETION] a photograph of Norman 3X Butler,
who was arrested by the Police Department for the killing of
Malcolm X as one of the persons who participated in the shooting
of Malcolm X at the Audubon Ballroom.

On February 27, 1965, [BUREAU DELETION] advised that
[BUREAU DELETION] identified Talmadge Hayer and Norman
3X Butler, both now in the custody of the New York City Police
Department, as assassins in the killing of Malcolm X. Butler was
arrested in January 1965, for shooting a Correctional Officer who
broke away from the NOI and, at the time he was arrested for
killing Malcolm X, he was on $10,000 bail.

[BUREAU DELETION]
[BUREAU DELETION]
[BUREAU DELETION]

[BUREAU DELETION] identified Norman 3X Butler from
photographs as the man who was sitting [BUREAU DELETION]
and said "Get your hands out of my pocket" in the Audubon
Ballroom, just before Malcolm X was killed. [BUREAU DELE-

TION] cannot recognize Thomas 15X Johnson from photographs as being in the Audubon Ballroom on February 21, 1965.

On March 4, 1965, [BUREAU DELETION] stated that as of this date, Hayer, Butler and Johnson, all arrested for the killing of Malcolm X, have refused to furnish any information other than their name and age.

On March 8, 1965, [BUREAU DELETION] advised that [BUREAU DELETION] was interviewed by the New York City Police Department on the same date. According to [BUREAU DELETION] stated that he saw Hayer shoot Malcolm X and also observed Butler and Johnson in the Audubon Ballroom the day Malcolm X was killed. [BUREAU DELETION] saw Johnson run out the side exit after the shooting.

[BUREAU DELETION] stated that Johnson, when arrested, denied being in the Audubon Ballroom on February 21, 1965. [BUREAU DELETION] stated that [BUREAU DELETION] after the shooting, he picked up the shotgun used to kill Malcolm X and gave it to Rueben X Francis. He said he also picked up a German Luger pistol and gave it to another person to hold until the police arrived.

[BUREAU DELETION] stated that the German Luger was never turned over to the Police Department and this gun could probably account for the nine millimeter slug in Malcolm's body. [BUREAU DELETION]

On March 10, 1965, [BUREAU DELETION] advised that the [BUREAU DELETION] in conducting interviews of persons, particularly MMI members who were present in the Audubon Ballroom when Malcolm X was shot, seem to have the same "clear cut" story that they were in the ballroom when Malcolm X was shot and when the shots rang out they fell to the floor and never got a look at the assassins. [BUREAU DELETION] stated that the Police Department learned that [BUREAU DELETION] of the MMI in New York City, has instructed members of the MMI and the OAAU to cooperate with the Police Department but only say that they fell on the floor when the shooting started and cannot identify the person who shot Malcolm X.

[BUREAU DELETION] said the [BUREAU DELETION] is now shifting their investigation towards officials of the MMI

[BUREAU DELETION]. In reference to [BUREAU DELE-TION] stated that information has been received that [BUREAU DELETION] also was one of Malcolm X's bodyguards the day he was shot, and has been seen in the Harlem area "dressed to kill," "wearing one hundred dollar suits" and a "pocket full of hundred dollar bills" since the death of Malcolm X. [BUREAU DELETION] said that [BUREAU DELETION] has no visible means of support at this time.

[BUREAU DELETION] also stated that on March 10, 1965, the New York County Grand Jury handed down first-degree murder indictments in the killing of Malcolm X on February 21, 1965, against Talmadge Hayer, Norman 3X Butler and Thomas 15X Johnson.

The *New York Times*, a local daily newspaper dated March 11, 1965, contained an article captioned "4 Are Indicted Here In Malcolm X Case." This article states:

> A grand jury indicted three Negroes yesterday in the slaying of Malcolm X, Black Nationalist leader, and indicted Malcolm's bodyguard for shooting and wounding one of the trio.
>
> Charges of willfully killing Malcolm "with a shotgun and pistols" were made against Thomas Hagen, also known as Talmadge Hayer and Thomas Hayer, 22 years old, of 347 Marshall Street, Paterson, N.J.; Norman 3X Butler, 26, of 661 Rosedale Avenue, the Bronx; and Thomas 15X Johnson, 29, of 932 Bronx Park South, the Bronx.
>
> A separate indictment accused Rueben [sic] Francis, under that spelling and also as Rueben [sic] X, on one count of first-degree felonious assault for "aiming and discharging a pistol" at Hagan, two counts of second-degree assault and a fourth count of possessing a pistol. Francis, 33, has given his address as 871 East 179th Street, the Bronx.
>
> Hagan is in Bellevue Hospital's prison ward. Butler and Johnson, [who] are being held without bail, and Francis, whose bail has been set at $10,000, are to be arraigned in Supreme Court, tomorrow.

Almost certainly the Nation of Islam was involved in the assassination of Malcolm X, but from the outset, it appears, the FBI suspected groups other than just the NOI responsible for Malcolm's death. More than one informant hinted at the possibility that Malcolm's own people in the Muslim Mosque Incorporated were involved, as security was definitely lax at the rally that afternoon. Two other sources suggested that the FBI should check out the CIA, which, they said, "wanted Malcolm out of the way because he 'snafued' African relations for the U.S."

Within days of the shooting the New York Police Department had arrested three suspects with NOI affiliations. All three were indicted by a New York grand jury on March 11, 1965, and on the same day a year later all three were convicted of murder in the first degree. Only one of them, according to confessed assassin Talmadge Hayer, was guilty, and the men he identified as his accomplices—four other Muslims from the Newark mosque—were never apprehended. (The wrongly convicted Norman 3X Butler and Thomas 15X Johnson were paroled after serving twenty years of their life sentences. So was Talmadge Hayer.)

The following excerpt reconstructs the events of February 21, 1965, in light of Hayer's Newark connection.

from *Malcolm X: The Assassination*
by Michael Friedly
"The Assassins"

> "I had a lot of love and admiration for the Honorable Elijah Muhammad, and I just felt like this is something that I have to stand up for ... I was just the type of person that if I had to stand up for what I believe, I would do it, man."
>
> —Talmadge Hayer

The assassins were among the first to arrive at the Audubon Ballroom that afternoon of February 21, 1965. They got there early to ensure that they got the seats that they wanted, in perfect position to get a clear shot at the main speaker of the afternoon. The five assassins first met in Paterson, New Jersey, that morning, then drove to New York City. One of them told his wife that he was going across town to work on his father's car, but instead traveled to New York with his fellow co-conspirators. They parked their blue 1962 Cadillac on a street near the George Washington Bridge, several blocks from the ballroom, then got out and slowly made their way to the Audubon.

The five gunmen passed easily by the watchful eyes of Malcolm X's security staff. All wore long trench coats to cover the weapons that they carried with them. The security staff, told earlier by Malcolm X that the standard body searches of the guests were unnecessary, instead focused their attention on the impossible task of identifying those who looked as if they might want to kill Malcolm X. To this extent, they searched for members of the Fruit of Islam who might be trying to sneak into the ballroom. Most of the security personnel were former FOI members, all of whom would be able to easily identify their former colleagues. One Fruit of Islam member was identified in the ballroom that day; he had forgotten to take off his FOI pin before he entered the ballroom. He was questioned by George Whitney, one of Malcolm X's bodyguards, but after explaining that he was merely trying to hear what Malcolm X had to say, he was allowed to remain if he removed his pin.

But the actual assassins moved through the security unmolested. All of them, including young Talmadge Hayer, were members of the Newark mosque and had never been acquainted with the members of the New York FOI. The security staff, on the lookout for members of the New York FOI, let the assassins pass without a second thought. "There was a slight possibility" that they would be recognized, Hayer later admitted. "I was [from] out of town, for one thing. The other people that I was with, they was from out of town. Even though there was a few people now in Malcolm's organization that was also from Jersey. I don't know exactly how many. I don't recall seeing any of them."

Having gotten over the only possible hurdle in their way, the five assassins took their appointed places in the ballroom. Hayer and another Muslim brother named Leon made their way to the first row on the left side facing the stage, ready to fire away at the predetermined signal. Hayer carried a .45 automatic pistol beneath his topcoat; Brother Leon held a Luger. Behind them in the second row sat William X, who concealed a sawed-off shotgun under his overcoat. The shotgun was the insurance weapon. As long as it was fired directly at Malcolm X, it was virtually guaranteed to kill him. The two pistols were meant merely to finish the job, if necessary.

The other two assassins made their way to different parts of the auditorium. Neither of them carried weapons. Their job was essentially to run interference for the assassination. Brother Wilbur was charged with the responsibility of creating an initial disturbance that would distract the guards and allow Talmadge, Leon, and Willie to get a clear shot at Malcolm X. He also held a smoke bomb that he would throw to magnify the confusion. Ben took a seat in the second row, apparently also with the responsibility of running interference. The five men sat and patiently waited for the rest of the visitors to find seats and for the program to begin. They sat silently, confident that Allah had willed the death of Malcolm X and that they were merely carrying out His orders. Doubtlessly they contemplated the murder that they were about to commit and the controversy that made Malcolm X's death a necessity.

The conspiracy to kill Malcolm X began in the summer of 1964, as tensions in New York flared between Malcolm X's supporters and those of Elijah Muhammad. Muhammad was scheduled to arrive in New York, Malcolm X's home territory, for a rally in late June, and the war of rhetoric had escalated. Malcolm X had recently begun an offensive against a series of extramarital affairs in which Elijah Muhammad had indulged, and the Nation of Islam had responded with a slew of scathing articles in *Muhammad Speaks* that attacked the former Black Muslim. Death threats were circulated against Elijah Muhammad, and the Muslims responded with similar threats against Malcolm X. "There was a lot of talk in the streets of Harlem," Hayer said. "A lot of tension, a lot of conflict. Rumors was being said that Muhammad better not come to Harlem—y'know, a lot of crazy stuff going on." According to Hayer, ministers in the mosques encouraged the growth of the hatred against Malcolm X and indirectly encouraged his assassination.

> The talk was real heavy coming from the ministers at that time, man. Because I'll tell you the truth, man, I felt that it was really putting the FOI to a test, y'know. And it was never in most cases said directly, but it was like a seed planting.

According to Hayer, it was Brother Benjamin from the Newark mosque who originally organized the conspiracy sometime in June 1964. As the tension between Malcolm X and his former leader intensified, the decision was made to hatch a plan to kill the New York Muslim and remove the threat that he represented to the Nation of Islam. The exact origin of the decision to launch the assassination plot is still undetermined, but Ben was the first to begin recruiting others into his plot. Ben was a lower-level official in the Muslim mosque—a secretary or assistant secretary—which gave him the impression of authority that allowed him to recruit in the name of his higher-ups in the Nation. Ben's first recruit into the cabal was Brother Leon X, who similarly felt that Malcolm X had to be silenced. They formed the core of the group into which they would now begin the process of recruiting others, the first of whom being Talmadge Hayer.

Talmadge Hayer led the life stereotypical of many black children of his time. He was shaped in a world of white domination, in which blacks largely accepted and internalized their lower status in American society. This acceptance of inferiority in turn reinforced it, as blacks fell far behind in education and job training, unable to overcome the rigid racial caste system. Their self-doubt preyed upon them, as they convinced themselves that their role in society was destined, as unchangeable as the color of their skin. Beset by their inner hatred, they often turned not to self-improvement but to self-destruction, as violence and drugs became standard features of black neighborhoods, where strength and "toughness" became the standard of success. Although many became mired in the battle against their internal conception of worthiness, still others, such as Talmadge Hayer, finally sought to fight back against the true source of their difficulties, America's racial hierarchy. By joining the Nation of Islam, or by joining the struggle for civil and human rights, some blacks attempted to turn their self-denial into self-confidence by overturning an unjust system.

But the fight for civil rights could take place only after Talmadge Hayer and other blacks had resolved the battle within themselves. The realization that poverty and community violence were not immutable characteristics of black societies did not come easily. Like many other blacks, Hayer had lived in poverty. He was born in Hackensack, New Jersey, but soon moved to nearby Paterson, where he spent his childhood. His father was a construction worker and the supporter of eight children, of whom Talmadge was the second-oldest boy. Their mother was far too busy raising the children and keeping up the apartment to have time to bring in a second income; only after Hayer entered his teen-age years could she leave the house to get a job. "My mother's work was really just keeping the house together. That was really heavy on her. I still remember my mother doing a lot of heavy, heavy work. Just cleaning, man." His parents were originally from the South, somewhere around the Carolinas, and migrated up north before their son Talmadge was born. Both were religious and found a Baptist Church to attend in New Jersey when they migrated from the South. Hayer's mother was more religious than his father, and it was she who often pressured her children to go to church every Sunday. Talmadge went grudgingly, although he never gained the enthusiasm for Christianity that his mother professed. "I used to go to church," he explained. "But then after a while it just wore off. We stopped going. My mother used to encourage us to keep on going, but it just kind of lost interest."

But religion did have an effect on young Talmadge. To him, Christianity was a religion that promised bliss in the afterlife, but condemned "Negroes" to remain in their oppressed status until then. When he finally found the Honorable Elijah Muhammad and the Nation of Islam in his later teenage years, he finally discovered what he saw as a more equitable religion in Islam. According to Hayer, Muhammad told blacks that "they should be able to have something in this life and not after they die." Hayer was also deeply affected by the stories of his parents' plight in the South, as they were forced to live under far greater oppression and an even more rigid social hierarchy. "My mother and father used to tell my brothers and sisters and me about the hard times in the South," he said.

My mother and father always used to tell us about the lynching, y'know? The Ku Klux Klan. Hard work, hard

labor—all of these type of things that was happening to
black people at the time. I never could understand it, and
I used to always ask. I used to always say, like, "How
could you—if white people are doing all these things to
you, why can't *you* get a gun? If they're shooting you,
why can't you shoot back?" . . . And my mother used to
say, "Well, you just don't understand." And she was right.

Too poor to afford a house, the Hayer family first found
shelter in a railroad flat, until they were finally forced to move
after it was condemned. The elder Hayer worked long hours,
but his meager wages could barely feed his large family. Eventually, he was able to pool his money and buy a house for his
family in the ghettos of Paterson. They lived in conditions that
were far from ideal for raising children, but they had no other
choice, forced by money and race to remain in the New Jersey slums.

It was in Paterson that Talmadge Hayer first went to school,
in a nameless grammar school officially known as School Number
Four. It was, according to Hayer, "a pretty notorious school," and
fighting was the measure of a child's worth. Like the other children, the young Hayer developed a "tough-guy type of attitude" that hid his true self behind a blanket of fear. The
neighborhood around School Number Four was rough, and the
laws of the jungle were more appropriate than the laws of the
land. "Trouble," Hayer described it. "Fighting. Bad situation,
really, to grow up in." But when he moved from the railroad
apartment, Hayer left behind much of the violence and entered
a better school that more closely resembled education than day
care. "It was like night and day to me," Hayer said.

I had to adjust to the change. Teachers were different.
Students' attitudes were different, and it really made *me*
change. Matter of fact, my whole conduct was a lot better
at that school than at the other school I was going to,
y'know? I didn't have to have a tough-guy type of attitude
at this school. Which is what most of the kids had at
School Number Four. Pretty tough.

Talmadge soon graduated from grammar school and began attending high school. Increasingly, however, he lost his focus on schoolwork as he began to realize the apparent futility of his situation. Overcome by doubt over his self-worth, his goals faded into mere dreams. "I didn't have the right attitude when I went to high school," he said. "I guess I had a lot of doubts in myself." Like many black youths, before he ever got to high school, he began to revise his goals to fit his racial plight as he realized the station that was reserved for him in life by the hierarchical society.

> I remember even in grammar school, a teacher would ask, "What do you want to be, man? In life." And I remember I wanted to say something big. But I couldn't, y'know—I was afraid. So I said truck driver. My father was a truck driver. Man worked hard. . . . I don't know. I might have wanted to say doctor, lawyer. I don't know. I might have wanted deep down to say something like that. But I just, you know, didn't. I don't know.

Ironically, this childhood experience was quite similar to one of Malcolm X's memories, as he was forced to rethink his goals and his ambitions. Young Malcolm Little attended school in a mostly white classroom, where he was noticeably out of place and was often teased by his classmates because of his race. In the seventh grade, he was confronted by his white English teacher with a similar question about the future.

> He told me, "Malcolm, you ought to be thinking about a career. Have you been giving it thought?" The truth is, I hadn't. I never have figured out why I told him, "Well, yes, sir, I've been thinking I'd like to be a lawyer". . . . Mr. Ostrowski looked surprised, I remember, and leaned back in his chair and clasped his hands behind his head. He kind of half-smiled and said, "Malcolm, one of life's first needs is for us to be realistic. Don't misunderstand me now. We all here like you, you know that. But you've got to be realistic about being a nigger. A lawyer—that's

no realistic goal for a nigger. You need to think about something you *can* be. You're good with your hands—making things. Everybody admires your carpentry shop work. Why don't you plan on carpentry. People like you as a person—you'd get all kinds of work."

It was this event that in many ways shaped his future and was branded into Malcolm X's memory. The experience immediately became "the first major turning point of my life," Malcolm X later recalled.

For Talmadge Hayer, dropping out of high school seemed to be the natural alternative. "I realized that my mother and father couldn't get me the things that I wanted—y'know, as far as clothes and many other things. And I began to look for ways and means to make ends meet, so to speak. . . . I dropped out of high school and I went to work." He began taking random jobs, soon learning that he also could not provide the things that he wanted. He began by making $35 a week in Paterson's textile mills. Quickly he began getting jobs that paid slightly better—about $1.75 an hour—but he still made a meager wage that barely allowed him to make ends meet. "The realization really strikes home. You really learn things, and you realize that you still can't buy the things that you want." He worked in labor shops, learning how to operate the various machines and slowly creeping up the wage scale.

Hayer said he first heard about the Nation of Islam by reading the newspapers, which had reports about the progress of Islam in the nation's prisons. The budding influence of Islam in the penal system raised the concern of prison officials that the Muslim inmates would rise up against the "white devil" guards who maintained order in jail. This growing concern led to numerous struggles across the country as officials began refusing to allow Nation of Islam members to pray or otherwise express their religion. Although clearly unconstitutional, these measures served to restrict the Muslims momentarily, but it added pressure to the importance of the Muslim cause and indirectly encouraged greater inmate membership in the Nation. "I remember reading a couple of articles" on the prison struggles,

Hayer said. "The fact that these people were stand-up people, y'know, I couldn't understand. What is it about this that the establishment seems to be afraid of?"

The Nation of Islam seemed to be the natural direction for Talmadge Hayer. Lacking a religion and a philosophy, he was attracted by the assertiveness of the Muslims. His knowledge of his parents' experience in the South, as well as his life of poverty in New Jersey, pushed him toward a greater militancy than his parents had ever considered. "When I first heard anything about the teachings of the Honorable Elijah Muhammad . . . it just struck a bell. It made sense to me because even though I didn't realize it then, it just made a connection with many of the things that my parents had been experiencing and telling me anyway." He was attracted to the Muslim philosophies of discipline and regimen. "So many of the brothers that I grew up with, coming out of prison as Muslims—I couldn't even believe the difference myself. Y'know, I knew some of these guys before they even went to prison, and you would never think, man, that even God could save them. But these guys were coming out of prison dignified young men, respectful. And I couldn't understand it."

So Talmadge Hayer finally decided to open himself up to the philosophies of the Nation of Islam. "One thing led to another, and I went to check this out," he said. "I attended, and it just made a lot of sense to me." Before long, Hayer rid himself of his "slave" name, and devoted himself fully to the program and the teachings of the Honorable Elijah Muhammad. The faith in Islam burned strongly within the new recruit. As with many of the recently converted Muslims, Hayer was willing to go to almost any lengths to prove his allegiance to Elijah Muhammad and his religion. "I wasn't really operating on what you might say a wisdom base, though. I guess you might say I was just a good brother." He was so fiercely devoted to the cause of the Black Muslims that he made the perfect assassin: willing to kill not for money, but for principle.

Hayer officially joined the Nation of Islam in late 1962, only a year before Malcolm X would be suspended by the Honorable Elijah Muhammad for his "chickens coming home to roost" comment. Hayer soon received his 'X,' which all Black Mus-

lims adopted, after sending his requisite application letter to the
Muslim officials in Chicago, and became a member of the Newark Temple Number 25. Hayer had trouble adapting to the world
of the Muslims, not because he did not believe in the tenets of
Islam as preached by the Messenger, but because of what he
saw as the failure of others to believe as much as he did. His
first sign of this came as a fellow Muslim was suspended from
the Nation for getting himself into a shooting fight with some
non-Muslims. To Hayer, battling non-Muslims was part of the
point of being in the Nation of Islam. Why should a brother be
punished for doing what he was taught he should do? Increasingly distraught by the episode, Hayer temporarily stopped attending the Muslim services.

Unwilling to go back to his fellow Muslims, Hayer sank into
a deep despair. As he lost the discipline that was required of
the Muslims, he began moving toward crime. He hadn't spent
much time on the street before he was arrested for possession
of stolen guns. As he told Peter Goldman many years later,
"my life started coming apart." But he could not stay away
from the Nation of Islam for long. Convinced that rejoining the
Muslims would put his life back on track, he again went to the
Newark temple and resubscribed to the Nation's version of
Islam. But after only a short time back in the temple, his burning faith in Islam again led to his loss of faith in his fellow
Muslims. Eager to demonstrate his passion for Islam, he physically punished a fellow Muslim for violating the rigid rules of
the Nation. Expecting commendations, he received censure from
his higher-ups in the Newark temple. Again, he drifted away
from the Nation, only to rejoin it when his love for Islam and
Elijah Muhammad overcame his disappointment in the organization. When he came back the second time, he set himself in
a direction where he would eventually commit an even greater
sin, but one that was sanctioned by the Nation of Islam.

Ben and Leon first approached Talmadge not in the mosque,
but on the street in downtown Paterson, New Jersey. The two
conspirators drove up to Hayer in their car, then invited Hayer
to get in and have a talk with them. The three of them drove
around for a while, with Ben and Leon carefully probing Hay-

er's attitude toward Malcolm X. For security reasons, Ben and Leon had to know whether other Muslims would agree with a plan to kill Malcolm X before they revealed that they had actually created a plan to assassinate him. According to Hayer,

> That first conversation was more or less around my feelings in regard to [the struggle between Malcolm X and Elijah Muhammad]. Nothing direct at first—just general conversation as to how did I feel about it. And then it was realized that my feelings was pretty much the same as theirs—you know, like the Messenger was being slandered, man. And this has to stop.

So Hayer became the third member of the secret plot to kill Malcolm X. "I had a lot of love and admiration for the Honorable Elijah Muhammad, and I just felt that like this is something that I have to stand up for. This is what I believe," he said. "So that led to me getting involved to the extent that—you know, I would go all the way." Hayer was easily convinced that Malcolm X and his followers needed to be taught a lesson. After all, he had already followed his conscience once and ended up beating a brother in the mosque for going against the ways of Elijah Muhammad. There was no reason for Ben and Leon to believe that he would not do it again to someone whose sins were far greater: Malcolm X. "I was just the type of person that if I had to stand up for what I believe, I would do it, man, y'know?" Hayer said. "And maybe I was manipulated. Maybe I was a pawn. I don't know. I didn't see it that way at the time. I just believed, and that was my motivation."

Ben, Leon, and Talmadge then found two more Muslims fervent enough in their beliefs that they would kill Malcolm X to save the reputation of Elijah Muhammad. Willie X and Wilbur also readily joined the group, and the five of them began to plan the logistics of the assassination. At the time of the planning, tensions between Malcolm X and Elijah Muhammad were at an all-time high, with verbal assaults careening back and forth between New York and Chicago. Malcolm X and his former Muslim colleagues had recently confronted each other in a small

New York City courtroom as the eviction proceedings against Malcolm X got underway. Although Malcolm X still lived in the brick house that the Muslims had provided for him for the duration of the time that he was minister of the New York mosque, he still tried to fight the losing battle of convincing a judge that the house was actually his even though it had the Nation of Islam's name on the deed.

With anger piqued, the five conspirators set about their business, enthusiastically discussing the optimum method and time for killing Malcolm X. Time was of the essence, since Malcolm X's sins against the Messenger were increasing by the day, and no one was certain exactly what inner secrets the Muslim held. He had already dipped into the secret of Muhammad's adultery with a number of secretaries, by whom he fathered more children than he had in his already large legitimate family. Although the charge of adultery apparently did little to turn the tide against the Messenger, Malcolm X also held a number of even juicier secrets that he learned while serving as Muhammad's chief aide. If he chose to expose these secrets, the damage could have been extensive, or so the Muslims reasoned. Besides, there was always the threat that Malcolm X would be able to destroy the Nation of Islam by out-recruiting them, stealing their potential converts and bringing them into his Organization for Afro-American Unity.

So the five men continued to discuss plans to remove the dagger that they saw pointing at the heart of the Nation of Islam. They met in various places, generally either at Ben's or Leon's house. At other times, they simply drove around Paterson, discussing their plans as they went. But almost as soon as they began laying down their strategy, Malcolm X left the country for Africa, and the controversy began to simmer down. He left New York in the early part of July and did not return for more than 18 weeks. In his absence, the controversy subsided somewhat, and the talk of his death similarly disappeared. "Around the time that he left the country, it seems to have been a cooling-off period, if I recall correctly," Hayer explained. "Nothing was happening. So I thought that maybe things were going to get better, man."

But despite Hayer's hopes, this was not the case. When Malcolm X returned to the United States on November 24, 1964, the controversy returned to its previous level. So, too, did the desire to see Malcolm X killed. Just before he flew back from Africa, Malcolm X once again became the target of scathing editorials in *Muhammad Speaks,* one of which was written by Boston Minister Louis X (later known as Louis Farrakhan). Brother Louis challenged his former mentor to return to New York and "face the music" and warned Malcolm X that he would meet his doom if he returned. "And then everything started hitting the fan again," Hayer recalled. "So we got together. Said, 'Alright, we're moving.' "

The first order of business for the assassins was determining how they would kill their prey. The first instinct was to try to get to him when he was in a vulnerable position in his own home. Not only would this accomplish their goal, it would also send a message about the power of the Muslims. They would kill Malcolm X in his own territory, in his own house, a clear message to future traitors to the Muslim movement. So the five men piled in the car and made their secret pilgrimage to Malcolm X's house. "We went out to wherever he lived at, y'know?" Hayer explained. "But he was very heavily guarded, and we came back." Malcolm X and his lieutenants had long anticipated that the Muslims would try to murder him in his home. To hinder such an attempt, armed guards kept an eye on the house, with others periodically driving by to make sure that all was well. Clearly, the Muslims would have to find another location for the assassination.

But most of the conspirators had little time for following Malcolm X around New York, charting his schedule and looking for the optimal assassination site. "We were all working, far as I know," Hayer said. "I know I was. I couldn't just run around New York and ride around, man, y'know. I got a wife and a family." So the five assassins got together and decided that there was only one place other than his home that they knew that Malcolm X would repeatedly visit: the Audubon Ballroom. It was here that Malcolm X held many of his meetings, where his rallies for his Organization for Afro-American Unity were generally held, where five unknown assassins would have a good chance of slipping into a crowd and getting close to the "chief hypocrite" of the Nation of Islam. So it was decided as simply as that. The Audubon Ballroom would serve as the backdrop for the assassination of a major figure in the African-American struggle for freedom.

The five men then went about the process of setting up the assassination. They first went to a meeting of the OAAU in the Audubon to check for security. None of them held any weapons, just in case the guests were being searched. After this first meeting, the site was finalized, and the five men decided that the Audubon would be perfect. The Audubon had two major advantages other than the lack of security precautions. First, the large crowd that was expected would allow for enough confusion so that the assassins would be able to slip into the background easily and escape undetected. They could simply pretend they were ordinary audience members after the killing and run out in fear with the rest of the mob. Second, the murder of Malcolm X in front of his supporters and security guards would send the same message that a murder in his house would send. The Audubon was his own territory, and the demonstration of his vulnerability would serve as the ultimate embarrassment in front of his supporters.

The next step was to line up the guns for the assassination. This job fell to Talmadge Hayer, who had some knowledge of the gun market on the streets of Paterson. "I could get my hands on something that was available," he said. He soon lined up three weapons—the Luger, the .45 automatic, and the shotgun—and distributed them to his fellow plotters. He got them from one of the gunrunners he knew on the street, and paid for the guns out of his own pocket. "Nobody gave me money. Any money that I laid off was really money that I was making off my job. If I had to spend it, I would spend it." Hayer also assembled the smoke bomb that was used to create a disturbance. Actually, the bomb consisted primarily of flammable film rolled up in a sock, but it served its purpose: it turned people's attention away from the center of the action and allowed four of the five conspirators to get away.

On Saturday night, February 20, 1965, as Malcolm X slept in his twelfth-floor room at the New York Hilton Hotel, his assassins again set out to the Audubon, where a dance was scheduled to take place. After the dance, they felt confident that the assassination would be successful. "At that point there, it was already out that there was going to be a meeting [of the OAAU at the Audubon] the next day," Hayer said. "So then it was only a matter of following then what we had planned to do." The five men all went to sleep after the dance in their respective homes, then reassembled the next morning at Ben's house, where the decision was made to go ahead that day with the killing. "We got a strategy together—decided what we were going to do," Hayer said. "Who was going to do what. And that's pretty much how we came to the decision of what would happen from that point on." The plan was finalized, the role of each man determined, and the five assassins set out for New York.

Like many of the others who were present at the assassination, Hayer also reported a lack of police officers present at the Audubon that cold winter day, given the immediate threat against Malcolm X's life. "I don't recall seeing any [police]," Hayer said. This also worked perfectly into the hands of the assassins. While there supposedly was an entire detail of police officers across the street at the Columbia Presbyterian Medical Center, at that distance they could not have interfered with the plans of the five Muslims. With a lack of police, another enormous hurdle had been avoided by the assassins. Now, sitting in their assigned places inside the Audubon Ballroom, all they had to do was wait for their victim.

With the .45 automatic pistol nestled inside his belt, Hayer sat quietly and thought about the crime that he was about to commit. "I didn't know what to expect [at the Audubon]," he admitted. "You know. I didn't come with any expectations about this, that or the other thing. I didn't know what to expect. This was it, man." Hayer had a certain amount of fear as he sat there and waited for the event that would define the rest of his life. But the fear was overcome with a sense that he was doing what he thought was right. He was striking a blow for justice and carrying out the will of Allah and His Messenger Elijah Muhammad. "I don't want to sound like any kind of hero," Hayer said, "because in my life—I've been through some changes with this whole thing, y'know? I don't know. You just do what you have to do, and that's all I can say, man. You know. And that's what I did. I won't say that I wasn't afraid. I don't talk in terms of that type of thing, or sound that way."

So the five men nervously waited. A sizable crowd of about 400 finally arrived and took their seats for the beginning of the program. Benjamin Goodman led off the show, giving a thirty-minute speech designed to prime the crowd for Malcolm X's entrance. For the assassins, everything went almost exactly as planned. Malcolm X strode to the podium, and was barely given the opportunity to begin when Wilbur X jumped up from his seat in the back of the auditorium, screaming, "Man, get your hands out of my pocket." Taking his cue, Willie X quickly stood up in the second row, unnoticed by the audience whose attention had been diverted by the disturbance in the back. As the guards moved from Malcolm X's side, and as Malcolm X stepped out from behind the plywood rostrum, Brother Willie opened his overcoat, produced his shotgun, aimed, and fired. Hayer and Brother Leon followed suit, pulling out their pistols and firing away at Malcolm X's lifeless body.

As Hayer's smoke bomb erupted in the back of the audito-rium, the five men turned to flee. Wilbur and Ben, neither of whom took part in the shooting, easily slipped into the crowd and disappeared. Willie rid himself of the shotgun; then he and Leon also turned and fled. Only Talmadge Hayer, still holding his .45 automatic, failed to slip out the door unnoticed by the rest of the mob. "There was a lot of commotion and stuff. . . . I remember though—there was quite a few guns in that place being fired. I didn't even know I got shot in the left leg. Even to today I think I got shot in my right. Because there was this guy shooting at my right side. I didn't see how I got shot in my left side." As he ran, he tried desperately to clear the way for himself, but the more he tried, the more he pulled attention to himself. "I was just trying to make a commotion, man," he said. "I fired off a couple of shots."

Hayer said he didn't know if his friends got out of the ballroom safely. "There was one person, he was running in front of me. I think it was Leon," he said. "He came out before I did. Because I was shot in my leg so I couldn't move fast. I was only trying to get outside. He was the only one I could say [that] went out before I did. Other people I couldn't see. They must have been after me.

> There was one guy I think he said I shot in the foot or something like this here. For the most part, I was just trying to get out. And I was hit in the leg. I didn't see the guy that shot me, you know. So I just hopped, man. I was hopping with one leg, and I slid down the banister, fell on the ground and—I don't know. And don't ask me why and how—there was an officer out there. And it was fortunate, because my life was spared.

Hayer was immediately taken to the hospital, then to the police station for booking. In custody for the assassination of Malcolm X, Hayer was destined to spend more than twenty years in the New York prison system. In his mind, he had dutifully served his ultimate leader, Elijah Muhammad, but he could never reveal his inner motivations. To admit that he had assassinated Malcolm X to protect the Nation of Islam, he would have admitted the culpability of the Nation and its leader, the Messenger of Allah. To one whose entire life centered around the philosophy of the Muslims, this would be unforgivable. So he hid his knowledge of the assassination, at first claiming that he was merely an innocent bystander who was mistaken for the actual assassin. In so doing, he saved the Nation of Islam from blame and forced the world to wonder why Malcolm X had been killed.

"She was the spitting image of Malcolm. You could see some of Malcolm's spirit in her eyes, and her face would light up with Malcolm's wide smile," recalls Benjamin Karim, writing about the birth of Malcolm's first daughter and about her bloodlines. "Malcolm's mother had been born of miscegenation," he notes farther on, "her mother having been raped by a white slave owner. Malcolm bore his mother's color in his light skin and reddish hair and maybe, too, in the gray shadows of his eyes. He said sometimes he hated it. He hated the oppressor's whiteness of it. Malcolm wanted his skin to be the same color as his soul. Pure black.

"I've known no one more purely or more proudly black than Malcolm. He taught that pride to us all. Pride was what he was teaching us in his lectures on self-discipline and self-respect as well as in his personal example of continual self-improvement. Pride lay in discovering our capabilities and extending them. . . . It lay in obeying the law, in properly knotting a tie, in arriving on time. Pride brought real hope to the birth of a child. Our pride was black, and with Malcolm we learned to find it both in ourselves and in each other."

In The New Yorker *(October 12, 1992), reporter-at-Large and writer Marshall Frady also reflected on the life and career of Malcolm X, on the legend he became and the legacy he left behind.*

"The Children of Malcolm"
by Marshall Frady

"Do you know *why* the white man really hates you?" Malcolm X would ask his black congregations in the nineteen-sixties. "It's because every time he sees your face he sees a mirror of his crime—and his guilty conscience can't bear to face it." In the midst of what seemed the high moral adventure of Martin Luther King, Jr.,'s nonviolent civil-rights campaigns, Malcolm appeared as some marginal shadow-figure of wrath, always paralleling King's progress. A ghetto street hustler turned grimly austere evangelist for a racial subsect of Islam known as the Black Muslims, he became one of those unnerving black figures who periodically rise up before the eyes of white society as an image of its own systematic dehumanization, at once a casualty of and a judgment upon America's racism. In ghostly black-and-white news footage from that time, he can be glimpsed at street rallies of inner-city blacks—a long, lank, sober-suited figure, hatted and bespectacled—excoriating the white man in a level, measured tone with rapid licks of scorn: "We don't want to have anything to do with any race of dogs." Spearing his forefinger in the air, he cries, "Two-legged white dogs sicking four-legged dogs on your and my mother!"

Twenty-seven years after his sudden death, in a bedlam of gunfire in a Harlem auditorium, his presence still hangs palpably among us. It's not merely in the speckling of "X"'s on caps

273

and T-shirts which one now sees everywhere (even on Bill Clinton's jogging cap)—a ubiquitous pop rash that has anticipated the film biography by Spike Lee. In this cinematic Second Coming, Malcolm promises finally to pass, in one form at least, into the mythology of America. Of course, such theatrical reconstructions, like "JFK" and "Mississippi Burning," can work their own polemically simplistic vandalisms on the past, coarsening the collective memory from which our understanding of our own times is formed.

Beyond his ascension into the pop firmament, though, Malcolm abides among us in a far more elemental sense. From the turbulent black awakening of the sixties, two lines of descent—two temperaments, two potentials—have contended for the spirit of black Americans: a tension between the children of Martin and the children of Malcolm. Though King's perspective was far more radical than the eventual sentimentalism about him would lead one to suppose, it was suggested even in his day that his vision—of a transcendent, nonviolent struggle of moral confrontation that would shame a racist and essentially barbarous society into redemption—could never be more than a dream. But if it could be said that King's vision expected too much of the species, Malcolm's seemed a vision of humankind's nature reduced to the basest, most minimal terms of anger and retribution for abuse. Malcolm proclaimed to his black audiences that only fools "could love someone who had treated them as the white man has treated you." He demonized the abuser as a "blue-eyed white devil," genetically beyond any moral appeal, who would never consent to admit blacks into his company and was unworthy of such ambitions anyway—a predator who could properly be handled only with contempt and threat.

To no small degree, Martin and Malcolm were projections of two separate black cultures. King, the son of an eminent minister, had grown up in the comfortable insulation of Atlanta's black gentility—part of that black establishment eager to join in a civil-rights coalition with the nation's white liberal community. Malcolm, on the other hand, arose from the lowest reaches of the black urban underclass. In "The Autobiography of Malcolm X,'' narrated shortly before his death to Alex Haley, Malcolm acknowledged, "I know nothing about the South. I am a creation of the Northern white man and of his hypocritical attitude toward the Negro"—an attitude closer, actually, to that of the nation as a whole.

It is now clear that Malcolm was in communion with submerged heats of anger far more widespread in the black community than most whites ever suspected. Peter Goldman, in his discerning 1973 biography, "The Death and Life of Malcolm X," reports that when he was a newspaperman in St. Louis in the early sixties "a bewildered cop told me that even the hookers and boosters were calling him a blue-eyed devil and would only talk to his black partner." Concurrent with King's nonviolent campaigns in the South was the emergence around the country of such guerrilla militants as the Black Panthers and radical young activists like Stokely Carmichael and H. Rap Brown, with their cries for "black power!" What disturbed some observers about this new phase of the movement was a contraction of its moral terms to a bitter cynicism that saw the human lot as one of hopeless racial alienation. I was covering the civil-rights movement in the South then, and one summer night in Greenwood, Mississippi, as King was conducting a mass meeting of fifteen hundred blacks in a local church, I sensed Malcolm's effect even there. King's voice pealed over the gathering, "We have a power that's greater than all the guns in Mississippi, greater than all the bombs and armies of the world—we have the power of our *souls!*" From several young partisans of the Student Nonviolent Coordinating Committee scattered around the back of the church, there arose a counterpoint of derisive hoots: "Oh, de *Lawd!* De *Lawd,* now!"

If, all these years later, the tensions between the visions of Martin and Malcolm have endured in the black community, it can sometimes appear that Malcolm's flat, blank anger has carried the day—and not merely in a certain style of attitude, as evidenced by the swagger and bluster of many rap artists. How Malcolm's presence far more deeply lingers among us was illuminated by the recent upheavals in Los Angeles, after the acquittal of the policemen tried for the beating of Rodney King.

But if the lasting racial alienations in America would seem to put King's high moral proposition in doubt, the irony is that at the time Malcolm was slain he had begun to move away from the fierce, implacable persona to which his mystique and his children have now fastened. He had broken with the Black Muslims, and in the last year of his life he had been venturing, however tentatively and unevenly, beyond the insular racial delirium of their doctrine and was approaching a more open and conciliatory vision—a vision closer, if still only in certain nuances, to King's own. James H. Cone, in his recent book "Martin & Malcolm & America," writes that "they *complemented* and *corrected* each other." Malcolm, in fact, was killed in the midst of a kind of metamorphosis. Just three days before his death, he confessed to a reporter, "I'm man enough to tell you that I can't put my finger on exactly what my philosophy is now." Charles Kenyatta, one of his followers at the time, recently told me, "All this hype now, they're trying to give the false image that Malcolm had come to be the Saviour of black people. But he didn't know himself who he was." In the end, he was groping, alone, for some different purpose, some different self-definition. Indeed, at no point in his life could Malcolm cease struggling, as if by dim but resistless instinct, for more light.

As Malcolm tells it in the "Autobiography," he was born into rage and despair, in the spring of 1925, in Omaha. His mother, Louise Little, was from Grenada—a lithe, erect woman of somewhat finely strung nerves, whose own mother, Malcolm claimed, had been raped by a white man, and who was herself pale enough to be taken for white. His father, by contrast, was an oil-black roisterous colossus of a man, named Earl Little— a one-eyed construction laborer and part-time Baptist preacher from Reynolds, Georgia, who had struck out on his own after finishing either the third or the fourth grade. A brooding, disappointed man, full of turbulence, he had become a discipline of Marcus Garvey, who, in flamboyant plumed uniforms with gold braid, was Harlem's aspiring black-nationalist Moses in the early years of the century. Garvey was imprisoned for mail fraud the year Malcolm was born.

From prison, Garvey had promised his believers, "I shall come back to you. . . . Look for me in the whirlwind or the storm, look for me all around you." Earl took young Malcolm to fevered meetings of Garvey's faithful, where such messages were regularly invoked. Because of Earl's devotion to Garvey, according to a somewhat melodramatic account of Malcolm's, Klan night riders with torches swept down on the family's house in Omaha shortly before he was born. Certainly, as Malcolm later liked to cast it, white harassment had pursued Earl Little in his migratory struggle to scrap out a living for his family; he moved them briefly to Milwaukee, then to Lansing, Michigan, where their home was burned—by white racists, Malcolm would claim. Earl Little finally moved his family to a rural plot two miles out of East Lansing.

There, in a drab and wintry countryside, in a tar-shingle house of only four rooms, each with a single naked light bulb dangling over a rugless board floor, Malcolm passed his boy-hood—a shabby and cheerless one, utterly unlike King's. His autobiography contains almost no mention of holidays like Christmas and Thanksgiving. His father ruled the family with frequent beatings, exempting only Malcolm, the fourth of seven children. Earl was particularly infuriated by his wife's scruples about diet: she disdained pork and rabbit. Once, Malcolm related to Haley, his father took a rabbit from the pen outside and ripped its head off with "one twist of his big black hands," then flung the body at his wife's feet, ordering her to cook it, and stormed out of the house. It was the last time any of them saw him alive. Late that night, police brought word that he had been found, mangled and dying, beside some streetcar tracks, where he had apparently fallen under the wheels. Malcolm was then six years old. He later insisted that his father's death had also been the work of white racist vigilantes.

If Earl was gentler with Malcolm than with his other children, Malcolm surmised in his autobiography, it was because "he was subconsciously so afflicted with the white man's brain-washing of Negroes that he inclined to favor the light ones, and

I was his lightest child." Of a brassy hue—"bright," it was sometimes called—he seemed tortured by the whiteness in him. He later told his followers, of the man he claimed had raped his mother's mother, "Yes, that raping, redheaded devil was my *grandfather!* That close, yes! My *mother's* father! ... If I could drain away *his* blood that pollutes *my* body, and pollutes *my* complexion, I'd do it! Because I hate every drop of the rapist's blood that's in me." There were moments, Malcolm said, when that most intimate of helpless outrages to his person left him "so choked up" that he would stalk the streets, solitary, late into the night.

After his father's death, his mother struggled on in a Depression poverty so stark that sometimes she had nothing to feed her family except stale surplus bread and boiled dandelion greens, and the children would be "dizzy" with hunger. Malcolm, at school, would huddle off by himself to eat a wild-leek sandwich. Before long, the remnants of the family began to disintegrate. "Some kind of psychological deterioration began to eat away our pride," Malcolm later said. At the age of nine, he began pilfering from stores in town. And his mother, sitting alone in a rocking chair chattering to herself with all window shades drawn, began to drift into insanity. The Christmas of Malcolm's thirteenth year, according to Bruce Perry's "Malcolm," a formidably researched biography that appeared in 1991, his mother was found wandering barefoot along a snow-dappled road, dirty and unkempt and clutching a baby, her eighth, this one illegitimate. Shortly afterward, she was delivered into a state mental hospital. Her children were scattered about as wards of the state, and Malcolm was briefly in a detention home.

Such hurt does not readily permit the inward grace for any sort of transcendent understanding like King's. Its only gift is, perhaps, a certain icy unsentimentality, a terrible bleak clarity of consciousness. At any rate, Malcolm never forgave white society for what had happened to him. By that time, he had reached the seventh grade, and was a tall, gawky youth, preternaturally bright and quick, but he was resentful even of being elected class president by his white fellow-students: as he told

Haley, "I was unique in my class, like a pink poodle." Not unaware that he held a special promise, he speculated to his English teacher that he might like to become a lawyer; the teacher advised him, amiably. "You've got to be realistic about being a nigger. . . . Why don't you plan on carpentry?" Withdrawing into a sullen and wordless isolation, he dropped out of school after finishing eighth grade and went to live with a half sister in Boston's Roxbury section.

There he swiftly moved into a night world of black bars and pool halls and dance halls, where, he recounted in his autobiography, "I met chicks who were fine as May wine, and cats who were hip to all happenings." He conked his hair to a sleek russet straightness with a scalp-scorching compound of lye, eggs, potatoes, Vaseline, and soap, and arrayed himself in billowy zoot suits of Crayola colors, with a long gold chain looped at the waist, a rakish wide-brimmed hat, orange bulb-toed shoes, and a pint flask in his inside coat pocket. He became something of a sensation on the ballroom floors for his abandon in dancing the Lindy. Before long, he was peddling dope, shooting craps, playing the numbers. After a time, he began keeping conspicuous company with a blond white woman, who regularly made expeditions to Roxbury's dance halls. He was then still in his mid-teens.

He managed to get a job as an attendant on Pullman trains between Boston and New York, and wound up staying in Harlem, which was, he remembered in his autobiography, "like some technicolor bazaar. . . . This world was where I belonged." There, as he recounted it, he became one of the snazziest of hustlers. He was called Red, or sometimes, because he came from Michigan, Detroit Red. Running numbers, steering men to prostitutes, selling dope, using dope. He carried automatics now, which he would flourish in random stickups.

Before long, sensing that the police and, more important, a gambling enforcer were closing in on him in Harlem, he returned to Boston, and set up a small burglary ring, enlisting the white woman there whom he was still dating, and her sister, to scout promising residences from their base, a rented apartment in Harvard Square. "Sometimes the victims were in their bed asleep," the "Autobiography" tells us. "In stockinged feet, we'd go right into the bedrooms. Moving swiftly, like shadows, we would lift clothes, watches, wallets, handbags, and jewelry boxes." It was as if he were exacting from all white society his own form of reparations. But a certain lunging recklessness had set in to his operations by now. It was only a matter of time before he was apprehended. And in February of 1946 he began serving an eight-to-ten-year sentence for burglary. He was not quite twenty-one.

Confined in Charlestown's Dickensian prison, whose closet-size cells had no plumbing, he kept himself in a constant rage, he told Haley, coming to be called Satan by his fellow-inmates, and spent much of his time pacing "like a caged leopard," railing aloud to himself. He had, he later reflected, "sunk to the very bottom of the American white man's society." And it was there that the Nation of Islam found him.

It came through the intercession of Malcolm's brothers and one of his sisters, who, in visits and letters to him in prison, told him they had converted to a faith they called the "natural religion for the black man." Its creed was that the white man was, quite literally, the devil—a pale, blue-eyed race genetically predisposed to a systematic devastation of "every race of man not white." It was an illumination that Malcolm compared to that of Paul on the road to Damascus—a blazing revelation that it was whites who had visited on him all the mortifications and torments of his past. He was so overcome by this discovery that, he recounted in the "Autobiography," he resolved to spend the rest of his life informing white people about their true natures, and he began by scrawling letters to the mayor of Boston, the governor of Massachusetts, and President Truman.

In that enterprise, he came to realize that he had lost to the streets what little schooling he'd had: "I didn't know a verb from a house." He began studying ferociously, copying out with a pencil on a blue-lined school writing tablet every word in the prison dictionary. He had taken a correspondence course in English, even one in Latin. In his cell at night, in the glow of the corridor light, he read digests of world history by H. G.

Wells and Will Durant. He read commentaries on Herodotus and Socrates, and he read Schopenhauer, Kant, and Nietzsche, volumes on linguistics and etymology. He later told Haley, "I didn't know what I was doing, but just by instinct I liked books with intellectual vitamins." In this prodigious exertion, he acquired the con's kind of enormous but eclectic, unproportioned learning.

This isometric amassment of scholarship was marked, particularly in its racial obsession, by odd gaps. In later life, he informed his audiences that blacks had been mistaken about their true enemies ever since they were brought captive to Jamestown "in the year 1555." In a 1958 newspaper article (included in Clayborne Carson's "Malcolm X: The FBI File"), he referred to "this Jesus who preached in Palestine, which is on the Arabian Peninsula." He once explained to Haley that Homer was among the Moors—"Homer and Omar and *Moor,* you see, are related terms"—who had been abducted from Africa by Europeans, blinded so they couldn't return, and forced to "sing about the Europeans' glorious accomplishments." He argued that Shakespeare's plays were written by King James I, the same King James "who poetically 'fixed' the Bible—which in itself and its present King James version has enslaved the world."

All this came to be mixed in with the Nation of Islam's racial theological history, which Malcolm earnestly subscribed to until almost the last year of his life. It was a kind of intellectual "Fantasia" that rivalled, in its fabulous loopiness, the racial anthropology of "Mein Kampf." Original humankind was black, appearing about seventy trillion years ago. A sublime civilization, which founded the city of Mecca, and even exercised dominion over Mars, it was presided over by twenty-four wizards, or "wise scientists," who created the animals and made the mountains, and even "deported" the moon from the earth. One of the wizards, a malcontent named Mr. Yacub, born about sixty-six hundred years ago and known as the "big-head scientist," because he had an oversized cranium, learned how to breed races scientifically. When, for his seditious agitation, he was exiled from Mecca to the Isle of Patmos—later famed for the Book of Revelation—he contrived as revenge, Malcolm explained, a means of creating a "bleached-out white race of devils." Mr. Yacub knew that black men contained two germs, black and brown, the lighter being the weaker. Through an eight-hundred-year process of genocidal culling—by means of needles inserted into the brains of unsuitably darker infants— that progressed from the black race to a brown, a red, and then a yellow race, the project at last produced a blond, pale-skinned, blue-eyed devil race, which wound up in the caves of Europe. In time, Malcolm reported. Moses was chosen by Allah to "civilize" these devils, the first with whom he succeeded being the Jews. But all the pallid devil race eventually gained ascendancy, through "tricknology," and finally seized into slavery a portion of the Original People, the tribe of Shabazz, who had been led into Africa fifty thousand years earlier to harden and toughen them for their predestined ordeal.

This entire historical panorama had been disclosed, in Detroit, in 1931, to the future Messenger of the Lost-Found Nation of Islam in the Wilderness of North America, Elijah Muhammad— then still Robert Poole, a slight young migrant from rural Georgia, with only a fourth-grade schooling. The source of the revelation was an enigmatic figure known as Mr. Fard, a small, beige man who was a peddler of silks and yard goods. Mr. Fard, whose real name, according to Bruce Perry, was Wallace Dodd Ford, described himself generally as a "brother" from the East, but at one point he confided to Robert Poole that he was "the Mahdi." In any case, after setting up the new Islamic sect in Detroit, he mysteriously disappeared. Some adherents believed he had returned to Mecca; others suspected he had been disposed of by the disciple into whose hands leadership of his little religion fell: Robert Poole, now calling himself Elijah Muhammad.

In 1952, after serving about six and a half years of his sentence, Malcolm was released on parole. He emerged from prison with his hair shorn close to his skull, in the Muslim fashion, and with only a ten-dollar suit; on his first day of freedom, he bought a new pair of eye-glasses, a wristwatch, and a suitcase.

He passed more or less directly from prison into the community of the Nation of Islam, which must have seemed to him, after the ferocities of his life up to that point, like arriving in a paradise of calm and order.

Its leader might have appeared, at first glance, a somewhat improbable mighty messenger of Allah. An elfin man of a delicate amber hue—a fragile bronchial asthmatic—Elijah had a peculiar daintiness of manner, with prim tightenings of the mouth, and he was usually dressed in a dull black suit with a black rubber-shiny bow tie and, on his head, a pillbox cap twinkling with a scimitar moon and radiant orbs and stars. But behind his wistful little demure smiles there lurked an unmistakable wiliness, and a cool deadliness of purpose: he reigned, after all, as the source and center of the Muslims' radio-active field of racial menace. Nevertheless, his message of a black Islamic elect of righteousness had effected wonders of regeneration among numerous souls lost, like Malcolm, in the spiritual desolation of America's ghettos. For his part, Malcolm would insist up to his end that he "believed in Mr. Muhammad more than [Mr. Muhammad] believed in himself." His slave name of Little was now replaced by a symbol for his long-lost and unknown African family name: he became Malcolm X.

Owing to his own rapt, consuming intensity, Malcolm was soon inducted into the Muslim ministry, and he was ultimately anointed by Elijah Muhammad to serve as a kind of peripatetic national missionary for the Muslims. Under his unflagging evangelism, the Nation of Islam swiftly expanded from a baroque and tiny variant of Islam, confined to about four hundred faithful who gathered mostly in storefront mosques, into, by 1960, a truly national congregation, of perhaps ten thousand registered followers, with some forty temples and missions spread across the country and a network of more than thirty radio stations. It formed a separate interior culture, with its own school system, its own economic complex of shops and service businesses, and its own religious militia of solemn, dark-suited centurion guards, called the Fruit of Islam.

In Harlem alone, where Malcolm now presided over the Nation's major mosque, he was addressing street rallies of fifteen

thousand for up to four hours. One of his converts from the
early years, Benjamin Karim, recalls, "He held me spellbound.
Listening to him, I began to understand how empty I was. And
he put in me, in place of that emptiness, knowledge. And out
of that came self-discovery, and pride." Malcolm moved ebul-
liently along Harlem's teeming sidewalks, a rangily tall, over-
coated figure, talking with everybody—one of Harlem's own
now returned, purged, to prophesy to his people. There was,
indeed, with his glinting eyeglasses, a certain priestly quality
about him. He lived modestly, in a succession of residences in
Queens (they were provided him by the Muslims), drove a blue
Oldsmobile, and dressed in staid funeral-director suits, with a
tie clip of a leaping sailfish, and unfailingly polished plain black
shoes. He was scrupulously—almost fanatically—punctual, and
ceaselessly entered notations with a red ballpoint pen in a red
pocket notepad. He had about him a tightly machined self-
containment. His only betrayal of excitement or anger, at some
moment of confrontation, was a rosy tinge rising, under his
brassy hue, from neck to face. "I was with him for seven or
eight years," Karim, who became one of Malcolm's assistant
ministers, told me. "I was as close as anybody could get to
him without burning up. But it was impossible to really know
him. Nobody could really get close to him." When one of
Malcolm's brothers—the very one who had first introduced him
to Islam in prison—later defected from the faith and then
lapsed, like his mother, into insanity, Malcolm commented, with
a strangely chill detachment, that "it was meant, for Reginald
to be used for one purpose only: as a bait, as a minnow to
reach into the ocean of blackness where I was, to save me."

Indeed, he could take on at times the grimness of a
Torquemada. He fervently observed the Muslim strictures
against not only the common carnal vagaries like fornication
but also dating, dancing, smoking, drinking, movies, gambling,
sports, and eating more than one meal a day. He usually slept
just four hours a night. About the only indulgences he allowed
himself were coffee and, late at night, tea. He permitted himself
to watch only newscasts on television. There was a fastidious
priggishness about him. He abstained from profanity and also

from slang, once reproving Alex Haley for referring to children as "kids": "Kids are *goats!*"

He was yet more forbidding when it came to the daughters of Eve. "All women, by their nature, are fragile and weak: they are attracted to the male in whom they see strength," he declared in the "Autobiography." Moreover, "you never can fully trust any woman. . . . Whatever else a woman is, I don't care who the woman is, it starts with her being vain." Karim remembers that Malcolm would admonish women about how to dress, telling them, "If you walking down the street with a piece of fresh meat in your hand, you can't blame a dog for snatching the meat. If you exposing meat, you either selling it or giving it away." At the same time, though, he would assure the women in his audiences that "the black man never will get anybody's respect until he first learns . . . to shelter and protect and *respect* his black women!"

For that matter, Malcolm kept himself an ascetic bachelor until, in 1956, he began to notice in the congregation at his mosque in Harlem a tall, dark-brown young woman named Betty Sanders. Born in Detroit, she had been an education major at Tuskegee Institute, in Alabama, and was now studying nursing at a New York hospital. She had not yet converted to Islam, but what struck her about Malcolm, she told me recently, was "his intensity." She said, "I thought, You can't play with this guy—he's serious." He also had what she calls "a high civility," and, she recalls. "When he used this high civility, a lot of girls took it to mean that he was interested in them. I was not going to be one of those fickle-hearted little females." She carefully maintained a sober tone in their first encounters, at a nearby restaurant. "However, there came a time when I thought"—and there she gave a girlish flip at the back of her hair with her hand—"I was *on*to something." When she indicated that she might do a lot of partying after graduating from nursing school, Malcolm reacted with an instant, visible alarm. When she eventually introduced him to her parents, who were Methodists, he struck them as "a marvellous young man—clean-cut, and he *knows* so much," but when she asked them if they would like him as a son-in-law "it was a little different," she says. In fact, they were horrified by the possibility that he might take her, their only child, away from them forever into the mysterious and alien world of the Muslims. Just over a year later; after Betty's conversion, and in accordance with a carefully and gravely deliberated arrangement sanctioned by Mr. Muhammad, they were married. Malcolm was then thirty-two. Betty's parents became estranged from her, and reconciled themselves to Malcolm only after she began bearing his children. "They finally accepted his 'difference,' " she says.

But marriage hardly mellowed the fury of Malcolm's obsessive pentecostalisms against America's devil rule: that mission had become the total meaning of his life. According to F.B.I. files, he declared, with an air of celebration, "We, the black men of the world, created the white man and we will also kill him. . . . Only in this way can there be peace on the earth." He named his first daughter Attilah, he later explained, for the Hun who "sacked Rome."

With the narrowed stare of his eyes giving Malcolm himself a vaguely Tatar aspect, he took on, for many whites, a sulfurous malevolence. Indeed, it does no service, either to the reality of Malcolm or to history, to try to moderate in memory the racial vituperativeness of his oratory then. "We don't want to integrate with that ole pale thing!" he would cry to black audiences, light flashing blankly off his glasses. "The dog is their closest relative. They got the same kind of hair, the same kind of skin, and the same kind of *smell*. Oh, *yeaaah!*"

It was a racial invective that was only an inverse, in fact, of that to be heard whinnying from the flatbed loudspeakers at any cow-pasture Klan rally of the time. Malcolm insisted this was only reflexive to four hundred years of white racism, but it captured him in the same cramped, black mentality, which placed a racial construction on all life. Malcolm readily professed that he shared the Southern whites' aversion to integration, as a sure prelude to miscegenation. As he declared, integrationists "want your wife and your daughter and your sister and—and your *mother*."

It is not, then, quite so bizarre as it might first seem that one night in 1961 Malcolm held a clandestine meeting with Klan chieftains in Atlanta, to solicit their support for the Muslim ambition to establish a separate country within the United States. He told the assembled Klansmen that the Muslims were as deeply committed to segregation as they were, and, according to an F.B.I. report, assured them that "the Jew is behind the integration movement, using the Negro as a tool."

Two years earlier, he had pronounced the Jews, "one of the worst of the devils," claiming, "He does more to take advantage of the so-called black people than any other and yet poses as being a friend." He averred at one rally, Peter Goldman reports, that "everybody talks about the six million Jews. But I was reading a book the other day that showed that one hundred million of us were kidnapped and brought to this country— *one hundred million.* Now everybody's wet-eyed over a handful of Jews who brought it on themselves."

In general, his fulminations seemed to carry an unappeasable malignance, which impossibly outraged white sensibilities. He declared that because of the genetically determined iniquity of all whites, in any race war it would be imperative to slay even their children. In 1962, not long after seven unarmed Muslims were shot, one of them fatally, in an altercation with the Los Angeles police, it happened that at Orly Airport, near Paris, a chartered jet bearing many of Atlanta's cultural élite crashed during takeoff. "I would like to announce a very beautiful thing that has happened," Malcolm told a Muslim rally in Los Angeles, according to the F.B.I. "As you know, we have been praying to Allah. . . . And I got a wire from God today." Allah "really had answered our prayers . . . in one whop," he went on. "He dropped an airplane out of the sky with over one hundred and twenty white people on it." And "we will continue to pray and we hope that every day another plane falls out of the sky." He could be just as pitiless about the deaths of white civil-rights workers. Goldman reports that when a white minister perished under the tracks of a bulldozer during a demonstration at a construction site in Cleveland, Malcolm told an audience in New York, "What he did—good, good, great. What he did—good. Hooray, hooray, hooray. . . . It's time some white people started dying in this thing."

In all, Malcolm was still operating from his old, street hustler's cynicisms. He contemplated the gathering civil-rights struggle, and its leaders, with the deepest disdain. The whole appeal for integration seemed to him craven, a spectacle of the abused who, out of some perverse compulsion, were "trying to unite" with their abusers. All that the movement was achieving anyway, as in Birmingham, was "promises that they will be able to sit down and drink some coffee with some crackers in a cracker restaurant," as an F.B.I. report quoted him. "Now, what kind of advancement is that. They still don't have a job." He particularly deplored the principle of nonviolence. "I believe it's a crime for anyone who is being brutalized to continue to accept that brutality without doing something to defend himself," he told Haley. "If that's how 'Christian' philosophy is interpreted, if that's what Gandhian philosophy teaches, well, then, I will call them criminal philosophies." He held a special contempt for King. Charles Kenyatta, who is now a Baptist minister in Harlem, remembers that, in private, "Malcolm had always said, when he met King, he was gonna hit him in the jaw and see just how nonviolent he really was."

Although, as some have pointed out, Malcolm never directly urged in public the initiation of any specific act of outright violence, his oratory fairly reeled with exultant anticipation of an impending racial Armageddon, some "maximum retaliation against racist oppressors" in a "racial conflict . . . that could easily escalate into a violent, worldwide, bloody race war." Kenyatta recalls, "I thought, the way Malcolm was talking, just had to be some unhidden guns and armies somewhere. He preached once, 'Anybody lays a hand on you when you go out of here, think five times.' And I told him, 'You done brought me all the way up here ready to kill somebody, what you mean 'Wait five times'?"

King, for his part, in an interview with *Playboy* did not conceal his misgivings about Malcolm's "demagogic oratory," saying of Malcolm's "litany of articulating the despair of the Negro without offering any positive, creative alternative" that he felt that "Malcolm has done himself and our people a great disservice." It was as if they were talking two different languages. While King refused to engage Malcolm in any open confrontation, he did occasionally indicate privately that he might like to have a conversation with him at some point. In fact, they encountered each other only once, and only glancingly—when both happened to be in the corridors of the Capitol during the debate on the 1964 civil-rights bill. Malcolm pounced to King's side. They exchanged amenities and briefly clasped hands, King's smile faint and tentative, Malcolm's a wide grin, in a flaring of flashbulbs. But that was it. They quickly parted and returned to their separate realms.

When Malcolm's startling separation from the Nation of Islam came about, in late 1963, the pretext initially given was that Elijah Muhammad had been dismayed by remarks of Malcolm's about the assassination of President Kennedy. Kennedy's slaying was "the chickens coming home to roost," Malcolm had said, and it made him "glad." He maintained that he had in mind, among other things, Kennedy's allowing the death, in a coup, of South Vietnam's dictator Ngo Dinh Diem. At the headquarters of the Nation of Islam, in Chicago, the day after he made these remarks, he was told by Elijah Muhammad, "That was a very bad statement. . . . I'll have to silence you for the next ninety days—so that the Muslims everywhere can be disassociated from the blunder." Malcolm initially submitted to this discipline, but he later asserted in his autobiography, "I hadn't hustled in the streets for years for nothing. I knew when I was being set up."

Charles Kenyatta, who was given the name Charles 37X, recalls, "Malcolm had become the money-maker. He had taken them out of the wilderness and brought them into the Promised Land, where all of a sudden they were being looked on as a very powerful organization." But tensions had been developing for some time, among those around Messenger Muhammad, over Malcolm's growing national conspicuousness. To be sure, Malcolm did seem to have become fascinated by his reflection in the media, white devils' instrument or no. He would willingly sit for three-hour interviews with the press. While he grumbled in the "Autobiography" that the media had "somehow" managed to filch his home phone number, he had actually slipped it to journalists himself. Kenyatta later lamented to Goldman that the media's bright mirror "really destroyed him," and went on to say, "He got drunk off it. He used to sit by the TV set and watch himself, and you could see how much he liked it." Increasingly, in the national eye, Malcolm himself became the Muslims. He had first attracted the attention of the F.B.I. in 1953, when it was informed that he might be a Communist sympathizer. But what sustained the Bureau's continued surveillance was a curiosity about him as an exotic racial incendiary. In any case, according to one F.B.I. undercover report, Elijah Muhammad finally complained to Malcolm that he had been constantly "hearing about MALCOLM this and MALCOLM that and even MALCOLM being called leader." Malcolm must never forget that he was "*ELIJAH'S* property."

Meanwhile, Malcolm, as his engagement with the world around him expanded, had been growing restive within the confines of the Black Muslims' righteous ghetto, the isolation of its millennial racial mythos. Despite all his berating of the civil-rights movement, he found himself increasingly stirred by the spectacle it presented, as the most powerful mass drama then unfolding in the black community. As many blacks saw it, he said, "Muslims *talk* tough, but they never *do* anything."

But there was more to his restiveness than that. Elijah Muhammad, he had heard earlier in 1963, had engaged in dalliances with a succession of young secretaries, and some of them were pregnant or had already borne what members of Muhammad's court delicately referred to as "divine babies." This news left Malcolm profoundly stunned. "I had discovered Muslims had been betrayed by Elijah Muhammad himself," he told Haley, as he described its effect on him in almost Shakespearean terms: "I felt as though something in *nature* had failed, like the sun, or the stars."

When word of Malcolm's reaction got back to the Muslims' inner councils, he was called to a session with Elijah Muhammad, beside the swimming pool of Muhammad's home in Phoenix, which had been acquired for him out of solicitude for his bronchial disorder. An implausibly frail and wheezy gnome to have disported himself so briskly with teen-age nymphs, Elijah explained that these activities had been an exercise Biblically imposed upon him. "You recognize that's what all of this is— prophecy," he said, according to Malcolm. "I'm David. When you read about how David took another man's wife, I'm that David. You read about Noah, who got drunk—that's me. You read about Lot, who went and laid up with his own daughters. I have to fulfill all of those things." Charles 37X was with Malcolm at this last session with Elijah Muhammad. "The old man told Malcolm"—at this point, Kenyatta stood and wagged his forefinger—" 'Son, go back and put that fire out. Or my followers are gonna hurt you.' But Malcolm had too much pride to do that."

Malcolm still viewed a final excision from the Muslim faithful with considerable reluctance and trepidation, however, and for some months he kept up a kind of furtive scrimmaging to ease himself back into a family whose elders had already effectively disowned him. Yet, at the same time, he began industriously distributing word of the Messenger's indecorous frolickings to others within the Nation of Islam, among them the future Louis Farrakhan, a natty and bright-eyed former calypso singer who was then presiding over the Boston mosque. He, along with others, relayed the tidings of Malcolm's betrayal back to Chicago. Then Malcolm, in escalating desperation, disclosed the matter publicly. Journalists hesitated to run the story at first, because of libel considerations. (One reporter told him, though, according to an F.B.I. wiretap, that he "wished to God he could print the bit about the divine babies.") Finally, Malcolm managed to persuade three of Muhammad's former secretaries to furnish affidavits, and two of them to file paternity suits.

In due time, Malcolm received a telegram from a captain of the Fruit of Islam of Chicago, stating, "Mr. Malcolm: We hereby officially warn you that the Nation of Islam shall no longer tolerate your scandalizing the name of our leader and teacher the Honorable Elijah Muhammad." A few months earlier, an F.B.I. wiretap had picked up a call to Malcolm's home by an unidentified person who instructed the woman who answered, "Just tell him he is as good as dead." Malcolm himself was confident that someone in the Muslim ranks would "take it upon himself to kill me as a 'religious duty,' " as he put it to Haley. But, he declared, what to him was worse than death "was the betrayal." Even at that point, "I could conceive death. I couldn't conceive betrayal." Indeed, when it became plain that he was now permanently cast out from the Muslims' midst, he wept.

The previous spring, perhaps not coincidentally, Malcolm set out alone on a pilgrimage to Mecca, and afterward he claimed to have discovered that the Black Muslim racial dogma had all along been an eccentric aberration, and no part of true, classical Islamic theology. At the airport in Cairo, among a multitude of other pilgrims headed for Mecca, he removed his western apparel and wrapped his waist and shoulders in two white cloths, his long rusty-skinned legs now extending bare and ostrichlike below, and he had shoved his large feet into sandals. On the flight to Jedda, he told Haley, he was awed to find the plane crammed with "white, black, brown, red, and yellow people, blue eyes and blond hair, and my kinky red hair—all together, brothers." On the verge, as it were, of a second release from a captivity—this one a release he had never anticipated—he was filled with exhilaration to note that "the whole atmosphere was of warmth and friendliness." He said, "The feeling hit me that there really wasn't any color problem here." Upon reaching Mecca, he found himself eating "from the same plate . . . with fellow Muslims, whose eyes were the bluest of blue, whose hair was the blondest of blond, and whose skin was the whitest of white." In all his life, he said afterward, it was "the first time I had ever stood before the Creator of All and felt like a complete human being."

His wonder and elation over such commonplace cordialities somehow hinted at the childlike simplicity—innocence, even— that had lurked all along under the ferocities of his racial exhortations back in America. Exorbitant or not, this euphoria— "Why, the men acted as if they were brothers of mine!"—now prompted in him, he declared, "the start of a radical alteration in my whole outlook about 'white' men." If there seemed an

oddly poignant naïveté in his jubilation, a part of that naïveté
was also a capacity for belief so instant and total, as the actor
Ossie Davis would tell Peter Goldman, that "when he saw
something, he embraced it. . . . It was *wow! a truth!* and he
grabbed it."

He returned to New York—with a scanty goatee, and wearing
an Astrakhan hat—no longer the Malcolm X of his Black Muslim years but with a new name, honoring his completion of the
pilgrimage: he was now El-Hajj Malik El-Shabazz. He held a
press conference at Kennedy Airport—a pandemonious convo-
cation—at which he announced his enlightenment and his transformation. "In the past, yes, I have made sweeping indictments
of *all* white people," he said, but, after what he had experienced
in Mecca, "I never will be guilty of that again," and he added,
"A blanket indictment of all white people is as wrong as when
whites make blanket indictments against blacks."

Over the following months, it did seem that he had moved
significantly beyond his old simple racial fixations toward what
he described in his autobiography as "a new insight": that "the
white man is *not* inherently evil, but America's racist society
influences him to act evilly." And it was less a matter of economics than a "historical neurotic pathology—the abiding and
almost limitlessly complex permeation of society by the legacy
of slavery, a "political, economic, and social *atmosphere*." His
mission now was "to help create a society in which there could
exist honest white-black brotherhood," and in which "both
races, as human beings, had the obligation, the responsibility,
of helping to correct America's human problem" and, ultimately, "to change this miserable condition that exists on this
earth."

It is easy to make a bit too much of this development in
Malcolm: it was, at most, only the beginning of a transmutation.
He never became able, for instance, to accept the ethic of nonviolence; in fact, in the very press conference in which he proclaimed his new racial illumination he had also recommended
that blacks form rifle clubs and otherwise arm themselves in
case of attack. Neither had he lost his essential mistrust of the
whole concept of integration. Even in Mecca, he contended in

the "Autobiography," there was "a color pattern to the huge crowds. . . . I saw that people who looked alike drew together and most of the time stayed together." More dismally, there continued to gutter in him the old, acrimonious suspicions that "so many Jews actually were hypocrites." As for whites: "Let sincere whites go and teach nonviolence to white people!"

But now, in his striving to free himself from other thralls in his past, he found that, in contrast to his almost immediate and total new birth in prison, he had to develop and define this regeneration extemporaneously and on his own. Peter Goldman, in a recent conversation, spoke of Malcolm at that time as being in "a period of explosive and chaotic growth, re-creating himself on the run." Benjamin Karim, his longtime associate, whose own memoir is shortly to be published, said that at the time he "saw a person who was trying to remake himself into another image, one that was not racially inclined—not to like or dislike a person according to his race. Committed to *brotherhood*, you know. Some of the people with him—because of ignorance, he had to deal with them about that." Malcolm even went so far as to propose what once, when he was a Black Muslim, would have been heresy—that blacks might use the vote to achieve political power. But he had wandered into a kind of thematic no man's land, caught between the simple clear rancors of his past and his still unformed mission for a more hopeful future. Charles Kenyatta says he cautioned Malcolm, "You can't tamper with another person's God if you don't have another to give them." Karim, who left the Muslims with Malcolm, says, "He had to shift into another gear he didn't know about. He never found that gear. He never came into focus. And that was right down to the last day." Malcolm had lost the simple certitude that is vital of any leader, and he was balked on every side: the civil-rights movement rejected him as too militant, and the militants discounted him as too moderate. He once blurted to Haley, "They won't let me turn the corner! I'm caught in a trap!"

Now that he was outside the society of the Muslims, he found that, for the first time since emerging from prison, he no longer had any real place. He improvised two organizations of his own—Muslim Mosque, Inc., and a more secular operation, which he called the Organization of Afro-American Unity. A good two years before the widely heard calls for "black power" and the eventual, now commonplace invocations of "community control," he called for a form of black nationalism that was his own variation on the Muslims' concept of self-contained black neighborhoods, taking their own economies and politics into their own hands. Beyond that, he sought to develop an active bond between the black society in America and the Mother Continent—a sort of Pan-African black Zionism promising a massive liberation of spirit for America's black minority as it identified with the world's overwhelming dark majority. In turn, he exhorted African nations to call the United States to account before the United Nations, for the oppression of its black population—as they had called South Africa to account in November of 1961, in the wake of the Sharpeville massacre. This was all an inspiration that had evolved from two journeys he made through Africa in the months following his pilgrimage to Mecca. To him, those journeys had seemed the ultimate spiritual homecoming, a return at last to the lost Eden of the Old Country. In those visits, as he forged about, looped in cameras and ceaselessly, greedily taking pictures, he was welcomed by governments there with much pomp and celebration, as if he were a visiting exofficio head of state.

At the same time, though, some Africans were a bit disconcerted by the pallor of his skin, and assumed he was an albino. He tended to be considered more an American than an African. Most of all, the African governments he had entreated to indict the United States before the United Nations later proved singularly reluctant to oblige him, and thereby jeopardize the considerable American aid they were receiving.

In a sense, then, in moving beyond the Muslims—"the only group that really cares about you," he had been taught—Malcolm found that he had moved into a kind of void. Benjamin Karim remembers that at the time "he was living on the edge. Before that, he had everything set up for him. Now he had to do it on his own. For the first time, he became very edgy, very sensitive." What was particularly painful, Malcolm was repudiated by Muhammad Ali, whom he had tutored in the Muslim faith over a period of three years, while Ali was still Cassius Clay. In the first days of Malcolm's suspension by Elijah Muhammad from public speaking, Ali had invited him and his family down to his training camp in Miami Beach before his heavyweight title fight with Sonny Liston—a kindness for which Malcolm remained passionately grateful. But at the time of Malcolm's final, open break with the Muslims, Ali told Haley, "You just don't buck Mr. Muhammad and get away with it. I don't want to talk about him no more." When their paths happened to cross in Africa, Malcolm addressed Ali as "Brother," but Ali, according to an F.B.I. report, remarked to his entourage afterward, "Man, did you get a look at him? Dressed in that funny white robe and wearing a beard and walking with a cane that looked like a prophet's stick? Man, he's gone so far out he's out completely. . . . Nobody listens to that Malcolm anymore."

In the meantime, the high pageantry of the civil-rights movement continued to sweep past, oblivious of him. He became, in fact, a familiar figure looming tall and alone at the margins of its rallies and demonstrations, again thickly hung with cameras and earnestly taking pictures of the proceedings. "He wanted so much to come on in, to be a part of it," Kenyatta remembers. "He had always this dream to belong." From abroad, he had directed an aide to write letters to leaders of the movement, offering his hope that his "new position" might be "attractive to you." Back home, he made blurting attempts to reach out to them more directly. Once, when I was covering King's campaign in St. Augustine, Florida, in which his marches were undergoing Walpurgis Nights of Klan mayhem, I learned that Malcolm had sent a telegram to King, assuring him that, on his word, "we will immediately dispatch some of our brothers there to organize our people into self defense units . . . and the Ku Klux Klan will receive a taste of its own medicine." King's reaction to this overture was, as I recall it, one of appalled dismay.

While King was in jail during the Selma demonstrations, Malcolm was invited by Snick partisans, for their own mischievous designs, to address a mass meeting in a Selma church. Malcolm wound up seated on the podium beside Coretta Scott King. At one point, he leaned close and whispered to her— with what seemed an apologetic and wistful urgency, Coretta later recalled—"to let Martin know he was not causing trouble or making it difficult, but that he was trying to make it easier," that he simply wanted to confront whites with "an alternative" to King's appeal. In his address, he made no equivocation about his own aversion to nonviolence but pointed out that whites "better be glad Martin Luther King is rallying the people because other forces were waiting to take over if he fails."

But his past would not turn him loose. He began to see everywhere, he said, on the streets and in elevators and in passing cars, "the faces of Muslims whom I knew, and I knew that any of them might be waiting for the opportunity to try and put a bullet into me." Of this period Kenyatta remembers, "We were on the move, one place to another, trying to dodge the bullets." Malcolm was also floundering financially, sustaining himself on loans and lecture fees and the less than imposing collections at his services, and finally, toward the end, on advances on his autobiography. Furthermore, a court had found for a claim by the Muslims that they were the legal owners of a house in East Elmhurst, Queens, occupied by Malcolm and his family—a house, Betty Shabazz still insists, that had been given to her by Elijah Muhammad himself as a wedding gift. And there now drew close the harrowing near-certainty that Malcolm, his pregnant wife, and their four daughters would be evicted from their home.

Malcolm had often claimed that his earliest memory was of waking up, when he was four, amid the flames and chaos of the fire at his home in Lansing and of his father shooting at two white men fleeing into the night. Now, some thirty-five years later, he found himself on the eve of a virtually inevitable court denial, in a Monday-morning hearing, of his last appeal to prevent the Muslims from flushing him and his family out of their home and repossessing it. And in the black early-morning hours of that Sunday there was a boom and a glare of flames around the house, and once again he was standing amid his family, in pajamas, with children crying, out in the yard, watching his home burn. Dawn showed that about half of it was scorched and spottily charred, from two fires—one that had exploded in the front parlor, the other at a back window.

In a service at the Audubon Ballroom, in Harlem, two evenings later, Malcolm declared, "My house was bombed by the *Muslims!* . . . I wouldn't care for myself if they would not harm my family!" However, it is not readily apparent why members of the Nation of Islam, whatever their general balefulness, might have wished to terrorize Malcolm out of the house by burning it, on the eve of the almost certain affirmation of an eviction order that they had already obtained. "We own this place, man," a Muslim chieftain protested. "We have *money* tied up here." The Nation of Islam asserted that the fire had been Malcolm's own handiwork—what might seem a manifestly absurd suggestion, since his four small daughters were sleeping in the house at the time.

Nevertheless, close scrutiny of some of the evidence does make it appear at least a peculiar affair. An F.B.I. summary of police and Fire Department reports states that while Betty told the firemen that she had been the first to awaken and had roused Malcolm, he stated that he awoke himself and discovered the fire. According to the summary, the only alarms came from two chance witnesses, a neighbor and a passing taxi-driver, who heard the window glass shatter but saw no one outside the house either in front or in back. Shortly after the fire was extinguished, investigators found the neck of a whiskey bottle containing a scorched cloth wick in the back yard, about fifteen feet from a broken bedroom window with a scorched venetian blind. Oddly, though, as Bruce Perry noted in ''Malcolm,'' the window glass had scattered only into the yard, not into the room, and a fan pattern of burned weeds suggested that the bottle had actually been thrown from inside the house. A whiskey bottle containing a small amount of gasoline was found on the unburned front porch, which led firemen to suspect that gasoline from the bottle had been first splashed around the parlor and set afire, and the bottle left broken on the porch. Even more suspicious, the summary reported that "a quart whiskey bottle filled with gasoline was located standing upright on the dresser" in a rear bedroom, and that "this bottle had a screw cap which was intact and did not have rags attached to it." Malcolm afterward attested that it was his wife who had first called the firemen's attention to the bottle. And, according to Perry, when a fireman picked up the bottle it left a clear circle amid the soot from the fire which had settled on the dresser top—evidence that the bottle had been set there before the fire. After stories appeared about the discovery of this gasoline-filled bottle, Malcolm maintained that it had been planted in the house, and postulated a conspiracy between the police, the Fire Department, the press, and the Black Muslims. The question is how the police or the firemen could have deposited in the room precisely the same sort of bottle that had been used to fire the house. It seems inescapable that the hand that set the bottle on the dresser was the one that had poured the contents of the others about the house and flung them out the windows. The difficulty with such a conclusion, of course, is that it assumes that Malcolm would knowingly put his children at risk.

Malcolm's mood at the time had become one of cornered frenzy. He told Haley that when he concluded that Elijah Muhammad had sanctioned his extermination "my head felt like it was bleeding inside." Some of the people close to him began to fear that he was approaching a psychic shattering. He seemed given more and more to a kind of blindly barging, barely contained berserkness, in which his resorting to such a personal scorched-earth recourse would not be wholly inconceivable—allowing him then to call down on the Muslims the vengeance at least of a public outrage and condemnation. As he declared afterward, "I'm waking up America to the great Muslim menace."

Moreover, Bruce Perry has discovered that the Lansing fire that traumatized Malcolm as a child—the fire he had always avowed to be the work of white racists—may have been set by his father, who, Perry found, had also faced eviction, and was briefly jailed for arson: a two-gallon oilcan that had contained kerosene was found under a bedspring in the basement; Earl

Little had purchased kerosene only hours before the Elmhurst
fire occurred at 2:30 A.M., and during the days following the
East Elmhurst fire rumor had it that Malcolm's wife appeared
visibly enraged at him. When I asked her about the fire recently,
she said, "I'm not gonna talk about all that now."

The week after the fire was the last week of Malcolm's life.
His protégé Louis Farrakhan had announced in a Muslim newspaper, with the scorpion vigor for which he later became more
widely noted, "The die is set, and Malcolm shall not escape. . . .
Such a man as Malcolm is worthy of death." The Chicago
elect, Goldman reports, issued a tape-recorded statement, to be
played for other temple memberships, that Malcolm was due to
be "blasted clear off the face of the earth." Malcolm said that
in the Nation of Islam "any death-talk for me could have been
approved of—if not actually initiated—by only one man." What
confronted him now was like the most primal of dreads—that
the man who had been his soul's true father wanted to kill him.
Kenyatta recalls that, even after all that had happened, Malcolm
"missed the old man more than the old man missed him. He
was so close to a breakdown that he wanted death, that's how
close he was." Malcolm declared, "Black men are watching
every move I make, awaiting their chance to kill me. . . . Anyone who chooses not to believe what I am saying doesn't know
the Muslims in the Nation of Islam." He seemed to move slug-
gishly, fitfully, in a trance of doom. "Each day I live as if I
am already dead," he told Haley, and kept assuring others,
"I'm a dead man." And the irony of this inevitability did not
escape him: that the Muslim faithful could be trusted to deliver
on their threats "because I taught them myself." It was as if
he were ambushed from the past by his own hand. In the end,
for all Malcolm's apostleship of wrath over the years, the only
violence his message ever demonstrably precipitated was upon
himself.

The Audubon Ballroom in Harlem was on the second floor
of a building with an arcing roof that looked from outside like
an airplane hangar or a civic gymansium. A frumpish, musty
relic from the dance-hall years of Malcolm's past, it had been

converted into an auditorium for his post-Nation of Islam ministry, with folding chairs for a congregation of four hundred. On the mild afternoon of Sunday, February 21, 1965, it was filled with a wan wintry light.

As had become Malcolm's policy, despite the miasma of threats surrounding him now, those entering the ballroom were not searched at the door. Moreover, the New York City Police, who had provided a twenty-man uniformed guard detail, were asked to post all but two of them outside. Charles Kenyatta was standing in the back of the ballroom and noticed the absence of police. "I said to two or three of the brothers, 'What is this? What's goin' on?' They said, 'This is the way he wanted it, didn't want any security.' He had come to long to die. That's the reason he pulled those guards. Seemed he was just asking for it. I told him, 'We can't keep on goin' like this. Got to be some fightin' back. You lost your street knowledge.' But Malcolm said, 'You have lost your faith in Allah.' Thing was, Malcolm felt under a stroke of fate." Kenyatta paused for a moment, and continued, "Listen, he was lonely. That's why he wanted to die. He wanted to be a martyr. He knew."

Earlier that morning, in his room, at the midtown Hilton, where he had stayed overnight, Malcolm put on a dark-brown suit over, despite the unusual balminess of that February day, long-john underwear. He talked to Betty on the phone, telling her not to come to the rally. But before leaving he called her back, saying that he did want her there. Malcolm had also asked several community notables and ministers, and also the Ossie Davises and Martin Luther King's attorney, to join him on the platform for the afternoon's service, but when he arrived at the Audubon he learned that none of them would be coming. In a small anteroom offstage, he barked sharply at a young woman there, an O.A.A.U. assistant, and then, according to Haley, a little before going out to speak he apologized to her, saying, "I'm just about at my wit's end."

Benjamin Karim was chosen to introduce him. As they waited in the anteroom, Karim recalls, "it was absolutely weird. Standing there looking at him, I felt he really couldn't go any further. But he had come to a point where he still couldn't see his goal.

I didn't know he was going to be assassinated, but it was like looking at a man who had been physically lifting logs, and had lifted the last log he could lift. The burden had become too much. He was very drawn. He looked like he had already begun moving out of life.''

Appearing on the platform to an explosion of cheering and applause—that familiar tall and gangling figure, his face wrapped in one of his spacious grins—he waited for silence, and then offered the Islamic greeting. *"As-salaam alaikum*, brothers and sisters,'' and the audience chorused in turn. *"Wa-alaikum salaam.''* At that instant, about eight rows back in the crowd below him, a man leaped to his feet crying, "Get your hand out of my pocket!'' As heads turned and Malcolm's security guards at the foot of the platform began moving toward the distraction, Malcolm lifted both arms and called, "Hold it! Hold it! Don't get excited. Let's cool it, brothers.'' But now a man was scrambling toward him, hunched forward over a long glint of metal. And, with Malcolm's arms still lifted in that becalming gesture, a shotgun blast blew him backward with a perfectly circular seven-inch pattern of holes over his heart. He toppled, with blood spattered across his face and shirt, down through two empty chairs to the platform, his head hitting with a loud thunk, and the shotgun, a sawed-off double-barrel twelve-gauge, blasted him again where he lay. Now two other men, in overcoats, at the foot of the platform, were clattering away at him with pistols—a 9-millimetre and a .45 automatic. "It looked like a firing squad,'' one witness recalled. Betty, sitting near the stage with her daughters, saw the original disturbance out of the side of her vision, and when she heard the shots, she says, she had an instant certainty: "I knew there was no one else in there they'd be shooting at.'' She turned to see Malcolm falling, and immediately threw the children under some chairs and covered them with her body. "They never actually saw it, what had happened,'' she says.

The auditorium had become a storm of howling people floundering for cover in a tumble of chairs, some of which were flung through the air as two of the gunmen fled for the door. In a continuing clangor of gunfire, some of it now from Malcolm's guards, the two gunmen made it down the stairway to the street, but there one of them, who had been shot in the leg, was overhauled by the crowd, and came close to being beaten to death before he was claimed by hastily arriving police.

Meanwhile, back inside the ballroom, Betty, crying, "They're killing my husband!," attempted to rush forward to where Malcolm lay. "I wanted to give him mouth-to-mouth resuscitation, but a person was holding me back," she says. A stretcher was finally brought from a nearby hospital, and Malcolm was borne away, his face fixed, in death, in a fierce grimace of bared teeth—almost as if he had been at last reclaimed by the old, irreconcilable rage of the Malcolm X who had been pursuing him all these many months.

Today, recalling that Sunday afternoon at the Audubon Ballroom, Betty Shabazz says, "I still carry it with me all the time. I prayed for years for it to be taken away, not to be able to remember it." She had even refused to take the children to the funeral, for fear "they'd see him there prone, not moving." She says, "But my consciousness expanded, so I can live with it." In fact, she has become, like Coretta King, the public keeper of her husband's memory. (According to her, it was Malcolm who suggested to Haley that he look into his ancestors' past in Africa—a suggestion that led to "Roots.")

After Malcolm's death, Betty earned a doctoral degree in education, and she is now an administrator at Medgar Evers College, in Brooklyn. She is an imposing dowager of a woman, with a round, full face that has a stately impassiveness. During a recent conversation, she began by declaring, with a forefinger spearing upward, much in Malcolm's old preacherly manner, "To understand Malcolm, you must understand his mission"— which she is now constantly explaining to audiences across the country. "He's called a racist—no, no, no! Sometimes you have to exaggerate in order to get people to see. What did he do? He held up a mirror. Sometimes you don't like what you see in a mirror." She added, quietly, "When he's away, he's here. I still feel his presence. He still lives with me. The guy was *so strong*."

*   *   *

Not long after Malcolm's death, Elijah Muhammad consented to receive the press—even those members with blue eyes and chalky skins—in a vast chamber of his mansion in Chicago. Tiny and solemn amid walls hung with white silk, he declared, in a fluting voice, "We have not, as I said, never resorted to no such thing as violence. Way I see it, Malcolm is the victim of his own preachin'. He preached violence, and so he becomes a victim of it." But Peter Goldman reports that to a gathering of his believers four days later he said, between coughings and wheezings, "He tried to make war against me. . . . It's wrong to even stand beside the grave of a hypocrite. . . . Malcolm got what he was preaching." Two of Malcolm's brothers were presented, to denounce him one last time as "a man who was no good."

Three black men—all Muslims, as it eventually proved—were arrested, and in a two-month trial nearly a year later were found guilty of the slaying and sentenced to life in prison. Two of them are now out on parole. The third, Talmadge Hayer, who was the gunman apprehended immediately outside the ballroom, confessed at the trial but declared that the two others had not been involved. They have continued to maintain that they had nothing to do with the shooting. In prison, Hayer admitted to Goldman that Malcolm's execution had been plotted by five Muslim street regulars, under the inspiration of the Muslim leadership, as retribution for the discomfort that Malcolm had afforded Elijah Muhammad. The message in comments heard by the faithful from some of Muhammad's close courtiers, such as "If you knew what Malcolm said about the Dear Holy Apostle, you'd kill him yourself," was as unmistakable as Henry II's legendary complaint about Thomas Becket.

Norman Butler is one of those convicted of Malcolm's murder who still denies he participated in it, but he nevertheless told Goldman that, beforehand, "security people rolled in from everywhere—captains from all over the country. . . . And New York was made to look bad," and he quoted one of them as saying, "What we got to do—bring in people from all over to take care of your business?" These words came, Butler said, from a member of Elijah Muhammad's own household in Chicago, who elaborated, "Cut the nigger's tongue out and put it in an envelope and send it to me, and I'll stamp it approved and give it to the Messenger." Butler told Goldman, "And that, at that time, was *death*. Back then, that was an *order*." It was not as if defectors and apostates from the Nation of Islam hadn't been killed before, and for considerably tamer affronts than Malcolm's. Charles Kenyatta says today, "They were nothing but a Mafia operation." As Elijah Muhammad's somewhat more benign son, Wallace, was later appalled to discover, at least ten believers who were simply restless about the overbearing manner of the Fruit of Islam had also been killed. All those who investigated Malcolm's assassination were convinced that, beyond the three convicted, at least one person and possibly three more people were involved.

Other speculations have since swarmed: suspicions—invigorated by subsequent disclosures about police operations against other perceived menaces, like the Black Panthers—that swiftly turned into certainties about complicity by the C.I.A., the F.B.I., the New York police, or all the engines of the state combined, choreographed from Washington, and including a possible betrayal by one or several of Malcolm's own. Malcolm's film biographer, Spike Lee, has written, "We all live in a wicked country where the government can and will do anything to keep people in check. . . . I see the F.B.I., C.I.A. and the police departments around this country as one and the same. They are all in cahoots and, along with the Nation of Islam, they all played a part in the assassination of Malcolm X. Who else? King? Both Kennedys? Evers?" It testifies to a curious superstition about the omniscience of federal agencies to maintain, as Lee does, that "the Bureau knew Malcolm's every move, knew he was being hunted down, but stood back."

In reality, Malcolm was warned by the F.B.I. of threats against his life, and was assured that the F.B.I. would supply witnesses if he wished to take the Muslims to court. And he was repeatedly offered protection by New York's Police. One was a formal offer of a twenty-four hour police guard, and he had received as many as seventeen offers to station uniformed officers at his rallies at the Audubon Ballroom—offers made, to be sure, with the anticipation that Malcolm would almost certainly refuse them, as he mostly did. The only probable complicity of the F.B.I. and the police in what happened would have been that, knowing a strike at Malcolm to be almost certainly impending, they chose not to intervene any more actively to avert it.

The case for some larger official conspiracy to execute Malcolm proceeds from the supposition that at the time he presented a serious concern to the custodians of the national interest, both internally and abroad. Evidence cited for such a conspiracy includes the claim that, during a journey of Malcolm's to Cairo to try to persuade the African Unity Organization to take America's racial policy before the United Nations, he was, while staying at the Nile Hilton, "poisoned." But, having partaken of the fare of Cairo, including that of the Nile Hilton, on several visits of my own there, I can say that I have been poisoned on at least two occasions myself. The truth is, the notion that the national authorities had become so hoodooed by Malcolm that they would actually engage in a plot to eliminate him rather exaggerates the perception of his threat at the time. Though he did eventually attract more interest from the F.B.I. and the C.I.A. with his transmutation from a Black Muslim isolationist into a militant advocate of a Pan-African black nationalism that interest never seems to have ranged much further than his potential for embarrassment. What unease about black militancy had gathered in government agencies was focussed principally on King, with his incomparably larger following. Malcolm's true danger to the nation's management—that he was creating a radical new consciousness of pride and assertiveness in the nation's black community—was a phenomenon still inherently beyond the institutional imagination.

To be sure, Malcolm himself once said to Haley, "'The more I keep thinking about this thing, the things that have been happening lately, I'm not all that sure it's the Muslims. I know what they can do, and what they can't, and they can't do some of the stuff recently going on." Nevertheless, his expectation of assassination was fixed, for the most part, on the Muslims alone. One Muslim operation to exterminate him, he reported afterward, went awry only when one of the participants had second thoughts and came to warn him.

In the end, much of the speculation about a conspiracy arises, as in the case of Kennedy's death, from a reluctance to accept the absurd disparity that so much could have been destroyed through any circumstance so paltry and mundane. In Malcolm's case, an obscure internal religious war on the fringes of the black community seems impossibly out of proportion to his life and its meaning now. But one should always be wary of explanations that are far more arabesque and fantastical in detail than the paradoxes they're trying to explain.

In the years after Malcolm's assassination, and Elijah Muhammad's serene expiration, in 1975, Elijah's son, Wallace, diverged with some Muslims into a far milder and more conventional version of Islam, in the process quietly discarding his father's claim to have been Allah's Messenger. He even began restoring Malcolm as a venerated figure of the faith, and eventually renamed the Harlem mosque in Malcolm's honor. (There has also survived a straighter line of doctrinal descent, from Elijah Muhammad to Louis Farrakhan, who now occupies Elijah's mansion in Chicago.)

But beyond the single personal testament of his autobiography, Malcolm, to all appearances, left little behind him that was measurable. Both of his organizations had already fallen into ramshackle disarray, on the verge of dwindling away altogether. His grand Pan-African political offensive had evaporated against the cold calculations prevailing at the United Nations. He remained little more than a kind of garish rogue figure on the edge of the ongoing surge of the civil-rights movement. But Malcolm's true epitaph has turned out to be much like a fulfillment of that old invocation of his father's great hero, Marcus Garvey: "I shall come back to you.... Look for me in the whirlwind or the storm, look for me all around you."

Shortly after his death, as the civil-rights movement shifted to the urban North, speculations arose that Malcolm would become an increasingly formidable figure in the black consciousness and that King would be forced to adapt to Malcolm's message. The suggestion, though, that Martin and Malcolm were actually converging, in their widening campaigns against poverty and the dehumanization of American policies, seems ultimately illusory: they held two profoundly different understandings of humankind. King was animated by a vision of how things could and should be; Malcolm operated within a flat, rancorous acceptance of things as they were. "This is an era of hypocrisy," he declaimed. "You pretend that you're my brother and I pretend that I really believe you believe you're my brother."

But the duality between their visions is an abiding one, reaching beyond both Martin and Malcolm, and it has become, if anything, even more pertinent in what seems now yet another quickening of America's old racial travail. Specifically, the government's—and the society's—bland obliviousness of the plight of the poor in the last decade seems only to have placed more pressure on the racial fault line in the national community. Beyond that, there are those who have even proposed that racial turmoil may well be the coming theme of international history, as the world contracts into an ever more intimate neighborhood: that ethnic or tribal conflicts like those today in the remnants of Yugoslavia and the Soviet Union, in Sri Lanka and Somalia, to say nothing of the Middle East, will replace the long historical kinetic force of state nationalism and ideology and economic contention—that the real conflicts that will occupy governments and their armies will be as primitive a matter as the clashings of races.

In this country, at least, the implications of the increasing bitter estrangement of the children of Malcolm (in his latter days he noted, "Thicker each year in these ghettos is the kind of teen-ager that I was") can be nothing less than a deepening dissolution of the old dream of a common, egalitarian American neighborhood. To an extent, Malcolm incontestably emancipated a form of black pride: he himself claimed, with considerable fairness, that he had acted "to revolutionize the American black man's thinking, opening his eyes until he would never again look in the same fearful, worshipful way at the white man.'' Jesse Jackson, who as a college student once drove from North Carolina to Harlem hoping to meet with Malcolm, remembers that ''he was able to cut down the enemy with his tongue—that was his excitement for black people. Martin's liberation was his public movement, opening up the system to blacks. But Malcolm's was personal—he somehow removed the fear in blacks' personal encounters with whites.'' Ossie Davis proclaimed in his eulogy at Malcolm's funeral, ''Malcolm was our manhood, our living, black manhood . . . Our own black shining prince!'' He is still hailed by many as the most authentic voice of America's vast black underclass. In this he was actually ahead of King. Virtually by his oratory alone, he helped call forth the dawning of black consciousness in America; a cultural decolonization of the black spirit.

But it has been his earlier incarnation to which his posterity has somehow clung: to Malcolm's own slayer, in effect. On book covers, and on posters that have proliferated throughout the black community—in university black-student unions and inner-city bookstores—it is the image of Malcolm during his Muslim days that glares out, in his old finger-spearing racial judgment and malediction; it is, as the myriad profusion of ''X''s shows, still Malcolm from his Nation of Islam years. For that matter, most of Malcolm's children may now have only a dim impression of him, as a fearsome black orator who was once the nemesis of white America.

It was his own hope, he told Haley, that ''one day, history may even say that my voice—which disturbed the white man's smugness, and his arrogance, and his complacency—that my voice helped save America from a grave, possibly even a fatal catastrophe.'' But the true tragedy of Malcolm's life would be if, along with his inner emancipation of blacks, his gift to his people should also become, from that grimmer evangelism which finally claimed him in the Audubon Ballroom, the lurid liberation of their anger in the moral nihilism most recently beheld in the firestorm of Los Angeles. The rage after the acquittals of the Los Angeles police officers who had been seen on video systematically beating Rodney King was much in the spirit of the old Malcolm X. It is a matter of some irony, then, that Rodney King himself, around whom the rage of the children of Malcolm had billowed, turned out to be consummately one of the children of Martin when he appeared before cameras and, pained and stunned, ventured the appeal, in a halting, stumbling voice that yet had an eloquence beyond all the roaring of those days, "Can we all get along?"

It was toward that simple but ultimately civilized sentiment that Malcolm was making his last pilgrimage. He undertook it against fearful odds—odds that, after all these years, still confront his people. For the rest of us, then, the parable of Malcolm X should serve as an urgent warning. We must at last come by the recognition, the conscience, and the will to somehow make it possible for Malcolm's children—the still dispossessed descendants of America's aboriginal crime of slavery—to continue the journey that he began.